BEIJING BOUND

A FOREIGNER DISCOVERS CHINA

BEIJING BOUND

A FOREIGNER DISCOVERS CHINA

GLEN LOVELAND

Published in Australia by Sid Harta Books & Print Pty Ltd,
ABN: 34632585293
23 Stirling Crescent, Glen Waverley, Victoria 3150 Australia
Telephone: +61 3 9560 9920, Facsimile: +61 3 9545 1742
E-mail: author@sidharta.com.au

First published in Australia 2024
This edition published 2024
Copyright © Glen Loveland 2024
Cover design, typesetting: WorkingType (www.workingtype.com.au)

The right of Glen Loveland to be identified as the
Author of the Work has been asserted in accordance with the
Copyright, Designs and Patents Act 1988.

This work depicts actual events in the life of the author as truthfully as recollection permits and/or can be verified by research. Occasionally, dialogue consistent with the character or nature of the person speaking has been supplemented. All persons within are actual individuals; there are no composite characters. The names of some individuals have been changed to respect their privacy.

All rights reserved. No part of this publication may be reproduced, stored in a retrieval system, or transmitted, in any form or by any means without the prior written permission of the publisher, nor be otherwise circulated in any form of binding or cover other than that in which it is published and without a similar condition being imposed on the subsequent purchaser.

ISBN: 978-1-922958-78-5

'Write your book,' she said when I returned.
For my mum.

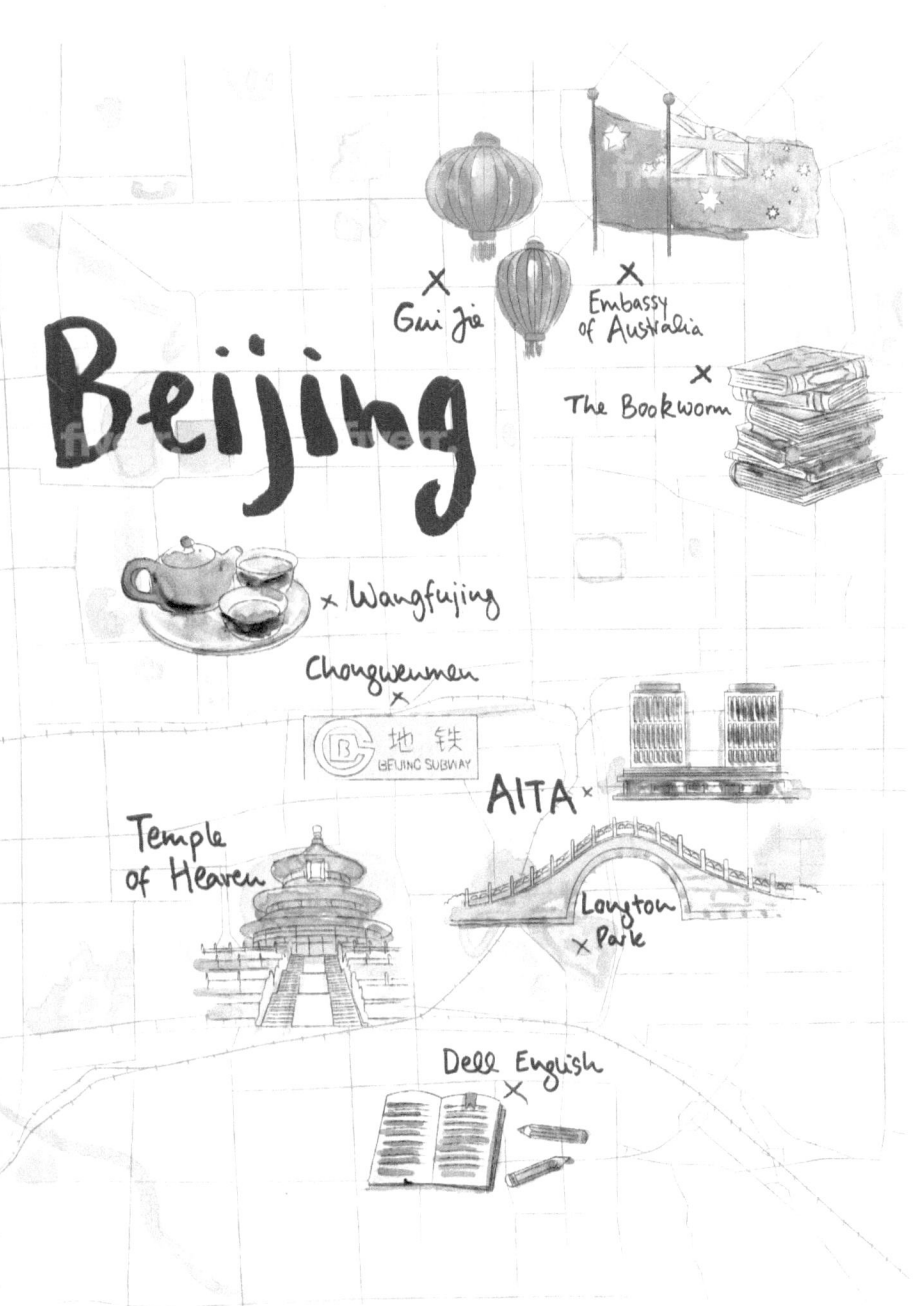

AUTHOR'S NOTE

April 14, 2024

In May 2020, as I set pen to paper to begin *Beijing Bound*, the United States and indeed the entire world found itself grappling with the Covid-19 pandemic. Amid the fear and uncertainty, the Trump Administration sought to exact revenge on China, the pandemic's origin. Proposals were floated to ban Chinese-owned apps such as TikTok and WeChat and longstanding cultural exchange agreements were unceremoniously discarded.

Watching US-Sino relations deteriorate to alarming lows, I couldn't help but ponder the future. What would the relationship between these two superpowers look like a decade hence? Would younger generations of Westerners struggle to comprehend why China had ever held such appeal, such promise? Were we destined to become lifelong adversaries?

Concurrently, China found itself firmly under the control of Xi Jinping's regime. Its priorities diverged sharply from the increasing openness that had come to define the nation in the modern era. The welcoming, globally minded China I had grown to love was fading away. This was made all too clear in November 2019 when the Bookworm, a beloved English-language bookstore that had long served as a cultural hub, announced its closure due to pressure from authorities.

A Chinese friend confided in me, his words echoing the unease that had settled in my heart, 'A different kind of cultural revolution is coming.' It was a chilling sentiment, one that presaged a future where the vibrant exchange of ideas and the warm embrace of foreign influences would be supplanted by a more insular, controlled environment.

As I reflected on the profound changes sweeping across the globe, I felt a deep sense of obligation to capture the essence of the Beijing I had known, a city that had captivated me with its vibrancy, its spirit and its unbridled potential. It was a rare and dynamic place, a testament to the resilience and ingenuity of the Chinese people who are so often misunderstood by the outside world.

The world watched in horror as images emerged from China's Covid lockdowns, painting a grim picture of empty streets, shuttered businesses and citizens imprisoned in their homes. The draconian measures, ostensibly implemented as a public health response, seemed to mark a new era of repression, a stark departure from the vision of hope and possibility that had once defined the 'Chinese Dream'.

I felt duty-bound to the countless individuals who had welcomed me into their lives and shared their stories during my time in China. In the pre-Xi era, the nation had seemed poised on the brink of a new and exciting future, a time when the 'Chinese Dream' represented a beacon of optimism and potential.

I knew I had to capture the essence of that China, to paint a portrait of a country on the cusp of change before it succumbed to the grim reality that now consumed it under Xi's rule.

My thoughts turned to the many Chinese friends and expatriates I had known during my time in Beijing. They are

Author's Note

now scattered across the world, a new kind of diaspora born of the realisation that there is no longer space for them in Xi's China. They carry with them the memories of a different time, a different dream, and the hope that one day the Beijing we knew and loved might rise again.

Throughout *Beijing Bound*, I use the terms Mandarin and Chinese interchangeably when referring to the official language of the People's Republic of China. It is important to note that while China is home to a diverse array of languages and dialects, Mandarin serves as the standard language for official communication and education.

When discussing money, I refer to the renminbi (RMB) with its primary unit being the yuan (CNY). In casual conversation, Chinese people often use the term 'kuai' interchangeably with yuan, similar to how Americans use 'bucks' for dollars.

To provide context, here are some currency conversions between Chinese yuan (CNY) and US dollars (USD) for 2007:

100 kuai = $13.22
1000 kuai = $132.20
5000 kuai = $661.00

By sharing these details, I aim to enhance the reader's understanding of the cultural and economic landscape in which my experiences took place, ensuring that the narrative is accessible and informative.

In *Beijing Bound*, I endeavour to capture the essence of the China I knew, the one that had captivated me and countless others with its rich history, dynamic cities and warm, welcoming people. By sharing my experiences and observations I hope to preserve a glimpse of this exciting pre-2008 Olympics-era China.

I invite readers to join me on a journey through a time of transformation, to bear witness to the hopes, dreams and challenges of a nation and its people on the cusp of a new and uncertain chapter in their history.

— Glen Loveland

Following the sun, we left the old world.
— from Eduardo Galeano's *Genesis*

DESTINATION: PEK

Saying goodbye to my corgi, Sir Nigel, was tough. As I scratched behind his floppy ears one last time, his brown eyes stared up at me quizzically. He tilted his head, puzzled by the suitcase in my hand. My vision blurred as I realised he did not grasp I was leaving him for good.

As I loaded my bags into the car, Nigel barked and whined, his stubby legs prancing in circles. Mum came up behind me and squeezed my shoulder. 'Don't worry, we'll take good care of him,' she said. I glanced back to see my sister hugging Nigey, giggling as she rubbed his tan belly. He'd be in good hands.

The flight attendant's announcement crackled through the cabin, *'Nǚshìmen Xiānshengmen, wǒmen jījiāng jiàngluò zài Běijīng.'* English had been sparse on this China Eastern flight, but judging by the time and passengers fastening their seatbelts, I guessed we were descending into Beijing.

My grip tightened on the worn pages of my *Frommer's Travel Guide*. Months of research, late nights poring over dog-eared sections, highlights mapping my journey—it had all led to this moment.

I still used the name Glen Loveland on that brisk March day in 2007. America had been the scene of my birth thirty-one years earlier and stamped me as one of its own in ink upon my passport. Yet I understood that identity runs deeper than any label or paperwork. As a gay single man without a mortgage I felt untethered and able to go wherever I wished. I chose China.

After seven disillusioning years on Capitol Hill, the rose-tinted glasses were off. I was craving adventure, meaning—anything to shake up my humdrum life. China was dynamic, modern and sexy; in other words, everything that America was not.

I tumbled out of that jetway into a maelstrom, all sound and fury. Beijing Capital Airport was alive with humanity, tides of it crashing and receding around me. Garbled Mandarin announcements reverberated from overhead, incomprehensible yet strangely melodic, while an army of bodies swarmed past in perpetual motion. Their chatter enveloped me in tongues I could not unravel.

I stood anchored in place, buffeted by the currents of foot traffic but unwilling to be moved. My fingers curled into a vice-like grip on the manila envelope, now damp and soft from my sweaty palms. Each passing face yielded no revelation. Where was the driver? Had I misread the vague instructions from my new company?

Through the chaos, I finally saw him—an elderly Chinese man in a flat cap, an unlit cigarette dangling from his lips. He was slender with kind, crinkly eyes. In his hands he held a weathered placard reading 'Loveland, Glen' in clumsy handwriting. Relief washed over me. I approached with a tentative *'Nǐ hǎo'* and received a silent nod in return as he gathered my bags and spun on his heel towards the exit. I hurried to keep pace.

When I tried to lift my overstuffed suitcases into the car, he leapt forward, waving his hands and clucking in protest. He motioned for me to step aside, then hoisted each bag in himself with a dramatic grunt.

The driver slammed the boot shut, revved the engine and peeled away from the kerb. Laying my head against the foggy window, I watched the glowing lights of Beijing streak past in a blur through half-closed eyes. The details of my new reality here would come into focus soon enough.

A thick haze shrouded the streets, diffusing the headlights into halos. The air held a bitter charred scent, as if a bonfire had only just been extinguished. So the rumours of Beijing's infamous pollution were true—this was truly an assault on the senses.

Beijing unfurled before me in an endless sprawl of twinkling high-rises and contrasting landscapes. Even at this late hour the city pulsated with energy, its scale far exceeding anything I had pictured. The ancient capital felt worlds away from the forest of towering cranes and half-finished buildings looming through the smog.

Finally, we pulled up to a nondescript apartment building. The driver led me inside, unlocked an apartment door and ushered me in. As he busied himself turning on lights, the realisation dawned—this was no random airport transfer. He must work for my company. A personal chauffeur, perhaps?

A few small cockroaches scurried across the floor. Their tiny bodies appeared harmless. The lingering smell of cooking oil hung in the air, clashing with the tidy order of the apartment. In spite of these issues my new home for the next twelve months surpassed my expectations.

The living room contained the basics: a small dining table, a worn sofa facing the TV and a bicycle parked in the corner. The driver gestured encouragingly towards it, miming riding motions. I smiled politely, envisioning navigating the streets where the road rules were so alien to me. Maybe someday.

The driver grunted as he lugged my suitcases down the narrow hallway. I trailed behind, poking my head into each cramped room we passed. The kitchen had yawning empty cupboards. The bathroom was hardly big enough to turn around in, with just a toilet crammed next to a showerhead and no tub in sight. I guessed the water splashed all over the floor. Then came three closet-size bedrooms, each holding barely enough room for a bed and desk. The driver wrestled my luggage through the doorway of the last room, dropping it with a heavy thud.

'*Xièxiè nǐ,*' I managed to sputter, tripping over the unfamiliar Mandarin phrase. He beamed regardless, waving away my thanks before replying, '*Bú kèqi.*' Don't mention it.

I watched from the window as the tail-lights of the company car faded into the night. Outside, darkened windows in row after row of high-rises stared back at me. The clock read 2:15 am, but the streets still hummed with activity—distant horns echoed through the canyons of concrete and glass. Beijing slept little, it seemed.

Sinking into the lumpy sofa, I grabbed the remote and flipped through channel after channel of Mandarin broadcasting. Finally I landed on CCTV-9, the country's sole English news network. The anchor's polished voice washed over me as images flickered across the dated television—athletes triumphant on podiums, cheering crowds waving Chinese flags. Was I already being brainwashed—or rather, inspired?

Jet lag settled over me like a blanket. Clicking off the television, I shuffled to the darkened bedroom. The mattress consisted of a sheet of plywood covered in thin padding.

After months spent imagining this moment, here I was

in the heart of bustling Beijing. Tomorrow would inevitably bring plenty of missteps and confusion. For now I was content simply to be. As my breathing slowed and consciousness ebbed, a small smile touched my lips. The adventure had begun.

CHÓNG WÉN MÉN

I woke around 10 am to find myself alone in the apartment. Quiet filled the rooms. My new coworker, Scarlet, whose flight was delayed, had not arrived with me as planned. With nothing else to do I eased open the curtains in my bedroom and peered out. Squinting, I spied an elderly Chinese woman and a young boy, perhaps her grandson, in the courtyard. I studied them for a moment and quickly shut the curtains. What if I did something wrong? What if I offended them? After a long moment I peered through the curtains again. Beijing beckoned.

I soon discovered the city is a clashing mosaic of old and new, a capital striving to fuse ancient traditions with modern ambition. At dawn, parks and public squares came alive with people exercising. In the city's *hútòng,* tangled warrens of grey brick alleyways, one could spy the covered archways of courtyard homes built centuries ago during the dynastic days of emperors long turned to dust.

But the hutongs were disappearing, bulldozed away as modernity arose in their place. Across the inner city the ominous character *chāi*—demolish—was scrawled on walls, spelling the impending erasure of history.

Change marched onward, unsentimental and relentless. I had arrived at the end of an era, witnessing a city shedding its past and hurtling towards the future. The Beijing of old still persisted in shaded corners, but it was fading fast. I could only hope to glimpse it before the city transformed once more.

In little more than a year tourists would flood the capital for the 2008 Summer Olympics.

My apartment had no Wi-Fi so I spent the morning unpacking. As I put away my clothes I studied the washing machine and wondered if I would one day navigate all the Chinese characters running around its dials and buttons. Over time, I would realise most Beijing apartments shared certain commonalities—gas stovetops but no ovens, washing machines but no dryers. The arid climate dried clothes in minutes, making dryers unnecessary.

The apartment decor was sparse. Some folding chairs, cardboard boxes waiting to be unpacked. The sole modern furnishings were a handful of ready-to-assemble pieces from Ikea. By the afternoon, restlessness had set in. Where was Scarlet? Surely she would arrive soon.

A knock at the door jolted me from my thoughts. I opened it to find the driver from yesterday, gesturing eagerly for me to grab my coat. He mimed eating, saying, 'Afternoon!' though whether we would eat now or tomorrow I couldn't tell.

We waited at the bus stop, breathing in diesel fumes as traffic roared past. Before long our bus lumbered up and wheezed to a stop. My driver gestured for us to board, slipping a protective arm around my shoulders to indicate we were together.

We squeezed down the crowded aisle. I was struck by the height of the passengers. A lanky youth standing next to me towered at more than six feet, and myself at six foot one didn't stand out. Northern Chinese skewed taller than their southern counterparts, attributed in something I'd read to wheat-versus-rice diets.

Glimpsing athletic builds and broad shoulders all around, I realised Yao Ming, the NBA star, wasn't an anomaly—tired stereotypes of short, slight Asian bodies crumbled before my eyes. As we jostled down the aisle, a kaleidoscope of faces turned to observe me with frank curiosity. I absorbed each new perception, feeling my understanding expand.

A young woman turned to me, speaking animatedly. 'I like Hillary Clinton. You think she will become president?'

I nodded. 'She has an excellent chance.' She wanted to know the name of 'the other party'. I enunciated the unfamiliar word slowly.

'Re...pub...li...cans,' she sounded out, brow furrowed. 'And the war in Iraq—you support this?'

I hesitated. 'Actually, most Americans oppose it. We shouldn't have gotten involved.'

Shock rippled across her face. 'You do not like this war?'

I explained the growing dissent back home, the calls to withdraw. Her eyebrows peaked as I spoke and she nodded along slowly, taking in each word. When my voice trailed off, her eyes remained fixed on me, unblinking.

I felt suddenly responsible, an unofficial ambassador accountable for my nation's actions. The complexities were not so black and white, I realised.

After a quick ride, we pulled up at a modest tower called Ling Hang International. Inside, a fine dust hung in the air, stirred up by ongoing renovations. We rode the elevator up and stepped out to a reception area marked with the company logo. Nearby, an Australian flag fluttered above brochures beckoning to international paradise. The ceilings were exposed, with silver pipes slithering above the office space. Needing to use the restroom, I wandered down a dim hallway lined with doors emblazoned with indecipherable characters. Selecting one at random, I stepped inside and froze. Gone were the Western-style toilets to which I was accustomed. In their place stood several shallow porcelain basins set into the floor—the infamous Asian 'squatters' described in my guidebook. I eyed them warily.

The office hummed with activity as workers wove between desks, their voices rising in Mandarin and accented English. Phones jangled, fax machines whirred and beat relentlessly. Everyone looked Chinese—no foreign faces that I could detect. It was a hive of productive chaos.

The driver introduced me to Tan Lu, the cheerful office manager, her hair in a bandana like a Chinese Julie Andrews in *The Sound of Music*. When I asked about Wi-Fi, she chuckled and led me to a cramped room tucked away in the back. A map of the world dominated one wall, time zones zigzagging across oceans.

I logged into my email and tapped out a quick missive to assure everyone back home that I'd arrived intact. As I clicked send on that first message from Beijing I glanced around at what would become my new office.

The driver directed me to a dingy sofa in the corner. I sank into its lumps, thankful for a moment's respite from the constant stares of new colleagues.

Heavy footsteps announced the boss's arrival. Michael Guo was tall, with a sleazy handsomeness, his cheap brown suit straining to contain a slight beer belly. Though he wished to present an image of refinement, the frayed edges of his improperly tucked shirt betrayed the hastiness of his preparation.

'Hello, Glen!' His Australian accent rang out. I jumped up to shake his hand eagerly.

'So excited to be here, Michael.'

We sat. 'Tea?' he offered.

Not wanting to impose, I reflexively declined. His face hardened instantly. My first cultural misstep—tea was a gesture of hospitality. 'Oh, uh, if it's no trouble, that would be lovely.' The words tumbled out in a rush, my hands raised in apology. I felt my cheeks flush hot with embarrassment.

He studied me for a moment before giving a slight nod, the hardness in his eyes softening.

Michael's tone shifted as he switched from English to Chinese. His words came out sharply, like cracks of a whip aimed at the young receptionist. What had she done to provoke his anger? She placed a paper cup of steaming green tea in front of me, leaves still swirling inside. I took a cautious sip, wary of revealing any displeasure. I sensed dealing with Michael would require a delicate touch.

He informed me I'd have the weekend to recover from my journey. With a brisk gesture, he summoned me to follow him on a tour of the office. He swept past the rows of employees without acknowledging them. At his approach, they shrank over their computers, cradling phones between hunched shoulders, plainly curious about me yet needing to look busy for Michael.

A smug smile spread across Michael's face as he paraded me around. The tour seemed less about orienting me and more about showing me off. Flaunting his foreign hire boosted his status in their eyes.

We settled into his preferred domain, a spacious conference

room dominated by a lengthy table surrounded by ten metal chairs. The walls were cluttered with photos of him grinning beside various personages. It was clear Michael had cultivated an impressive web of political connections in Australia and New Zealand. These photos were his credentials, displayed to convince sceptical Chinese clients.

'Let me finish up a few things and we'll go to dinner tonight,' Michael declared. I smoothed my jeans self-consciously as Michael's eyes tracked up and down my casual attire. My sneakers suddenly felt woefully underdressed for dinner. I opened my mouth to apologise but Michael cut me off with a dismissive wave of his hand.

'It doesn't matter.'

The brusque words offered little comfort. My limited knowledge of Chinese customs left me anxious that I'd unknowingly committed some dressed-down faux pas. Michael clearly didn't care what I wore, but I felt inadequate. Best play it safe with slacks and loafers on Monday.

The driver reappeared from the back hallway where he was no doubt sneaking a cigarette and gossiping about me with the others. At Michael's command, he brought the car around. I took the front passenger seat while Michael and his top managers, Ms Xu and Mr Zhao, slid into the rear. Ms Xu spoke rudimentary English, though she preferred not to use it. Mr Zhao spoke only Chinese.

Beijing's rush hour roads terrified me. If traffic laws existed, they were rarely enforced. Cars merged lanes arbitrarily, while others swerved wildly to avoid collisions. I watched dozens of bikers narrowly escape being hit. My heart nearly stopped when we almost clipped a toddler perched in the basket of a bike. In New York there would have been middle fingers and cussing, maybe even a shot fired. Here the near-victim simply blinked, barely processing their brush with death. The patience of pedestrians amazed me.

Michael and the driver erupted in a shouting match as our car careered between lanes. No longer satisfied with being a passenger, Michael commanded the driver to pull over so he could take the wheel himself, despite indignant protests. Once in the driver's seat, Michael's rage was palpable—his hands clenched the wheel and his face flushed crimson. He drove like a man possessed, weaving recklessly through traffic.

I clutched my seatbelt, silently praying we would make it to the restaurant in one piece. Ms Xu and Mr Zhao seemed unperturbed, likely used to Michael's temper. I wondered how often he pulled stunts like this. The timid driver shrank into the corner of his seat, wisely keeping quiet.

Finally, we arrived ... somewhere. It was a street crowded with restaurants, red lanterns swaying overhead—the China of movies and imagination.

'Where are we?' I whispered, climbing out of the car.

'Gui Jie,' Michael replied. 'Foreigners call it Ghost Street, but that's not right. The pronunciation is similar, but the characters are different. Anyway, let's eat here.' The restaurant was bursting at the seams. My senses reeled, assaulted from all sides—a sea of faces chatting in indecipherable tones, unfamiliar aromas wafting by. People smoked freely at their tables, diners bellowed for servers, beer bottles clinked and an endless parade of dishes emerged from the kitchen, bearing little resemblance to the orderly Chinese buffets back home.

Clearly the driver was in charge of ordering as he became

embroiled in a heated debate with our waitress, who volleyed right back. I watched their spirited exchange, bemused as to the cause of contention. Michael, Ms Xu and Mr Zhao carried on a side conversation, unperturbed—this was business as usual. Noticing my bewilderment, Michael explained, 'This restaurant is renowned for its spicy fish.' As if on cue, the waitress returned with a plastic bag that thrashed wildly in her grasp. I realised with horror that the fish we would soon be eating was still alive inside, presented for our inspection. The driver peered into the bag and with a simple nod signalled his assent. This was China in its rawness, no concessions made for foreign sensibilities.

In all my preparation for this move—the Mandarin lessons, vaccinations, history books—I'd made one glaring omission: learning to use chopsticks. Another major faux pas. The driver was especially perturbed by my clumsy manoeuvring and repeatedly showed me the proper technique. Perhaps even more objectionable would have been my left-handed grip. A Chinese seatmate on my flight had informed me that left-handed children were still forced to use their right hand here. As a chopsticks novice, I thought it wise to follow this unspoken rule.

The parade of dishes arrived in a spectacle of colours and aromas, each plate an edible work of art. As guest of honour, it was my duty to be the first to sample these masterpieces. Fish rarely tempted my palate but the sea bass topped with a chilli peppercorn sauce proved a revelation. Not a hint of the dreaded fishiness, only perfectly cooked flesh yielding to the fork. The garlic sang in harmony with the chilli peppers, leaving my lips tingling with their invigorating song. Though no stranger to spicy fare, never before had I experienced such an inspired use of these simple ingredients.

Next I was presented with the fish head, staring up at me. I picked at it with my chopsticks, then gingerly took a bite. To my surprise, it was delicious. One of my fears about moving to China stemmed from my distaste for American-style Chinese food. But in that moment, eating the prized fish head, I realised how little I truly understood about the breadth and complexity of Chinese cuisine. Everything I thought I knew was wrong. Maybe that extended into other corners of Chinese life.

As dinner progressed, Michael began to open up. With no other fluent English speaker at the table, I was grateful for the conversation. He explained he'd been born in Beijing but immigrated to Australia later. Surprisingly, he'd moved back a decade ago. I'd assumed anyone who went through the ordeal of gaining citizenship elsewhere would stay put. Many had left China over the years due to politics or to seek better opportunities. Perhaps the country was changing?

Michael laughed. 'Australia is where you retire. Beautiful but dull. Beijing is where you live when you're young.' His parents also remained in Beijing and he needed to help care for them. Only his brother, Steven, stayed in Australia. He revealed that he was married, with two small children. I was startled to learn his wife, Vicky, also worked for the company. I wondered why she hadn't joined us for dinner. He described her job and childcare duties briskly, without affection.

'Ah, enough about me,' Michael said, holding up a Yanjing beer bottle. 'Want one?'

I wasn't much of a drinker, but I also didn't want to offend again as with the tea. I explained apologetically, 'No thank you, just water for me. I'm still jet lagged.'

Michael saw through my flimsy excuse. His tone shifted, not angrily but with genuine concern. 'Glen, in China beer is used to communicate, especially in business.' I nodded, chastened.

After the meal, cigarettes emerged—evidently part of wrapping up the evening. The driver tried sticking one in my mouth but I stood firm in my refusal, hoping my rejections of smoking and drinking hadn't come across as standoffish.

Michael seemed unfazed, downing his beer and laughing with Mr Zhao. Ms Xu gave me a sympathetic look. I made a mental note as we left the restaurant: next time, drink the beer.

I had much to learn about Chinese social customs and fitting into this new culture would require some compromises. Finding that delicate balance between assimilation and staying true to myself would be an ongoing challenge.

The driver dropped Michael at his apartment, not far from the office. Ms Xu and Mr Zhao exited at the parking lot, leaving me alone for the ride home. With only silence between us, the driver switched on the radio. A melodic narration came through the speakers, perhaps a historical drama or classic like *Journey to the West*.

My apartment was still empty when I opened the door. No sign of Scarlet yet. Though I'd been in China just twenty-four hours, jet lag lent a sense of momentousness to everything. But I'd survived this first full day, even done better than expected, barring the missteps with the tea, beer and cigarettes.

As I replayed the evening's events, I realised a question Michael had put to me at dinner demanded a proper answer: 'What brought you to China?'

MORE THAN THIS

Ambition drove me to China. America had come to feel devoid of meaning, numbing in its emptiness. I don't mean to imply that my compatriots were living in a collective trance. Certainly, many led lives of purpose and contentment, but I was merely existing, not truly living. Most days I was not depressed yet knew there must be more than this. What was the point of it all?

My plan to move to China sprang from a desire to run toward something. For nearly seven years I had worked as a congressional staffer in Washington, DC. Those years under George W Bush's regime were dark ones for me. I bore witness to epochal events: Bill Clinton's final year in office, the Bush-Gore election purgatory, 9/11's horrors, the hurried Patriot Act, the inexplicable anthrax attacks. So much transpired so swiftly. New wars launched in distant Afghanistan and Iraq. Then came Hurricane Katrina, exposing government failure as the floodwaters rose. Throughout it all, there was ironclad Republican control of Congress and the White House.

I toiled in vain for a congressman in the shackled opposition, unable to advance any substantive shred of our legislative agenda. I saw then how broken Washington had become, how warped its towering institutions truly were. This so-called 'Great Experiment' of America was rotted through in practice, however high-minded its ideals.

We put forward trivial Bill after trivial Bill, trying to keep the lights on at some nearly abandoned post office or renaming a federal building. Meanwhile, the people cried out for justice, for jobs, for healthcare, for their voices to be heard over the din of bombs and bluster. But the Bush administration had stopped listening.

As press secretary, I had to schedule TV interviews for my boss to react to the president's annual State of the Union address. These speeches were pivotal nights in Washington, with reporters eager for congressional responses to the president's priorities. Members of the president's party sang his praises; the opposition cried about lack of vision.

The intense security surrounding the State of the Union meant arriving at the Capitol early. One year, in the maze of corridors I opened the wrong door and found myself face to face with Colin Powell and Donald Rumsfeld, the secretary of state and secretary of defence. I slammed it quickly, red-faced. Moving on, security forced me through another mystery door. And there before me stood all one hundred senators, lined up by state, waiting to enter the House chamber. The gravity of that room left me awestruck.

Few moments in Washington gave me such chills, however. Bush rode a wave of post-9/11 patriotism to reelection on 2 November 2004, erasing the tainted Supreme Court victory of 2000. He had won a clear mandate now. Worse, Republican majorities in Congress expanded on his coattails. I felt despair seeing the electoral map bleed red that night—the system I revered seemed irreparable. Many friends quietly turned to antidepressants in those days.

That election shattered my idealism. As a boy I'd joined the annual seventh-grade pilgrimage to DC and was captivated by Georgetown and Monticello. Now, the country I loved seemed gripped by an irrational fervour.

I was also lonely. At home I would read the *Congressional Record* and spend hours watching C-SPAN. My DVR overflowed with shows to fill the time—especially Martha Stewart, teaching me to bedazzle pumpkins and pipe cupcake frosting. I must have hit Target three times some weekends, seized by the urgent need for Windex or something to fill the void.

In many ways, I was living the stereotypical American Dream—from an Albuquerque Starbucks to congressional press secretary. Weeks flew by in a blur of 5 am arrivals and midnight departures. By the end of my time in America I couldn't stomach the dysfunction anymore. Staying would mean complicity and my soul could bear no more of that toxicity. I yearned to shake things up, to find a bold new direction.

At first I thought escape meant simply fleeing Washington and its poisoned Potomac waters. But in truth a far greater change called to my spirit. I yearned to move abroad, to see new horizons. As a curious child, the world beyond American borders had held endless fascination. I'd gaze nightly at the stars, imagining unknown eyes staring back across the cosmos. A romantic, ever an optimist—how I cherished those pen pal letters from the Philippines, Australia, Switzerland, England, India, their exotic stamps and tales of bigger lives than mine. There existed a wider world beyond America's shores.

I knew my next move had to be a dramatic change. I had always felt wanderlust but had never acted on it. Childhood vacations at my grandparents' condo in Mexico were the extent of my international exploits. We had lived in Washington State when I was young, ferrying to Victoria for fancy afternoon teas.

As I contemplated my next chapter, one theme persisted: China ascendant. This giant dominated the headlines. But what did I truly know of this civilisation beyond the Great Wall? I was thirteen when the Tiananmen Square incident happened. Amid the seismic upheavals of 1989, it seemed but one tremor among many.

While I cannot recall the exact instant when China cemented as my destination of choice, certain vivid images stand out in my memory: photos of Shanghai's glittering Bund skyline in *Businessweek*, futuristic cityscapes from *Wired* depicting China's booming metropolises. This gleaming tomorrow beckoned not from some distant horizon but over the crest just ahead. China's inexorable rise summoned those seeking new frontiers. Life-shaping experiences can await in many diverse lands across the globe. For me, only China made sense.

One blog that drew me in was by an American teaching in rural Zhejiang province. Jim's adventures trying donkey meat or navigating local markets enthralled me. He didn't sugarcoat the experience; the language barrier made everyday tasks tough. But over time, locals recognised him, sparing him from his faltering attempts to order in restaurants. They knew his preferences.

Though isolated and frustrated at times, glimpses of connection kept him going—sharing a meal, stumbling through a conversation. Villagers greeted him by name on his walks, practices becoming familiar rituals. He was carving out a place, however tenuous.

Of course, the small town offered little excitement. The

noisy bus to Hangzhou took ninety minutes. But the landscape was beautiful, the pace of life slower. He could walk for hours on quiet paths without seeing another foreigner. This solitary existence took some getting used to, but it also offered perspective. Away from the glittering expatriate bubbles of Beijing and Shanghai, he was immersed in the real China.

Finding a suitable job posed the biggest hurdle for me. With seven years of public relations' experience, I hoped to find a related opportunity. So, I posted a simple ad on an expat job board: *'Experienced American PR professional seeks role.'*

Next morning a flood of replies greeted me as I rubbed the sleep from my eyes. More than thirty responses cluttered my inbox, each one extending an invitation to teach English. Scanning through the list of unfamiliar city names, I realised that instructing eager students was the go-to gig for expatriates seeking work in China. Places like Qufu, Yiwu and Zhangjiagang—cities I had never encountered before—called out to me, their foreign syllables enticing me with the promise of untold adventures.

Surprisingly, my lack of teaching experience didn't deter them. If anything, they were more interested in my photo, seeking visual confirmation that I was a native English speaker.

Expat teaching blogs vented about constant frustrations, however. Communication was inconsistent, extra classes were sprung on them at the last minute. Cross-cultural challenges overwhelmed many teachers. It was common for disgruntled foreigners to sneak away or pull 'midnight runners'. Their abrupt departures only increased the burdens on the remaining teachers.

Now I understood why jobs teaching English were so

abundant. High turnover was clearly the norm. But I figured that with the right attitude I could withstand the challenges. My personality would win over colleagues and students. I imagined lively classes and weekend adventures with fellow expat teachers.

The sloppiness of the initial HR contacts worried me. I accepted typos, but the overall casual approach raised red flags. Could these companies properly support me overseas? Secure my visa? Understand my concerns? I was not sure I'd be an effective teacher either, with zero experience. What did I have to offer students? Even so, I started to picture myself inspiring kids à la *Dead Poets Society*. Teaching seemed the only avenue in.

'Do it for a year,' I reasoned. 'Learn Mandarin, then transition to a real career-track job.' I just had to get my experience in front of the right companies. Employment agencies that vetted Chinese firms could help.

I found one in Chicago run by Keith, an American who had previously lived in China. His barebones website didn't inspire confidence, but he had on-the-ground experience I lacked. After reviewing my résumé, he guaranteed me a job within six months for a fee of $2000. I hesitated briefly, then gave him my AmEx number, nearly giddy with excitement.

I plunged into books—John Pomfret's *Chinese Lessons*, Da Chen's *Colours of the Mountain*. At a travel clinic I shelled out more than $1000 for every recommended vaccine, even those for obscure risks such as Japanese encephalitis. I wanted to prepare for anything. Learning Mandarin was essential too. I got Pimsleur audio programs based on memory techniques and originally developed for the CIA.

I immersed myself in all things China. Even my dreams became saturated with Chinese imagery and phrases, reinforcing that this move was meant to be. Like most Generation X Americans, I'd begun knowing only superficial stereotypes of the country. Now I yearned to grasp the nuances beneath.

A month before my departure, Keith called with 'good news'. A Beijing firm, the Australia International Trade Association (AITA), needed a PR professional—the type of job I'd wanted. Living in the capital was a dream opportunity.

While the notion of an American working for an Australian firm in China may have seemed odd, it wasn't so strange for me. A pen pal relationship as a teen unexpectedly sparked a friendship with Australian sisters my age. Through airmail letters and crackly overseas calls I discovered Vegemite sandwiches, Tim Tam biscuits, Violet Crumble candy bars and the soapy intrigue of the show *Neighbours*. Mimi and Jeannette invited me into the fascinating Australian pop culture taking the world by storm, from the coy wink of Dame Edna Everage to cinematic classics like *Strictly Ballroom, Dead Calm* and *The Adventures of Priscilla, Queen of the Desert*. I was smitten. As a high school graduation gift, my parents even footed the bill for a ticket to Melbourne, where I lived with my adoptive family for an enchanting two months, relishing the lack of tipping culture and singing along to Dannii Minogue's *This Is It*. Long before I ever set foot in China, 'the Lucky Country' had already worked its Aussie charm on me. I was a 'Yank' prepped and primed for the adventure ahead.

My role would involve trade delegations between Australia and China. Another American, a young woman from New

York, would also be hired and we'd live together. When I pressed for more specifics, Keith reassured me I'd get all the details upon arrival. A sliver of doubt crept in but I tamped it down, unwilling to let scepticism taint this long-awaited fresh start.

I rushed to check out AITA's website, hungry for clues about this mystery firm. The verbose text trumpeted achievements since 1990 fostering Australia-China ties in trade, agriculture, education and more. Through its extensive network of government contacts and members, AITA facilitated major delegations and partnerships. It proudly touted support from both major parties, naming bigwig Aussie politicians who had led past trips.

The offer, Keith said, was 5000 kuai monthly plus free lodging ($650 in 2007)—perfect for someone not yet conversant in Mandarin. I would receive no health insurance or other benefits and was allowed to bring only two suitcases. It represented a huge drop in salary and lifestyle—truly madness to willingly accept such instability.

'Perfect,' I responded immediately.

Soon came a breezy email from Michael Guo, copying my new coworker and roommate-to-be, Scarlet. He welcomed us aboard, providing no further details.

Scarlet replied swiftly, asking about the office dress code and what to bring. Her email went unanswered. But we now had each other's contacts. Our call revealed that Scarlet was twenty-one years old, an eager Korean American college grad. Her enthusiasm was contagious. We discussed packing lists and coordinated visa timelines.

Despite our age and experience gaps, I felt better knowing

Scarlet would be there too. We were in this together, come what may.

In those final weeks, we speculated endlessly about the mysteries awaiting us. Michael remained vague in his sporadic replies so we filled the information void ourselves. In my imagination, AITA was a thriving firm where we'd make influential connections. Scarlet pictured a glamorous new social circle in Beijing's cosmopolitan core, maybe even a boyfriend.

Finally, Keith sent flight details: we would leave the US together on March 7. He included photos revealing AITA's office as plain and cramped but at least came furnished with computers and folding chairs. After months of suspenseful waiting our departure was imminent.

Though escaping America, my decision was as American as apple pie. Only boundless optimism enables such leaps into the void. The future was China's and I yearned to play a part. The Bush era was ending while China's star continued its rise. As one chapter closed, I stepped boldly into the dawn of the next, greeting its surprises with an open embrace.

SCARLET

I glanced up from my guidebook again, peering out the window of the cozy Beijing apartment. Though it looked brisk outside, I was snug with the heat cranked up high. So high that I'd slipped into shorts and a tank top. Scarlet was set to arrive any minute.

My eyes drifted to the bilingual sign on the back of my door, chuckling at the clumsy English translation. As long as Scarlet and I followed the rules outlined there, I had a feeling we'd get on just fine.

Please every staff notes:

1. *Maintain the wall clean. Do not paste any picture randomly on the wall or nail drawing pen.*
2. *Does not huddle the goods.*
3. *Keep the public place cleaning: the bathroom, the kitchen, the refrigerator, the ground health, and cleaning in turn.*
4. *Maintain the cleaning of oneself room and the living room.*
5. *Rinsing the curtains in time.*
6. *Need to maintain sanitation of the facilities such as the TV set. Save water, electricity and coal gas use.*
7. *Clean the trash up and put in special place. Do not put the trash for a long time in the room.*
8. *Regularly open the window to ventilate.*
9. *Avoid the air grime inside room.*
10. *Without the chief agreement, do not make the stranger to stay overnight in the apartment.*

As eager as I was to have a roommate in this foreign city, trepidation lurked. Eventually I would crave my own freedom. I came here to immerse myself in the culture and make Chinese friends, not transplant my American life. From what I could tell, Scarlet and I were vastly different people. She seemed like she was brimming with youthful enthusiasm that bordered on naivety at times. Meanwhile, I was a world-weary politico taking a break from the cynical DC bubble.

For better or worse, Scarlet was my new roomie. We'd have to find some common ground if we were going to make this odd couple pairing work.

I heard Scarlet's voice through the thin walls as she chatted with the driver, clearly asking if I was home. A gentle knock followed and I opened the door to find her beaming face. She immediately threw her arms around me in an enthusiastic hug as the driver looked on approvingly.

'You must be exhausted from your trip,' I said after she released me. 'Why don't you shower and rest a bit first?'

'No way,' Scarlet replied, already unzipping her suitcase. 'Let me just grab a warmer coat and we can hit the streets. It's way colder here than New York.'

I frowned slightly. 'But aren't you jet-lagged?'

'I'm fine,' she insisted, zipping up a puffy down jacket. 'I can't wait to explore Beijing. And I'm starving—let's get some food first.'

In our calls leading up to this, Scarlet's energetic personality had shone through. She barely paused for breath between sentences. Optimism seemed to radiate from her as she chattered about working in China for a year before grad school, like an extended gap year abroad. Having relatives in South Korea was an added bonus for her.

Some of Scarlet's friends had warned her about what she might encounter here. Since she had an Asian face, people would assume she spoke Mandarin. There was a chance some Chinese folks would insult her for being with me, a white foreigner, instead of with 'her own kind'. Interracial couples still raised eyebrows in East Asia, apparently. And she might face ridicule for being overweight in a culture obsessed with thinness. As if all that wasn't enough, Scarlet's American upbringing meant people could get offended that she didn't embrace Asian culture more. I felt bad that such prejudices existed, but Scarlet didn't seem worried in the slightest. She brushed off the warnings with optimism, insisting we would be fine if we minded our own business.

Though Scarlet didn't speak Mandarin, her frequent trips to Korea meant she was far more relaxed in Asia than I was. She recognised more cultural norms, had insider knowledge of East Asian societies and generally seemed in tune with the region. Without Scarlet, I doubt I could have survived those first few weeks in Beijing. She became an indispensable guide for me.

We decided to grab some lunch and I was going to show Scarlet how to take the bus. But given the sudden turn in the weather, we opted to walk instead. An ominous brown fog had rolled in overnight, obscuring the buildings that yesterday had been clearly visible. It was an eerie, murky scene. I lamented the poor timing. Scarlet's first day and she could barely see two feet in front of her.

The fog lifted just in time for us to spot an ornate pavilion tucked away in Longtan Park near our apartment. We paused at the carved wooden door, emblazoned with calligraphy reading 'Private Club'. Our first foray without local guides and already we faced uncertainty as to whether we'd even be allowed into this elegant bastion. Around us, the parking lot glittered with Ferraris, Rolls Royces and other luxury vehicles that hinted at the clientele within. Clearly this restaurant was the haunt of Beijing's elite.

Two hostesses in *qípáo* gowns pulled open the imposing doors to greet us as we approached the entrance. They immediately addressed Scarlet in rapid Mandarin, naturally assuming she was a native. Her tinkling laugh and helpless '*Duìbùqǐ!*' (sorry) made them pause and reassess the odd foreign pair before them.

With polite smiles, they ushered us inside to a lovely table by the window. Only one menu arrived, presented to Scarlet—the server deducing that I was the guest.

Later I learned it was customary for the host to receive the menu and order for everyone, much as our driver had the night before. But for now we simply shrugged and fumbled through the elaborate menu together. Luckily, photos accompanied each dish, a boon for illiterates like us.

We ordered liberally: juicy pork and leek dumplings with soy garlic dipping sauce, an unfamiliar but enticing duck dish, and warming soup. Fragrant green tea arrived, leaves drifting poetically. Delectable cashews too, and one mystery plate. Some alien sea creature? Scarlet gasped, hands flying to her mouth, 'It's chicken feet.' Indeed, four yellow claws leered up at us. Scarlet prodded one hesitantly. I stifled a shudder, plastering on a polite smile. We would simply have to be adventurous.

The Peking duck, *kǎo yā*, arrived next. Scarlet navigated her chopsticks with precision, plucking aromatic morsels of duck with graceful movements honed through years of practice. As steam rose gently from the lacquered skin, she gestured for me to mimic her mastery. My clumsy hands fumbled with the smooth sticks, the slippery implements colliding haplessly as I chased the shreds of tender meat around the plate. Scarlet's smile radiated encouragement as she gently adjusted the angle of the sticks in my grip. After further struggles, I finally claimed a small victory—grasping a sliver of duck and delivering its rich flavours to my tongue. Scarlet nodded approvingly as I savoured the complex blend of spices. Though my chopstick skills remained an amateur imitation of Scarlet's, it offered a window into her Asian-American tradition.

When the bill came, payment fell to me as Scarlet lacked local currency and foreign credit cards were useless. I wanted a moment to review the bill, being inexperienced with the currency, but our hovering server denied me the chance. She stood sentinel until I surrendered the money, our awkward cultural impasse broken only by nervous laughter.

The large banknotes felt like play money in my hands. Back home, such sums seemed enormous. But with the exchange rate, I could be handing over anything from $20 to $200. It was all Monopoly money to me so far.

As Scarlet's number one priority was obtaining local currency, we set off for the nearest bank.

As we turned the corner, the massive pillars and imposing grey marble of the China Construction Bank came into view, the blue logo above rows of tinted glass doors declaring its identity. I felt small passing into the cavernous lobby, our footsteps echoing off the high ceiling. Stern-faced guards tracked our progress from behind tall counters set along the walls, the velvet ropes before them separating staff areas from customer zones.

Salvation came in the form of the 'lobby host', identified by her official sash. I pointed urgently at 'exchange rate' in my Mandarin phrase book. Nodding, she clacked at her calculator and flashed us the magic numbers. Next, I pantomimed a money exchange. Another nod and she summoned us forth.

Moments later, passports and dollars were relinquished and mysterious forms were filled out in triplicate. Then, success! Crisp RMB banknotes were counted into Scarlet's eager hands. The transaction complete, we scurried out in relief.

Our next quest was procuring mobile phones. A shop window promised all the latest gadgets, posters tantalising us with deals we could not comprehend.

Behind the counter, two attendants presided over phones encased in glass. One approached speaking Mandarin that was beyond us. Relief arrived when his English-speaking colleague emerged.

Alas, our vocabulary for modern telecommunications proved lacking. 'SIM card?' 'Phone card?' I grasped desperately for the proper terms. The patient clerk persisted, equally frustrated at the linguistic barrier between us, yet utterly patient, wanting to serve his customers well.

After what felt like an eternity, we finally settled on our new phones—a slick Sony Ericsson for me and a shiny Nokia for Scarlet. Pretty advanced for the pre-iPhone era. But our tech troubles weren't over. China's pay-as-you-go phone card plans were a total mystery. Where could we buy more minutes?

How much per call? Would we get new numbers each time? Our questions in broken Mandarin were met with blank stares.

An hour of mounting frustration later, Scarlet and I completely lost it. We burst into hysterical, jet-lag-fueled laughter that we couldn't control. Probably not the best cultural ambassadors for America, but we were at our wits' end. The patient clerks watched our tearful meltdown, no doubt wondering what was wrong with these foreign nut-jobs. In truth, it was the first of many occasions where I would feel guilty for not being able to speak the language effectively.

We finally emerged as the evening rush hour descended. Hordes of cyclists and jam-packed buses ruled the streets. We squeezed aboard one bus, me uncomfortably aware of standing out as a foreigner. I felt every eye studying me, though not unkindly. Simply an unexpected curiosity in their daily commute.

Alighting at our stop, Scarlet and I knew we had to stock up on essentials to make our sparse apartment feel like home. We found a little shop selling cleaning supplies and bottled water—the basics. With no baskets in sight, I grabbed the lone bag for purchase.

Soon we'd amassed a mountain of goods to the bemused stares of the shopkeepers. The choice of brands we recognised was paltry compared to home. Why make everything in China yet sell so little of it here? A puzzling disconnect. Among the few foreign brands, such as Colgate and M&Ms, one toothpaste, Darlie, featured a beaming black man. One of Asia's top sellers, I later learned. Our cashier laughed in delight at our haul, summoning help to tally this retail windfall as customers openly gawked.

My legs ached from more walking than I'd done in ages. But it was a good ache, proof of my progress. I now had a China Mobile phone SIM card, Peking duck in my belly and I was managing to navigate the immense city. With every passing day I was becoming a Beijinger.

WORK

My alarm went off at dawn, startling me awake. Outside, the sounds of Beijing already throbbed even at this early hour. At the bus stop crowds jostled and pushed, everyone anxious to cram onboard. It seemed like hundreds of people were waiting there, the divisions of bus lines unclear, destinations unknown.

March came in like a lion that year, with bitter winds that cut through my inadequate layers. I shivered in my thin coat as we waited at the bus stop, ignoring the looks of pity and concern from the locals swaddled in their down jackets and wool hats. Workers monitored the boarding, helping to direct confused riders like us. One shouted sharply at a rambunctious child darting about instead of boarding his bus. I caught the words *xiǎo hái ér* (little kid) and felt a glow of accomplishment at understanding even that snippet of Mandarin amid the chatter swirling around me. My Chinese was still painfully limited, but moments like those gave me hope I might someday grasp this perplexing language.

Our commute was short, just five stops to our office in Guǎngqúmén Nèi on the southwest corner of Guangqumen Bridge in the Chongwen district.

Across from me, a boy sat bawling, distraught over going to school, I guessed. His father repeatedly pointed in my direction until finally the boy lifted his tear-stained face, startled at the sight of a foreigner before him. Seeing me up close made him briefly forget his distress, though unease still lingered in his wide eyes.

'Hello,' I repeated gently while he gazed back in silence. Wanting to cheer him up, Scarlet reached into her purse for a chocolate bar. But I signalled 'No'. In China, giving candy to a stranger's child could easily be misconstrued.

That first day on the job felt strangely familiar, like starting any new position back home. We went through the motions—reading manuals, meeting colleagues, trying to look busy. But my new Chinese coworkers revealed cultural differences. Their work ethic astounded me. They were disciplined, focused and deliberate in every task. Punctuality reigned supreme. Lateness brought fines and no one risked their job with lax behaviour. The office was devoid of the usual American workplace indulgences—no casual web surfing, no personal calls, no idle water cooler banter—it was all business.

AITA occupied the entire fifth floor, with Scarlet and me stationed in an office near the large conference room. At first I wondered about our odd placement by the entrance, so removed from the other offices. In time I came to see the method in it. We were positioned to be seen, a strategic move by Michael. With me seated prominently at the front, my white face signalled international collaboration and expertise to visiting clients. Our firm leveraged my foreign status for credibility, hinting at global connections.

A bilingual message was taped to the glass door of our office:

> AITA Rules and Regulations:
> AITA employees are not allowed to have private chat on office phone or internet, not allowed to send or

read emails or faxes unrelated to AITA business, and not allowed to surf unrelated websites or play internet games during working hours;

AITA employees are not allowed to do anything unrelated to AITA businesses [sic] during working hours, such as working carelessly, abusing working power, interrupting other employee's work, reading newspapers, chatting freely, or eating; employees who break the above rules and regulations;

Employees of the Department of Project Development will get fined 500 RMB for the first time, 1000 RMB for the second time, dismissed for the third time, and announced at the AITA conference; employees who damage the AITA image or cause huge economic losses to AITA for personal reasons will get punished according to the actual situation.

AITA 2007-1-15

Meeting our new Chinese colleagues was enlightening. Phoenix, the team leader, greeted us first. Petite, bespectacled, hair in a tidy bun, she had a warm smile that put me at ease. Her fashion choices surprised me though. A bold purple miniskirt with over-the-knee boots struck me as more Julia Roberts in *Pretty Woman* than professional office attire. Phoenix had studied in Australia and spoke the best English, earning her the leadership role. My first impression was that she was an earnest and diligent woman, if somewhat reserved. I was later shocked to learn of her secret life meeting men online for trysts, which was so at odds with her studious outward persona.

Sally, or Niu Qing, was next. She too had studied in

Australia, but her shy nature and quirky hairstyle instantly evoked Ally Sheedy's character from *The Breakfast Club*. At first I thought her English skills were lacking as she rarely spoke. I eventually realised she simply preferred silence to chatter. But when Sally did laugh, it was with her whole self—pure, full-bodied delight untainted by self-consciousness. She had an innocent authenticity that was refreshing amid the polished city dwellers. While others rushed to judge me, Sally took her time, watching carefully until she was ready to open up.

Then there was Judy. On our first meeting, she barely registered. Her diminutive stature and mousy demeanour made her presence almost forgettable. Her tired T-shirt featured some garish graphics proclaiming FLASHY CARNIVAL! She too had done her requisite overseas study stint in Australia but clearly failed to return with the sheen of cosmopolitan glamour. Her teeth were slightly crooked, which gave her character. She was the latest addition to the team and the most reticent so far. But watching Judy out of the corner of my eye as we made stilted small talk, I sensed depth beneath the shy exterior.

Finally we met Nick, the lone male colleague in our little office. At first glance he struck me as the archetypal Chinese man—sturdy build, cropped black hair, flashing a warm grin. I noticed his belt didn't quite fit, looped awkwardly around his lower back. Did they make belts in only one size here? A decorative ornament hung from the ill-fitting belt, likely meant to convey personality but only exacerbating the comic fashion faux pas. I had to smile at his well-intentioned style attempt gone slightly askew.

Nick admitted in hesitant English that his language skills

were limited. Yet his steady presence lent our office a feeling of reassurance. When Nick was there, we felt secure, bolstered by his attentive energy. In his absence, we all missed that warm watchfulness. He became like a big brother figure, looking out for us newcomers. His guidance and good humour helped ease our transition in those early days.

At first, I scarcely understood the deeper bond linking Phoenix, Sally, Judy and Nick—all hailing from China's northeast lands. This sweeping territory near the borders of North Korea and Russia has long been marked by turmoil. Over centuries, Manchus, nationalists, Soviets, Japanese, communists—so many—vied for control of its strategic position, mixing traditions through years of struggle.

While most Chinese cling proudly to their provincial roots, those from the *Dōngběi* region shared an affinity transcending hometowns. Theirs were hybrid lineages—fused customs and resilience forged collectively during eras in flux. My colleagues moved effortlessly between local dialects, conversing in an intrinsic shorthand. So when Phoenix named Dōngběi as her home, not any specific town or province, I began to appreciate the primal magnetism of this community welded through shared history.

I discovered a pile of past newsletters waiting on my desk, soon to become my responsibility. With my PR background I was tasked with crafting the English version—a monthly communiqué showcasing AITA's activities and successes. These were designed as marketing collateral, meant to impress clients and partners. The pages brimmed with photos of VIPs at gleaming banquet tables, men in suits exchanging hearty handshakes, and prominent officials visiting the office. It portrayed an organisation deeply embedded in political and business circles across China, Australia and New Zealand.

Reviewing AITA's materials, I grasped the depth of the firm's Chinese government ties—even meetings with the vice minister of the publicity department. This promise of insider access excited me. Although I came to China ready to leave politics behind, I now found myself simply approaching it from a new angle. AITA's robust connections were central to its success. As an American outsider, I occupied a unique position.

Beyond PR, Scarlet and I were brought onboard to provide research support, scout potential new business, draft memos, polish our colleagues' English and essentially serve as Michael's right hand. The role was broad but the opportunity clear. This would be a crash course in an entirely different market and culture.

At noon, our new colleagues led us downstairs to a waiting van where a woman dispensed mysterious little boxes—our first foray into *héfàn*, the traditional Chinese lunch box. Watching the quick exchange of cash for containers, I felt momentarily transported to some back alley drug deal. I soon learned this was standard procedure. For mere pocket change—six kuai, or less than a dollar—office workers across Beijing survived on these portable boxed lunches.

Back upstairs, we cautiously removed the plastic lids to reveal the meagre lunches beneath. The sad excuse for a meal consisted of tiny piles of bony mystery meat, a few dull vegetables, plain white rice and a wilted side salad without a speck of dressing or sauce to enliven it. It was less a meal than a ration designed to fuel the workday and nothing more. My colleagues ate indifferently as they browsed online, headphones silencing the world.

When the empty boxes were discarded after barely twenty minutes, I realised lunch here was less about nourishment or pleasure and more about simple efficiency. At 1:30 pm heads immediately dropped to their desks for nap time, another pragmatic ritual. The sight was oddly endearing. In this frantic, modernising society these small moments of rest felt nostalgically old-fashioned.

Drinking water came from towering dispensers, purified for safety yet scalding hot. Filling my cup after lunch, I glimpsed a dark speck bobbing inside. A baby cockroach. Revulsion gripped me but my officemates merely giggled at my horrified reaction.

Nick assessed the bug sombrely. 'Not very good,' he declared.

Judy urged me to inform Tan Lu, our office manager, yet my complaint was met with laughter. 'Very common,' Tan Lu shrugged, bemused by my squeamishness.

The office furniture offered no concessions to comfort or ergonomics. We sat on tiny metal stools at desks set at a uniform height, no adjustments allowed. My six-foot-one-inch frame towered awkwardly. The concept of customised workspaces had not yet arrived.

Relief washed over me when I saw the keyboard bore familiar English letters instead of endless Chinese characters. Yet navigating the computer system itself proved impossible with everything in Mandarin. Each click felt like a shot in the dark and one wrong move could wreak havoc. Begging Tan Lu to switch the system to English got an anxious laugh.

'Just Chinese here. You'll figure it out.'

It's just Chinese ...

Unable to read Chinese websites, I clicked aimlessly through Baidu, China's Google equivalent, to glimpse this parallel online world. The pages seemed crowded compared to the elegant minimalism I was used to. Baidu's homepage was a solid-black expanse but links led to a dizzying kaleidoscope of images, characters and flashing animations in seizure-inducing colours. Not an inch of restful white space remained. My eyes needed frequent breaks from the visual circus.

Nick cocked his head when I asked about the assaulting aesthetics. After grasping my confusion, he explained gently. For the Chinese, white space represented empty, wasted nothingness. Density was desirable—more content, more value packed into each page. Likewise, bright colours and stimuli attracted attention, accentuating the vibrant abundance on offer. To my Western sensibilities all that visual clutter felt suffocating, desperate even.

'In China, people won't trust a website that looks too simple,' Nick went on. 'They will think maybe the company does not have enough money.'

I realised then that this visual busyness reflected deeper cultural values about status and success. Unlike in the West, subtlety and restraint suggested instability. The crowded offices, packed web pages—it all signalled prosperity, abundance, strength.

China was modernising at a dizzying pace, with fortunes being made overnight even as tradition clung on. Business was ruthless, precarious, uncertain, so visible demonstrations of wealth and activity inspired confidence and trust. It mattered less whether such displays accurately represented reality. Perception was power.

In some ways, Scarlet struggled to adjust more than I did. As a brash New Yorker her volume defaulted permanently to eleven. When she hollered questions across our cramped office you could see our colleagues visibly startle before exchanging looks. *What is this alien creature?*

Scarlet's decibel level gradually lessened around the office. She observed how I softened my voice, slowed my speech, chose my words carefully. Bridging the culture gap required adapting our most basic modes of interaction. It wasn't enough to simply transplant ourselves. We needed to grow roots in this new soil.

The next morning, Scarlet messaged me on my computer as we settled in at our desks. 'OMG,' she typed, 'everyone is wearing the SAME thing as yesterday.'

I did a quick scan of the room and had to admit she was right. My heart sank a little thinking maybe our colleagues were struggling financially if they had only one set of work clothes.

I shot an email to friends back home going on about how blessed we are as Americans with overflowing wardrobes while these poor souls probably had so little.

Eventually I realised it wasn't about money but about practicality and not being wasteful like Westerners. Why put on a new outfit if the old one isn't dirty? Frugality and pragmatism ruled the day.

That Friday we all went out to celebrate surviving week one. No menus, no guessing games—our Chinese colleagues ordered a feast. Scarlet made the mistake of asking if anyone had siblings. A frosty reminder about the one-child policy killed that line of chatter. We sat there awkwardly as the truth sank in: some topics were verboten.

Judy's stern gaze fixed on Scarlet. 'Well? Do you think it's harsh or not?' Scarlet's shoes shuffled and tapped an uncertain beat.

'I mean, it's complicated, right? Cultural differences and stuff ...' Her voice trailed off under Judy's unrelenting stare. An uncomfortable silence descended on the group. No one looked convinced or satisfied by Scarlet's non-answer. It would only be later that we learned the full complexities of the policy—mainly targeting urban couples while rural families could have two children. Ethnic minorities like Tibetans were exempt too. But in that moment none of those nuances and exceptions were clear to us. All we felt was the weight of Judy's disapproval hanging thick in the air.

Out of the blue, Judy asked if I was German, seemingly offended. I explained I was mostly English-Irish, but she struggled with the concept of mixed ancestry. My instinct said being German was bad, given their World War II ties to Japan. Later I would learn the opposite was true—the Chinese respected German prowess and quality manufacturing. Most importantly, the Germans had owned their war crimes, unlike the unrepentant Japanese.

We were floundering through a cultural minefield, grasping for diplomats' nuance. But open minds and cultural literacy would eventually replace missteps with mutual understanding.

After work Scarlet and I skipped the bus, cutting through Longtan Park on our walk home. Two kuai got you through the gate—small change for an urban oasis like this. Come summer the paths would be packed but that bone-chilling March we had the place to ourselves. Rowing boats bobbed empty on the lake, amusement rides sat silent in the gloom.

Pollution made Beijing's sunsets pulse angry shades of crimson and rust. I'd never seen anything like it—spectacular but ominous, especially with everyone wearing face masks. It made me wonder what the locals knew that we didn't. Some mornings I'd wake up and feel my skin peeling like a chemical burn. The air was stripping me raw.

But in the park our troubles slipped away. Willows whispering, water lapping—no horns blaring, just a pocket of perfect peace. We savoured a few stolen moments of quiet before diving back into the maelstrom of Beijing. However imperfect this city, I was learning to seek out the beauty hidden beneath.

NICK

Over lunch, Nick told me of his hometown, Harbin. Once the Russian imperialists carved their railway across Manchuria in 1896, Harbin became the Moscow of the East. By the 1910s, Russian fur trappers and traders outnumbered the local Manchus and Han Chinese. In the early 1920s, a community of aristocratic Russian exiles settled in Harbin. Known as the 'White Russians', these displaced members of the former elite imported a taste for European food, fashion and culture to northeast China well before similar trends took hold in Shanghai.

The globetrotting White Russians brought a touch of old-world panache to Harbin with their vintage luggage and Continental manners. Their cafés, serving Russian fare like creamy borscht and sweet *syrniki* pancakes alongside Chinese dishes, attracted locals and foreigners eager for a taste. The White Russian community gave Harbin an unexpected cosmopolitan flair, shaping the city into a melting pot on the China-Russia border with European, Russian and Jewish influences.

For most present-day Chinese, Harbin was less about unique history and more about its famous ice festival, first staged in 1985 amid temperatures plunging to −38.1 °C, owing to its location near Siberia and North Korea. Lasting more than a month, this sparkling frozen wonderland attracted hundreds of thousands of visitors. By night, lamps illuminated elaborate ice castles and pagodas in parks. By day, tourists wandered along the frozen Songhua River with its pop-up amusement parks offering ice slides and skating. While Chinese visitors flocked to sample the far north's extreme cold, Nick felt Harbin's garish tourist spectacle failed to reflect the rich, complex history of the city.

Nick's grandparents regaled him with tales of the past—of stylish Russian babushkas promenading down the cobblestone lanes, of Orthodox onion-domed cathedrals rising beside Confucian temples, of Chinese warlords and Cossack militia standoffs in the streets. But that was before the Japanese invasion, before Chairman Mao's relationship soured with the Russians, shutting off their influence for a while.

The tinny MIDI rendition of *We Will Rock You* that emitted from Nick's TCL mobile phone was the first hint that he was different. He had escaped to the big city with dreams of getting rich. His pragmatic parents had urged him to stick with the stability of army life but the barracks held no allure for a guy like him.

So here Nick was, crammed into an apartment with three girls he barely knew, his 'own' room costing nearly his entire monthly salary. The space could barely fit his bed and a shelf that held a faded photo of his grandmother and a certificate from the accounting classes he took on weekends.

On the subway each morning, Nick watched the flashy Beijingers around him chatting on their sleek phones. He would smooth his ill-fitting suit and promise himself that someday soon that would be him. For now he would dutifully ride the packed train to his job at AITA where he hoped his expertise with numbers would eventually translate to a promotion.

In the evenings Nick sometimes splurged on a bottle of *báijiŭ* from the corner shop before heading home. Later, as he drifted off in his little room with the Muzak strains of *We Will Rock You* lulling him to sleep, I imagined he would dream of the riches that awaited him in this new city.

The first time I heard my name emerge from Nick's mouth, it came out as 'Flan'. An odd nickname but English pronunciation often tripped him up. He stared at my mouth when we conversed, his brow furrowed in concentration as he tried decoding each syllable. One afternoon as I passed his desk after weeks of this I finally made out my true name being formed carefully by his lips—he'd been attempting to say it accurately all along.

I had first noticed the wider staring after the 'Flan' incident. Now when I passed his desk, Nick would turn fully in his chair to examine me, eyes narrowed as if seeing me clearly for the first time. One afternoon, he conferred excitedly with Sally, gesturing animatedly in my direction. I only made out 'Flan' and 'Nicolas Cage' among the foreign cadences. At the mention of the Hollywood actor, Sally pivoted to study me with the same intense appraisal.

The truth emerged when Scarlet demanded to know why they kept assessing me so seriously. Nick broke into a grin, announcing with delight, 'Flan looks like Nicolas Cage.' My heart sank. Of all the movie star resemblances, it had to be him. Sensing my dismay, Nick added reassuringly, 'Nicolas Cage very handsome.' I later glimpsed my reflection and had to admit I saw the similarities in our angular features. Amusement flickered across Nick's face whenever we passed each other now, as if marvelling, *Wow, the resemblance really is striking*. I almost preferred being called Flan.

Nick took his role as my lunch benefactor quite seriously.

Each day around noon he'd faithfully appear at my desk, eyebrows knitted with concern as he asked in Chinglish, 'What you want eat?' My usual reply was noncommittal. This never satisfied Nick. So when I finally agreed to accompany him to the parking lots to pick up the boxed lunch, his face lit up. As we walked downstairs, he confided that he knew of a secret spot, even better than his usual parking lot offerings. I was game. After all, discovering hidden local eateries with Nick was much more appealing.

As we walked, Nick peppered me with his usual questions about America. Did all Americans own cars? I explained that in cities like Washington DC, many people relied on public transportation instead. He looked genuinely astonished. 'I thought every American had a car.'

Nick plainly relished these chances to teach me about his homeland. I didn't always grasp the cultural nuances—like why a host should never fill a teacup to the brim, an act representing the phrase 'leaving room for the heart.' But I nodded along, soaking up his lesson on hospitality.

The conversation turned to the Chinese zodiac and I revealed that I was a rabbit year. Nick's eyes widened in surprise. 'People in America know this?' I explained how many American Chinese restaurants incorporated the calendar and animations into their decor and menus. He chuckled, delighted that a piece of Chinese culture had taken hold across the ocean.

Nick's pace was gentle yet firm as he led me into the shadowed alley. The passage narrowed, the ground underfoot smoothed by centuries of foot traffic. We brushed past storefronts, the vendors' curious eyes following this unfamiliar sandy-haired face. Nick turned to make sure I was keeping up. '*Lǎowài* okay?' he asked, eyebrow arched with amusement. The locals' whispered repetition of that term—foreigner—trailed us as we delved deeper. Nick seemed oblivious.

The alley opened into a small courtyard dotted with a few wooden tables and bench seats along the periphery. At the centre, a makeshift grill wafted scented smoke, its chef cradling skewers of glistening fare unlike any market food I had seen. No other *lǎowài* filled the seats.

Nick motioned me inside with a proud grin, clearly delighted to expose an outsider to an authentic slice of local life unseen by tourists. The menu board loomed in indecipherable characters. I peered over shoulders at plates on nearby tables, finally pointing to a tantalising dish. 'I'll have that,' I told Nick, placing my trust in his hands.

As we settled onto a bench, Nick gestured with pride—this treasure was now mine. In his beaming grin, this outpost became singularly ours, if only for the faded red lanterns to bear witness.

As we ate, Nick watched me closely, asking if I liked the food and insisting I tell him if anything was not to my taste. I assured him all was delicious. With Nick, meals were more than just sustenance—they were a cultural exchange.

As the waiter placed sealed chopsticks packets on our table, I instinctively reached for one to tear it open. But just then, Nick said something to our server and swiftly, loose chopsticks appeared without the wrapping. Puzzled, I peered at Nick as he gave a knowing smile and dived into an explanation—it seemed the sealed parcels were a bit of a hygiene 'premium' in local perception, though unnecessary by his standards. With a wink, he told me one simple trick was to request the unfussy cutlery and save a little money. An endearing glimpse into everyday Beijing life.

As I fumbled to position the wooden sticks in my fingers properly, Nick graciously reached over to adjust my hapless grip. 'Like this, look,' he offered kindly, carefully manoeuvring my hand into a better poise. After some amused efforts mimicking his movements, he gave an approving nod at my progress and I flushed with gratitude at his patient guidance.

'You must be missing your KFC by now,' he remarked. 'We have many here, you found them yes?'

I nodded, my mouth full. He waved his hand dismissively.

'Too much oil, not enough flavour.' He raised a skewer in toast. 'Real Chinese food, this you won't get back in America.'

I had to agree as I bit into another skewer, the juices bursting onto my tongue. Such care put into each homemade bite. A far cry from KFC.

'Americans love fast food, no? Always in a rush.'

I laughed, a bit embarrassed by our reputation.

On our walk back, Nick asked if I had visited a place called 'Laughing Gas' in America. I racked my brain before realising he meant Las Vegas. Confirming I'd been, Nick nodded approvingly. Of course he knew Vegas was a premier American destination.

I told Nick he should visit the States himself one day. He grimaced, saying it was very difficult for Chinese citizens to go there. This gave me pause. I asked if he'd been to Hong Kong. He ruefully shook his head again—he didn't have a passport. When I asked if passports were difficult to obtain, his response was vague: 'Somewhat.'

I wasn't sure what to make of this. Perhaps the process was bureaucratic and tedious. Or maybe the cost was prohibitive. Nick's tight smile didn't betray much. I realised then how much privilege I took for granted as an American, able to cross borders with relative ease. Nick's world, for now, largely encompassed only this sliver of Beijing within the Second Ring Road.

One afternoon, Nick invited me to his favourite dumpling restaurant, enthusing about their renowned 'balls'. When we arrived at the tiny hole-in-the-wall shop, there wasn't an empty seat to be found—a shocking sight for Nick. He blinked in disbelief at the crowds crammed elbow to elbow around rickety tables, normally vacant during this hour. I speculated that the warming weather had enticed flocks of hungry office workers to dine out.

Unfazed, Nick marched straight towards two women chatting at a table and unleashed what I assume was a request to move. Chastened, the women hurriedly collected their belongings under his torrent of words. Nick beckoned for me to take one of the newly vacated seats.

I awkwardly avoided eye contact with the disgruntled diners displaced by Nick's demands. Focusing on the residue of sesame seeds and vinegar staining the tabletop, I could feel their gaze as I waited for Nick to return. The women slurped down their last dumplings hastily before moving on, no doubt informed their dining time was limited. I picked at the tabletop, an uncomfortable interloper in the weekday lunch rush.

The exclamation pierced through the din—'*Lǎowài!*' I glanced up to see a group of uniformed air force men entering the restaurant, their eyes fixed on me. The familiar cry, while not malicious, never failed to isolate me further. I fantasised about responding sarcastically in perfect Chinese, 'No way, I'm not from around here.' But the sentiment would be lost in translation.

As I sat scanning the filthy floors strewn with days of debris, a man nearby poured his leftover liquid unceremoniously onto the ground. I recoiled in disgust. This was the first truly no-frills local eatery I'd set foot in. When Nick returned, he slid a steaming bamboo basket before me with a flourish. 'Real Chinese food,' he declared. I watched, transfixed, as the vinegar pooled atop the dumplings' thick skin, the glaze slowly seeping in.

That first taste in the cramped dumpling shop stayed with me for years—the succulent meat, the soft chew of dough, the tang of vinegar. Long after, I made a pilgrimage to the original Gǒu Bù Lǐ restaurant. Waiting in line with locals, I recalled that magical Beijing afternoon with Nick. These were no mere dumplings, but *bāozi*, the hallmark of Tianjin cuisine.

I related the legend for my friends. How a young apprentice named Gouzi became renowned for steamed buns so addicting that crowds flocked for just one more. So devoted was he to his craft that Gouzi turned a deaf ear to all conversation, earning him the nickname that stuck—*Gǒu Bù Lǐ*, 'the dog doesn't care.'

As we strolled back from lunch, an unfamiliar fragrance wafted from a fruit peddler's cart—pungent, fermented. Nick made a face, warning me of a stinky fruit. Our colleague, Tan Lu, and others were browsing the nearby produce and called out to us enthusiastically.

Nick guided me to the suspect fruit, its spiky armour concealing flesh the hue of custard. I inhaled its complex aroma—sweet yet metallic, a whisper of vanilla but with an animal funk. The women giggled as I announced this puzzling specimen wasn't found in America. Nick nodded sagely, confirming that Westerners shunned its stink.

Days later, a newspaper article solved the mystery—the durian. Reviled and revered, its stench evoking rotting fish or garbage but its flavour heavenly. The more putrid the smell, durian devotees claimed, the better the taste. Nick's grimace now seemed fitting for this polarising delicacy.

I wondered if one day my palate might become sophisticated enough to appreciate the durian's allures, to find the scent that first turned my stomach into one that made me drool. Perhaps, as with learning to navigate a foreign culture, certain tastes required patience and an open mind. Had Nick been nudging me towards expanding my horizons in his own subtle way that afternoon? I smiled, making a mental note to seek out the durian once again should our paths cross in the future.

Nick was teaching me about China one bite at a time.

GREY AREAS

The cavalcade of black sedans rolled through Tiananmen Square. Inside one vehicle, Gough Whitlam gazed out at the crowds of Chinese lining Beijing's streets, their faces filled with curiosity and pride. The red flags fluttering overhead marked his arrival in the heart of Communist China, an unthinkable journey only a few years earlier. But now, in 1973, the Australian prime minister was about to shake hands with Chairman Mao Zedong himself, marking a tectonic shift in engagement between China and the West.

Thirty-four years later, in 2007, the fruits of that decision were evident. In Shanghai, Aussie entrepreneurs such as Michelle Garnaut carved out a niche, embracing the dynamism of China's transformed economy. Garnaut's popular M on the Bund restaurant, with its 1930s decor and hip Glamour Bar, had become a hotspot for expats and Chinese nouveaux riche alike. Meanwhile, Australian and Kiwi students flocked to China's universities, immersing themselves in Mandarin language and culture. In November that year, Australia even elected a fluent Mandarin speaker, Kevin Rudd, as prime minister.

Hordes of Chinese tourists spilled from buses into Australia's Red Centre, jostling to photograph Uluru's ancient monolith. Nearby, Aboriginal performers entertained with didgeridoos, their haunting tones mingling with Mandarin exclamations. At a Gold Coast resort, Chinese characters adorned the walls as hotel staff greeted arrivals from Shanghai and Guangzhou.

In Sydney Harbour, a Chinese naval fleet joined Australian counterparts in a parade of maritime might.

In tropical Cairns, Chinese delegates sat with Australians and Kiwis, negotiating accords on sustainability. Envoys paid respects in the halls of power in Canberra and Wellington, cementing ties between old allies even as a new giant rose in their midst. On distant Asian shores, Australian mineral shipments fed the furnaces powering China's industrial ascent. And in trendy cafés, young New Zealand baristas served flat whites to a generation for whom China was as familiar as their own backyards.

The threads between these Pacific nations and the Middle Kingdom now ran deeper than ever, transcending political systems and forging bonds of culture, commerce and cooperation. An unlikely journey four decades earlier had set it all in motion, when a bold Australian leader ventured forth to shake the hand of the People's Republic of China.

Working at AITA immersed Scarlet and me in histories we scarcely knew, making even routine tasks seem excitingly new. But Michael's unequal treatment of us soon proved to disenchant. Though Scarlet and I shared identical roles and pay, I soon realised Michael managed her far more closely, as if her Asian face merited only local wages. While he granted me autonomy, Scarlet endured constant scrutiny. Michael judged us on prejudicial perceptions. His double standards turned our crash course in Australasian history into a lesson in inequity closer to home.

The phone rang endlessly as Scarlet dialled company after company in Australia and New Zealand. The time zone differences meant their offices closed well before our workday ended. 'G'day mate' and friendly banter couldn't bridge the gap when she lacked local knowledge. Why was she cold-calling about obscure rubber gaskets anyway? Then it dawned on me: Michael had a Chinese client churning out these widgets. Any Aussie connection scored AITA a tidy finder's fee.

Scarlet's hands shook as she tallied the rows in her notebook, dreading Michael's interrogation. Two days ago, twenty-seven calls. Yesterday, thirty-one, with four requests for info. Was it enough? The clock ticked as she waited, rigid in her seat.

'Scarlet,' Michael's voice jarred her. 'Let's review your progress. How many calls made this week? Connections? Follow-ups?'

The conference room door clicked shut as Scarlet braced herself for Michael to unfurl his list of her failures—calls missed, targets unmet, expectations unfulfilled. She scribbled each criticism in her notebook, filling the pages with his accusations lined up like a shield.

When she presented her notebook with her neatly lined-up numbers, Michael scanned the pages, his eyes narrow. 'Hmm. Seems a bit low compared to Judy's outreach,' he said. His words pricked Scarlet's pride. 'Chase up the ones who didn't answer,' he told her.

As she snapped the notebook shut, Scarlet said she blinked back tears, stung that despite giving her all, Michael's impossible standards left her constantly on the defensive. His critiques meant she had to work twice as hard to overcome assumptions about her Asian face.

'Let's reconnect Friday on your plan to boost those call volumes,' Michael said, oblivious to her silent defeat.

When his scolding ceased, he casually leaned back and said, 'I'm headed to the hot springs this weekend with a friend, a colleague. Why don't you join us.'

Scarlet's stomach dropped at the invitation—a weekend getaway with Michael and another male colleague? She shifted in her seat, grasping for a way to politely decline.

'I'd feel more comfortable if Glen could come too,' she said finally. But Michael frowned, his eyebrows drawing together. 'No room. I'll pick you up Saturday at noon,' he replied dismissively.

Dismay flooded her as she hurried back to her desk, pulse thrumming. She instant-messaged me, hands shaking, 'Michael invited me to the hot springs this weekend—just us and another guy. What do you think?'

My response only increased her unease. 'Sounds like he's matchmaking. Can you decline?'

Scarlet slumped in her chair, dread sitting heavy in her gut. Rejecting Michael so directly could jeopardise her job. But accepting his invitation felt dangerous, like an abuse of power. This went beyond a kind gesture from her boss.

She had to find a way out. Scarlet composed and rewrote several emails, searching for the right tone and excuse. Finally crafting one she felt conveyed respect, she hit send:

Thank you for the invitation, but I just remembered a prior engagement on Saturday that I cannot miss without the other person losing face. My apologies.

She held her breath, hoping the vague justification would satisfy Michael without offence.

His terse reply appeared minutes later. 'No problem.'

Scarlet exhaled, relief washing over her. She had escaped for now, but Michael's intentions were hard to decipher.

After work, the aroma of coffee enveloped us as we sank into armchairs at Starbucks, exhausted from trying to make sense of what had happened. An innocent invitation, or something seedier? A Chinese woman at the next table leaned in conspicuously, eavesdropping on our hushed conversation.

After a few minutes, she said in halting English, 'I'm sorry, I don't mean to interrupt. I just came here to practice English.' She gestured at the English newspaper article before her. 'May I join you?'

Taken aback, we nodded hesitantly. The woman launched into reassurances about Michael's behaviour. 'He means no harm, just friendship. Some people good, some bad. You are a very clever girl to avoid the trip.'

Scarlet squirmed under the unsolicited praise. The woman prattled on, advising the use of wit to combat unsavoury characters.

For Scarlet, at twenty-one, the world held so much wonder and discovery. Yet some lessons arrive too soon, their meaning grasped only in hindsight. Was Michael's invitation simply cultural disconnect? The awkward fumbling of a work superior? Or a deliberate abuse of power? Scarlet could only feel her own discomfort and distrust. She sensed the situation was untenable but lacked the cross-cultural expertise to probe its deeper significance.

Scarlet was at the start of a journey, her eyes opened to dynamics she may have preferred not to see. But enlightenment brings obligation. Michael's actions were wrong—her inner voice said so, no matter how others labelled them. She refused to accept this as normal. The path forward was hers alone.

SCARLET'S CHOICE

For Scarlet and me, on the surface, everything was the same—we worked at the same company, lived together, spent most evenings chatting over dinner. But underneath, a deep divide separated us.

I was white in an Asian land; Scarlet, Korean American. Nothing could prepare me to witness the disparities in treatment she endured daily. I remained ignorant to this realm where my skin afforded undue grace. Superiors and strangers alike cut me slack, extending generosities I neither requested nor merited.

Yet scrutiny trailed Scarlet's every step, harsh judgments for daring to occupy her own skin. Especially given her curvaceous figure, which violated expectations for an Asian woman's body. Where my angular frame elicited praise, Scarlet's fuller silhouettes generated ridicule.

I knew it was only a matter of time before another culture clash occurred at the office. When it did, it came from an unlikely source—Judy. Sure, Judy wasn't exactly thin herself, but she was nothing if not blunt.

One morning Scarlet reached her breaking point. Stressed, she pulled chocolate after chocolate from her desk drawer.

Judy peered down her nose at the open chocolate box, nose crinkling as she read the wrapper. 'Oh, it's from that shop down the road,' she murmured dismissively, already shifting back in her seat. With a dramatic swivel, she fixed her gaze on Scarlet, thin lips pressed together. Her eyes blazed with scorn as they raked over Scarlet's figure.

'You really shouldn't eat so much of that,' she said loudly, tilting her head towards the surrounding women. Judy's blunt words echoed through the tense silence, punctuated only by giggling erupting from the circle of chairs. Oblivious to Scarlet flushing red, Judy ploughed on, 'And no sugar at all for you, at your size.'

The whispered laughter swelled as all eyes turned to Scarlet, who shrank under their smug, assessing stares. Judy flashed her a patronising smile before resuming her paperwork, confident in her authority.

I could see Scarlet bristle, but she tried to keep her tone light. 'Actually, chocolate has antioxidants, so it isn't as bad as people think.' Judy's comments must have felt like a slap in the face to Scarlet, who had only been trying to share a nice treat from her stash of chocolate bars.

A chill permeated the office for the rest of the day. The truth was, Judy hadn't meant to be cruel. In her mind, she was helping by directly sharing her opinion—that's how things were done here. But for Scarlet and me, it breached our American sensibilities.

Nothing cheered Scarlet up like the fried pumpkin beignets from our favourite lunch spot near the office, so I suggested we go there. The staff knew our usual order by heart—six piping-hot pastries, crispy on the outside and melt-in-your-mouth on the inside. With their pumpkin spice aroma and the indulgent drizzle of oil, they were the closest thing we could find to dessert in most Chinese restaurants.

We relished those sweet pumpkin treats as they were available year-round. No restrictive October-November pumpkin season like back home. Scarlet loved them so much she often got extras to go for weekend snacking.

As we sat and savoured our beignets, Scarlet suddenly perked up. 'Guess what? We're going to have dinner this weekend with Woojung and her friend Kuong,' she said.

Woojung was a South Korean exchange student at Peking University for the semester. They were already acquainted via a connection through family friends. Woojung's friend, Kuong, was also studying abroad but his home university was Boston College, where he majored in philosophy. I was so glad to see Scarlet smiling again after the morning's tension.

It was the most excited she had looked in a long time. I offered to plan the dinner for Saturday night. Most of our meals took place at Chinese restaurants so I thought Western food would be the best choice. I turned to my trusted Frommer's guidebook once again and found a place called Steak & Eggs. It opened in 2003, was owned by an American named Paul Astephen, and had won several awards from expat magazines which claimed it had the 'best' American food in the city. As much as we loved Chinese food, at Western restaurants you didn't feel you needed to apologise for not speaking the language.

That Saturday, Scarlet and I headed to our dinner at Steak & Eggs. We took the subway to Jianguomen Station, relaxing in the spacious cars—such a relief after the packed morning bus rides. Part of what made the subway interesting were the illegal vendors who set up shop on the stairs, ready to grab their wares and dash if the authorities appeared.

As we rode the escalator up, we passed an elderly woman holding a plastic bag bouncing with odd energy. A kitten's meows burst from inside. We froze, gaping at the woman, then the bag, then each other. With a grin, the woman held up the bag in offering. Scarlet had mentioned getting an apartment pet, but I refused, too busy experiencing China to care for a critter.

Steak & Eggs sat nestled in the original diplomatic district, Jianguomen. With so many foreigners here, Jianguomen had an international feel quite distinct from our neighbourhood of Chongwenmen. Starbucks, TGI Friday, Sizzler, Häagen-Dazs and the Beijing International Club dominated the landscape. Russian shops and restaurants also flourished with the boisterous Moscow Restaurant leading the charge.

Turning a corner, we stumbled upon a remnant of the past—a 'friendship store'. These stores once allowed diplomats to access familiar comforts unavailable elsewhere in rationed China. Chinese citizens were prohibited from entering. The two worlds were no longer so separate by 2007. Most friendship stores had since vanished as China's economy opened up. This one felt empty, its shelves bare. But some consolations remained—more international brands and convenient staples such as cheese and milk at reasonable prices. The store also stocked English books and foreign magazines—*The Economist, Time, Newsweek*. I made a mental note to return.

We met Woojung and Kuong at Steak & Eggs at six. Despite the rave reviews, the diner looked worn, practically derelict. This was the best American food in Beijing? Not a single customer filled the tables. But at least our Chinese server spoke English and thankfully we each received our own menu—no sharing required.

Scarlet shrieked with delight seeing they served breakfast all day and immediately ordered waffles. I regretted my breaded chicken strips, which tasted heavily fried. Woojung's chicken primavera looked limp and pallid. After one bite of his burger, Kuong sneered, 'Who found this place?' I kept mum, not volunteering it was my vaunted *Frommer's* recommendation.

We ordered the carrot cake the guidebook had praised. It arrived dense and dry, tasting of artificial flavours. Despite the disappointing food, for a moment we felt transported back to America. The company of friends made up for the lacklustre meal.

Our dinner was marred by the owner Paul's constant berating of his staff. Originally from Florida, Paul had plastered the diner's walls with photos and news clippings glorifying himself. His arrogance permeated the place. He hassled the servers all night. At one point he suggested a Chinese waitress try on a blonde wig to see if people treated her better as if it were a joke. I cringed at his callousness.

It struck me that even foreigners like Paul absorbed the same entitled attitudes as bosses like Michael after living in China long enough. The staff likely took these jobs hoping to work with Americans, only to deal with more mistreatment.

I shook my head, disgusted by Paul's behaviour. No matter how long I stayed in China, I vowed never to abuse authority like he did. The dinner was soured by his need to belittle those serving us. Their downtrodden faces reflected the invisible social divides that still lingered at this Western oasis in Beijing.

I'd been so engrossed in the conversation that I realised too late Scarlet had gone quiet. Her responses trailed off as she stared numbly into her glass, detached from our chatter.

When she finally spoke, her words dropped like a bomb. 'I'm going to quit.'

Quit? As in her job? I froze with my drink halfway to my lips, stunned. I never thought she'd actually leave so soon.

'Are you sure?' I asked gently. Across the table, Woojung and Kuong exchanged uneasy looks, concern creasing their faces.

Scarlet gave a resolute nod, mouth set in a tight line. 'I can't take it anymore.' Her voice cracked on the last word. 'The bullying, the harassment ...' She blinked rapidly, eyes shimmering. 'I just want to go home.'

I knew Scarlet's frustration had been mounting—the fat-shaming, that awful hot springs invitation. She deserved better. Though she'd enjoyed parts of this China adventure, she refused to finish her contract at AITA.

However, Scarlet loved exploring and wasn't yet ready to return stateside. But her decision posed risks. We didn't understand Chinese employment rules. Could people just quit their jobs? Could Michael report her to the police, affect her visa? The uncertainty made this more fraught. But Scarlet was determined, so we hatched plans.

Our apartment came with our jobs—no AITA meant no place to live.

'No problem,' Woojung said. 'You can stay with me until you find a room.'

What about money? Scarlet had some savings but not much of a backup plan. She promised to look for short-term gigs. It wouldn't be glamorous, but it would pay the bills.

'You could always teach English,' I suggested.

But Woojung shook her head. 'To the locals, Scarlet looks Asian—not a native speaker. It'll be hard to get hired, and if she does, they'll pay her less than white teachers and treat her like staff.' Just like at AITA.

We didn't know what was next for Scarlet, but she was taking that first step—the hardest one. She would figure the rest out. She always did.

On Monday morning, Scarlet went through the familiar routine of getting ready for the office. She also carefully packed the contents of her desk—the chocolates, extra pens, framed photos—into a small cardboard box. Keeping up casual chatter about the weather, no one seemed to notice when she tucked the box, brimming with her personal effects, into her bag.

After work, we packed her into a taxi with suitcases crammed around. Tears streamed down as we hugged goodbye. She blew a kiss as the cab pulled away, leaving me feeling numb. This marked a sea change for both of us. I couldn't imagine taking such bold risks at her age—I admired her strength.

I swept past Michael's assistant early on Tuesday as I threw open the doors to his inner sanctum. Michael sat enthroned behind his desk, gazing out the windows with the air of an emperor peering down at the teeming masses from his personal Forbidden City.

I planted myself commandingly in front of him and, with great ceremony, lowered Scarlet's letter of resignation atop his desk. His eyes flicked down briefly as it landed, mouth tightening. I let her apartment key clatter noisily beside it on the glass tabletop for good measure. The ensuing silence hung suspended as I gazed levelly at the tight sinews in his jaw, watching him refuse to meet my eyes.

To acknowledge my presence meant acknowledging his loss of *miànzi* in front of a subordinate. Turnover at AITA was rampant, yet the resignation of Scarlet carried extra significance. As a foreign employee, she had brought a certain international prestige that bolstered the leadership claims of Michael. Though she was there only briefly, her presence affirmed his credentials in the eyes of Chinese staff and clients. Her abrupt withdrawal served as an embarrassment, undercutting the air of exclusivity and elevation Michael sought to project. In a place where perception was power, optics mattered and this surprising resignation struck directly at how Michael was perceived inside his company.

Like a defeated emperor, he continued staring skyward while I drank in his subtle reactions. I turned on one heel to exit, my strides echoing across the floor. He could keep his precious dignity; my friend had reclaimed far more precious freedom this day. That was all that mattered.

When Nick arrived, stunned not to see Scarlet, I gently explained in simple English that she had quit. He just nodded.

I couldn't have survived those early days without Scarlet's guidance, despite our differences. We held on to each other, laughing at our faux pas and growing together. My memories of her are of smiles, laughter and zest.

And so she was gone. I found myself alone, facing the stark reality of AITA without her support. But in leaving, she also lit a spark. Witnessing her conviction filled me with inspiration. If Scarlet could firmly pave her own path, perhaps I could too.

SALLY

Strands of Sally's black hair curtained her face as she hunched over the computer monitor. Her eyes darted about like a cautious squirrel, afraid to meet my own.

When we passed in the hall, her lips would part as if to speak but clamp shut just as quickly. In meetings, I could hear the squeak of her chair as she shifted her weight.

She had spent a year studying English literature in Melbourne, imbuing her speech with lyrical Aussie inflections. But her voice rarely rose above a murmur around the office.

Once I glimpsed her smiling at a video on her phone, lips spread wide and cheeks rounding into apricots. But the Sally I knew was a timid creature who wrung her hands in her lap, eyes downcast as if willing herself invisible.

Yet when we were alone in the office, Sally swivelled to me, eyes alert, sensing an opening.

'Can you believe Phoenix took credit for my report at the meeting today?' she fumed, fist clenching a pen. 'I was up all night working on that thing.'

I nodded along, emboldened by this rare outpouring. 'She can be a bitch,' I said.

Sally's cheeks flushed crimson, her mouth drawing tight as a bowstring. She whipped back to her screen without a word, our momentary bond severed.

My cheeks burned too as I replayed my blunder. I had mistaken her casual venting for a closeness between us that was not there yet.

The office emptied like a bathtub, employees streaming out for lunch until only Sally and I remained. In the hush, words flowed easier without the pressure of so many eyes and ears.

We bonded over movies, dissecting plot twists and casting choices. Sally's eyes darted as she asked me to meet her in the conference room. I assumed it was to discuss my coming trip. But when she closed the door, her face was grave, eyes shimmering like pools.

She reached out, clasping both my hands in her own. I froze, startled by this sudden intimacy.

'South China is different,' she said, voice hushed. 'It's not like Beijing. You need to be careful.'

I pondered her words, moved by the concern that prompted this covert warning. I felt safe in Beijing, safer than anywhere back home. But clearly Sally knew dangers I did not.

Questions swirled in my mind about her motives, but I stifled them with a joking assurance I would be fine. She did not seem convinced, gaze still brimming with unspoken fears.

We stood in awkward silence until she slipped out, leaving me to puzzle over our strange encounter.

One night, my phone lit up with a message from Sally that jolted me from my drowsy bus ride home.

'I will probably leave AITA soon. I am not happy.'

I blinked. She had seemed content these last months, even cheerful on occasion. But obviously a deep discontent churned beneath that placid surface.

I was touched that she had confided this secret turmoil to me. Our lunches and chats must have watered the seeds of trust between us.

I knew AITA's sterile halls and Michael's overbearing

ways drained life from the place. As a foreigner, I had some immunity. But Sally did not have that luxury.

The next morning, Sally appeared at my desk, eyes averted as she extended a lunch invitation to her home that weekend.

I knew such an offer was no small gesture here. Sharing a meal meant opening her private world to me, unveiling the unfamiliar rituals of her family.

'That's so sweet,' I exclaimed, warmed by this sign of deepening trust. 'Yes, I would be honoured.'

Back in America, I had always been the Sanford to some Carrie, Samantha, Charlotte and Miranda quartet—the accessory gay bestie to every glamorous girl gang. We'd clink cosmopolitans after work as they obsessed over the latest celebrity heartthrob while I offered plenty of 'yases' and 'you go girls!' from the sidelines.

I was hopeful Sally might become my very first Chinese bestie. We could ditch our office drudgery every Friday for tipsy gossip sessions over lychee martinis. She could school me on all the absurdly handsome Chinese actors lighting up the cinema and tabloids, their names still a mystery to me.

Maybe one night after too many drinks, I might even get daring and ask about her romantic prospects. Surely a girl like her had a few eligible bachelors circling like sharks. A guy could dream.

I arrived at Sally's apartment complex just after 10:30 am, having wandered the labyrinth of buildings in search of her unit number. The compound stretched on, its paths and gardens meticulously groomed.

The apartment was dim and compact—two snug bedrooms bisected by a slim hallway. But every inch was fastidiously arranged, surfaces polished to a sheen.

Late-morning sun infiltrated the curtains, leaving rooms steeped in permanent twilight. Pale complexions were still prized here over the Western allure of tanned skin.

A bowl of mandarins adorned the table, perfuming the air with sweet citrus. I imagined sinking my thumbs into the thin peel, releasing a tangy spray as I pulled the flesh apart. The fruit's sun-kissed exterior hinted at the burst of flavour waiting within.

Sally glided in, mentioning her father still lived far north in Dōngběi, serving in the military. She parked me at her desk as *Forrest Gump* played tinnily on her laptop.

From the kitchen came the chop of a knife on a cutting board. I imagined Sally's mother prepping vegetables, folding thin slices of noodles into a bubbling pot.

These were the intimate rhythms of their private realm. Yet Sally had ushered me inside without hesitation, breaching the walls that separated their world from mine.

Sally's mother fluttered in sporadically, placing mystery morsels into my mouth with quick fingers. A velvety mushroom cap. A crunchy shard of lotus root. I normally recoiled from such casual handfeeding, but I held steady, not wanting to offend.

When Sally emerged clutching a shiny packet proclaiming 'Peking duck' in broad lettering, my curiosity piqued. That intrigue curdled slightly as she slid out an entire vacuum-packed waterfowl—ready to eat. My stomach lurched while my mind scrambled to reconcile this with notions of proper food handling. Ducks sold on convenience-store racks. Surely I was missing something that made this routine. I aimed to embrace new customs with an open mind, but staring down this particular duck tested my convictions. Clearly they had spent good money on this feast for me. Even the touches like *Forrest Gump* were to help me feel at home.

When Sally presented me with a glistening duck leg, I waited for her to turn before discreetly wrapping it in a tissue and burying it at the bottom of the trash. I wolfed down mandarins as cover, letting the juicy rinds tumble in to disguise my subterfuge.

I felt a pang of guilt at deceiving my gracious hosts. But I hoped my small sacrifice would nourish this friendship between us. I wanted to show I respected the sanctity of this day and honoured the gift of their welcome.

Sally's mother didn't utter a word of English, yet I immediately took a shine to this spirited woman. In her bedroom, a shapely mannequin prominently displayed where she would carefully style chic ensembles before nights out.

That afternoon, she breezed around audaciously in pantyhose ending scandalously above her knees—practically risqué attire for a woman her age. Meanwhile wallflower Sally had clearly inherited little of her mother's flair.

Honestly, this defiant lady seemed far more fun than her timid daughter. Behind the language barrier, I imagined the cosmo-fuelled gabfests we could enjoy roaring over handsome admirers.

What an odd couple this vibrant mother and retiring daughter made. I had to wonder if Sally's demureness was a mutiny against her mother's infectious zeal for life.

We eventually gathered at the small dining table, me already full but not wanting to offend by refusing more. Sally's mother watched intently as I picked at the feast before me.

Sally chimed in with translations as I dredged up a few Mandarin pleasantries, eliciting proud smiles from them both.

Between small bites, I took in the scene—this humble meal in close quarters. Sally and her mother moved in an unspoken choreography, passing dishes, topping up teas, anticipating each other's motions after countless shared repasts.

Everything about this ritual felt delicately balanced—the pace, the space between words, the equilibrium of giving and receiving. I was an awkward outsider here, unsure of the steps. But Sally and her mother waltzed through it all with grace.

After lunch, Sally led me to her bedroom as *Forrest Gump* droned on her laptop. I had plans that afternoon but reluctantly settled onto her quilt.

She reclined beside me and began stroking my hair. Her touch was gentle, almost reverent. But alarm bells rang in my mind.

I realised suddenly that our intentions here were tragically misaligned. While I sought only friendship, she clearly ached for more.

'I need to get going,' I said abruptly, bolting upright.

'Huh?' Sally blinked up at me, stunned. 'Already?'

I made excuses about a Chinese lesson. She offered to teach me instead, eyes pleading. But my mind was set on a hasty escape from this situation.

As I backed away, I glimpsed the hurt in Sally's face, her hand suspended in midair where my head had been. She reached out to bridge the gap between us, but I had already rebuilt the walls.

Yet my stomach churned, thinking of the care Sally's mother had put into this meal for her honoured guest.

In the living room, I bid the confused mother *zàijiàn*—goodbye—my regret surely evident in my eyes. Sally quickly explained the situation while I slipped on my shoes.

Part of me longed to turn back, to somehow make amends for this abrupt departure. But my feet carried me steadily to the door as a protective numbness set in.

I glanced back before leaving, taking in the apartment's warm glow. Mere hours before, I had revelled in the warmth they created there. I retreated into the central courtyard, sweltering in the midday heat. Residents milled about—playing mahjong, lounging in plastic chairs, observing life passing by.

Leaving brought relief, but also revelation. Even if I had felt drawn to Sally romantically, I was still too early in my China journey for commitment. Callous, perhaps, but true. I needed to keep my options open, see who else was out there. Too much remained unknown.

I envied these residents' rootedness in place and custom. My time here felt transient, a sojourn between other chapters. How could I plant roots when the soil still felt foreign underfoot?

But observing their ease, the grace with which they inhabited each moment, I longed for that sense of belonging. To be at home in the rituals of laughter, language and touch without fumbling or uncertainty.

Sunday night, Nick called—oddly urgent in the texting age.

'I need to ask you something, brother,' he said, laughing uncomfortably. He'd been drinking, perhaps. 'Sally's mum called me.'

I cringed, anticipating where this was headed.

'She doesn't speak English, so she asked me to ask you …'
'Ask what?' I said, though I already knew the dreaded answer.
'Do you want to marry Sally?'

I was floored. 'Nick, I …'

He explained arranged marriages were still common here. But I had to definitively shut this down.

'No, I don't want to marry Sally. Please tell her mother. I'm sorry, Nick.'

After hanging up, I collapsed back onto my bed, wishing I could disappear. The signs had been obvious, yet cultural cluelessness had blinded me. Sally had liked me from the start, but I never realised.

I thought back to our first lunch, her shy glances and nervous laughter. The gifts she left on my desk. Even her warning about my trip had been born of intimate concern.

This wasn't just culture clash—it was my utter naivety around dating itself. I had blundered in thinking she sought a best friend while Sally truly yearned for a husband. Now I had brought shame upon her family.

In hindsight, Sally's candid text had likely been a test of my feelings. Accepting her lunch invitation only fuelled her romantic hopes. I had been way out of my depth.

Perhaps declaring my sexuality on arrival could have prevented disaster. But I wrongly assumed same-gender attraction was still too taboo here. I failed to grasp how distinct orientation was from prospects of marriage in China. Ignorant, I blundered into calamity.

An icy chill descended at the office. For weeks, Sally refused to acknowledge me, her gaze passing through as if I were invisible. I kept my distance.

This taught me platonic male-female friendships remained rare in China, usually limited to old classmates or relatives. Intimate socialising generally signalled courtship intentions, a language I was ignorant of. Landmines lay everywhere for the oblivious foreigner like me.

Nothing could substitute for time itself, the slow accretion of knowledge as the years unfurled. Relationships required patience, not rushed choices made in haste. For now, all I could do was remain open and keep exploring.

The longer I immersed myself in this place, the more its secrets were revealed. With each new encounter, another veil lifted.

THE GREAT WALL

I rarely got food poisoning in China, but when I did, I caught it from American chains. The first time, I'd bought a vanilla ice cream cone from KFC—I'm not even sure it was dairy. At the very least, it didn't appreciate being eaten. A little while later, I visited the Starbucks connected to the friendship store across from the St Regis Hotel in Jianguomen. They had some samples of cheesecake out on the counter, so I grabbed one. It wasn't until I fell violently ill the next morning that I realised the cheesecake probably needed to be refrigerated.

There was no way I was missing out on a trip to the Great Wall. I rummaged through my medicine cabinet, downed some Imodium to settle my angry stomach and trudged into the office. The warm spring air felt amazing on my clammy skin as I walked. Though I felt miserable, seeing my coworkers' excited faces as we prepared for our adventure gave me a burst of energy. I wasn't about to let a little fever spoil my fun. The Wall awaited.

At 10 am we gathered outside, where two shuttle buses awaited. Coworkers chatted happily, ready for our outing. But nausea churned inside me.

Nick steered me onto a bus and into a window seat. The plush seats promised comfort, but with no bathroom onboard, I squirmed through a cheesy killer whale movie on the overhead TV. As we crawled through traffic, Beijing's vastness sank in. The tour guide's echoing microphone irritated me during the two-hour drive just to reach the countryside.

Nick interpreted the guide's spiel through his pocket translator, our bridge over the language divide. He had served two years in the military and was now a reserve soldier, barred from overseas travel—the government feared recruitment for espionage.

I typed, asking him his religion. 'Buddhist?' He said military service required devotion to the Party, precluding faith. But otherwise, personal beliefs raised no issue.

'Glen, I have a question, if you're comfortable,' Nick said. 'What do Americans think of China and Taiwan?'

My chest tightened. Certain topics held danger here. Was this a test? Despite Nick's affability, did he aim to suss out my views? Worse, an informed response eluded me.

I cautiously answered. 'Well, most see Taiwan as separate, but it's complex. People want peaceful reunification, however that looks. Selling them weapons means we're worried about attack, I guess. It's pretty sensitive.'

A DC press secretary's spiel—acknowledge issues without taking a stand. Though I doubted it satisfied him, I couldn't risk more. I made a mental note to study the One China policy.

Nick leaned in. Expectant, I braced for follow-ups but they never came.

Arriving at the Great Wall felt like entering another world, Beijing's smog was a distant memory. Crisp blue skies stretched overhead, the very air scrubbed clean. Though a historic site, it felt like any rural village. Roadside fruit stalls, meandering tourists, the scents of spring optimism clung thick as honey after winter's chill.

Locals wore the weathered look of the countryside—rough hands, scrappy grins. They could handle anything tossed their way. Far from the city's sleekness, these were salt of the earth people.

I breathed deep, letting the country fill my senses—warm wind tousling my hair, birdsong, soil underfoot. Already I could feel the clutches of illness loosening.

We filed into a restaurant and anxiety gripped me. Public eating remained a trial as the sole foreigner. The Chinese entered a state of total focus when it came to food. Their chopsticks became blurred flashes, swirling and diving as they shovelled bite after bite into their mouths. Meals disappeared within minutes, the frenetic pace leaving splatters of oil in its wake. In this culinary frenzy, nothing else mattered. My skills left me scrambling for stray morsels during the whirlwind. Worse, the ceaseless toasting. You'd barely grab a bite before the next round began. Try as I might, their complex dance during meals eluded me.

The giggling girls from the office mockingly eyed my clumsy chopstick grip. I didn't know them well, but I could tell they were amused by my fumbling. Glaring back, I wielded the chopsticks defiantly, my pride stung by their laughter. Chuckles surrounded me as I fumbled with my food, but I was determined to show my mettle. Though my dexterity with the thinner noodles still needed work, I sought the broad, flat potato noodles—much easier for a chopstick beginner to grasp. The girls may have had a laugh at my expense but I had shown I could persevere. With practice, I'd be a pro in no time.

My tablemates asked constantly if I enjoyed the food. This weekend's refrain—'Do you like?' 'Are you happy?' Whatever my actual feelings, I always smiled and nodded.

After lunch came the touted hot springs; but my visions of natural outdoor pools were dashed when we entered a gym filled with hot tubs. No chlorine smell either. Alarm bells rang. Wise Judy skipped this trip; on Monday she asked if it was sanitary. 'Nope,' I replied.

Public restrooms loomed large. I avoided them when possible, unsure of the rules of engagement and wanting to avoid standing out. In Beijing, maybe half the restrooms had Western seated toilets. The rest? Squatters. Drop your pants, hover your tush and let loose into the hole below.

The locker room brought a new dread. My colleagues stripped freely, zero embarrassment even with workday reunions ahead. Mortified, I stood paralysed as they bared all. Nick had wisely made himself scarce.

A muscular guy nearby caught my eye as he changed into his swimming trunks, revealing a chiselled chest that made my pulse quicken. Acutely aware of my own body, I undressed at a glacial pace, taking an excruciatingly long time to remove just one sock. My cheeks burned when I noticed him and his buddies watching me, their laughter echoing off the tiles. But I sensed no cruelty in their amusement, only a sense of recognition at my obvious discomfort. The concept of needing privacy to change clothes clearly bewildered them, as if they couldn't fathom why I would feel self-conscious in the first place.

Part of me envied their carefree attitude. People were just people with the same needs, nothing too shocking here. If only I could embrace that simplicity. Instead tension gripped me at every flash of flesh.

In time, my rigid boundaries softened. Their joyful lack of

inhibition held an appeal. Bit by bit, I felt my mind expanding to embrace new possibilities.

Despite my swimming prowess, I felt uneasy here—my first indoor pool and cleanliness seemed dubious. I swam just enough to be polite, not wanting to seem above it all. But my manoeuvring was for naught—I got booted for lack of a cap.

Approaching a hot tub, the grey water gave me pause—I sunk my legs only briefly into that murkiness before retreating. The sauna became my refuge instead. I'd always loved sweating out toxins and after being immersed in Beijing's smog, a detox felt overdue. Taking a deep breath, I leaned into the dry heat, letting it cleanse me.

I raced back to be first to change, emerging with Nick before the others. We took a walk around town, with him tutoring me on culture as we went. Each lesson began with 'In China ...'

We paused at the entrance to a shop, a guardian pair of stone lions flanking the heavy wooden doors.

'The one with the ball is the male,' Nick said, drawing my attention to the statue on the left. His fingers traced the carved contours—the lion clutched an engraved ball under one sturdy paw, its fanged mouth curled into a permanent snarl. 'According to Chinese tradition, he protects the building.'

His female companion stood watch on the right, her own mouth frozen in a soundless roar. One claw rested gently atop a playful lion cub, symbolising nurturing feminine energy and the cycle of nature.

Though no lions had actually roamed the lands of ancient China, diplomatic envoys returned from Central Asia with stories of the magnificent beasts now captured in stone.

The early carvings blended these legends with native myths, incorporating the tiger's stripes and horn of the mythical beast *qílín*. Over dynasties they evolved, first guarding only imperial tombs before creeping slowly into everyday spaces—bridges, gardens, homes. Though once defenders against invisible evils, they persisted now as figures of luck and prosperity, Nick said.

I gazed at the weathered pair with new admiration. These icons carried centuries of history in their simple forms, a new lens to uncover the layers of culture and meaning. Nick was opening my eyes, shining light on a profound world I had never glimpsed so close to the surface before.

Nick embodied the caring mentors I would need, illuminating without condemnation what I could not yet see. I had so much more to understand—and he represented where my journey would lead. Teachers like him would slowly unwrap the mysteries before me, one 'In China ...' at a time.

Exhausted from the day's activities, I drifted off to sleep on the bus as our group headed to the next stop. I was jolted awake sometime later when we pulled up to an old farmhouse where we would apparently be spending the night. Many farmers in this region rented out rooms for extra income, making for a quaint place to stay.

I awoke at dusk to find mountains surrounding us, with the Great Wall visible in the distance. The farm was overflowing with spring blossoms, choruses of yellow, pink and white trees bursting into bloom.

Our room held a *kàng*, the brick stove beds used up north. Nick, the driver, and another man would share it with me.

'Usually there's a fire below for warmth,' Nick explained. 'But it's warm tonight.'

I exhaled in relief, unable to fathom dozing atop a blaze.

Nick and I explored before dinner, wandering past roaming, eager village dogs. A mother German Shepherd nursed pups outside a barn. They'd skitter up, size us 'city folk' up and scoff.

Dinner was at the farmhouse and I delighted in the soulful meal. Sweet potatoes and cornbread—my colleagues deemed the fare quaint and novel to an outsider, repeatedly explaining its humble nature. Midway through, I realised we ate at the 'VIP' table, designated by ornate glass dishes being used. As my guide, Nick joined me for this honour, despite normally being relegated to lower tables.

Though the food was plain, homestyle country cooking, each bite brimmed with a wholesomeness that I appreciated. This loving family cooked with a deft hand and generosity of spirit.

As we savoured the tastes, I felt connected to generations past who drew sustenance from this fertile soil. The old stone *kàng* stove, the timeworn wooden table engraved with decades of memories, the farmer's weathered hands—history itself dwelled here. No fancy Beijing banquet could match this honest fare.

After dinner, Nick took me outside, sacrificing status to spare me the incomprehensible chatter. Under the stars, the night air was crisp and untainted, not possible to see in light-polluted Beijing. Nick pointed out constellations, apologising that he only knew the Chinese names.

'It's okay, I want the Chinese,' I said. He showed me *Běidǒu*, the Big Dipper.

I had loved astronomy as a child, even dreaming of it as a career before being scared off by the math. But the stars still enthralled me. Standing there with Nick by the ancient wall, learning new names for the familiar heavens, felt surreal, like childhood dreams made real.

I couldn't believe I was actually here. Who else across time had craned their necks at this sky? Now I too walked beneath its mystery, bridging ages and cultures to share the experience with Nick.

Some memories lodge in you forever. These images take root, growing over time rather than fading. That night would be one of them for me—the ancient snaking wall catching the day's last glinting rays, the sagging farmhouse still sturdy in its bones, the purple dusk sky strewn with stars that now felt familiar. I knew that when I glanced back years later, I would find my mind wandering to that humble meal swallowed in a chorus of crickets, that aroma of cornbread and soil, the quiet company of a universe glittering down without judgment or borders. This night had seared into my identity.

CALVIN

Security personnel may at times place foreign visitors under surveillance. Hotel rooms, telephones, and fax machines may be monitored, and personal possessions in hotel rooms, including computers, may be searched without the consent or knowledge of the traveler. Taking photographs of anything that could be perceived as being of military or security interest may result in problems with authorities. Foreign government officials, journalists, and businesspeople with access to advanced proprietary technology are particularly likely to be under surveillance.
—US State Department consular information sheet concerning China, 2007

I wanted to call it a nightmare, and I would have if there had been gods, monsters or anything like that in it. I couldn't call it that because it was just Calvin, and kind souls like Calvin don't show up in nightmares. So I called it a dream.

I had met Calvin for the first time earlier that day and the unexpected depth of our interaction took me by surprise. The meeting had been nothing short of a delight. My dream wasn't marred by any unpleasant event as it was by disappointment in how wrong I was.

The expectations I had ahead of arriving in China were

set in stone. After all, it was China—a Soviet-era police state, or at least something that resembled one.

Having extensively read—and visualised—countless stories detailing the experiences of Americans visiting the former Soviet Union, I had convinced myself that Chinese agents would monitor my every move. And when I arrived in China, I couldn't bring myself to stop looking over my shoulder.

It was the era when sunglasses paired with Bluetooth headsets were a thing, but chills went down my spine whenever I saw anyone sporting the look. The thought of being cornered and possibly dragged down an alley by someone with a code name had me double-checking anyone who came within five feet of me, something that made life difficult in a country with crowded public places.

I know that at first glance all this looks like needless paranoia or even a bit of xenophobia, but it didn't seem like an unreasonable stretch back then.

On the night I first met Calvin, it didn't take long for me to be convinced that he would confirm all my fears. He showed no hesitation in diving right into geopolitics or other sensitive topics. Calvin seemed to relish the kind of conversations that the majority of my other Chinese friends steered clear of because they were perceived as 'taboo' subjects. I suspected most of them weren't too interested in matters of international relations as their careers required more attention. Or perhaps they avoided those topics out of respect for unspoken boundaries, or maybe knew how apprehensive I already was and didn't want to make it worse. In any case, Calvin didn't care.

Calvin casually strode into my world through that obscure American doorway called *Craigslist*, a portal little known to locals in those days. When he replied to my personal ad about language exchange, he insisted we meet that very night.

'Calvin?' I asked, rising from my seat. He beamed in affirmation and shook my outstretched hand with enthusiasm that looked out of place in the sleepy atmosphere of Starbucks in Chongwenmen.

His sharp grey flannel and crisp pleats stood out among the sea of wrinkled khakis around us. As did his conduct towards me. The lines of his custom-tailored suit hinted at new money but his cocksure smile suggested there was more to him than buttoned-up conservatism. The fluorescent light caught a flash of his perfect teeth in a wolfish grin—dangerous yet charming. At first I wasn't sure whether to go ahead with the meeting or make a run for it. Thinking about it now, I'm surprised I stayed.

We had barely gone through our first cups of coffee when Calvin suggested we go somewhere more local, Houhai. He sprang to his feet like a man on a mission before the last sip of coffee completed its journey down our throats. I followed suit, infected by his agility. He flagged down a cab with an impressive single authoritative wave before giving the driver directions in what I'm sure were the fewest words possible.

Neon danced across the water in an undisturbed rhythm, the lake still and peaceful under the glittering lights. Establishments ringing the water's edge beckoned with music and laughter. But I lingered at the shore, taking in the quiet ripples at odds with the fiery beacons blazing all around. Calvin led me to a quiet Vietnamese restaurant, Nuage, explaining over dinner how the cuisine reminded him of his childhood in Guangxi Province, which bordered Vietnam.

'Canada was liberating, you know?' Calvin said, picking at his spring rolls. 'Those years changed how I see the world.'

I lifted my wine glass, eyes locked with his, listening to him spur on about Montreal's jazz clubs and European cafés while his family waited at home. I was surprised by how eager he was to dive right in, and I wondered what inspired a married father to seek out the company of an American stranger.

'China can feel claustrophobic at times,' he continued. 'Even working for an advertising firm connected to CCTV, I'm still just a cog.'

'Is that why you're on Facebook and Flickr?' I asked. 'To feel free?' I used to think feeling like an insignificant puzzle piece was an American thing, or at most a thing of the West.

Calvin laughed, a wistful look in his eyes. 'You understand. Most foreigners I meet just want to practice Chinese or make business connections with a local. But you ...'

I swirled the pale liquid in my glass, the candlelight dancing. 'But I what?' I was curious as to what he thought was different about me, mostly because I wanted to see if I believed him.

'You make me want to spill all my secrets.' Calvin raised a smouldering cigarette to his lips, gaze never leaving mine. 'Shall we order another round?'

There was an electricity about him that made me forget he worked for Beijing Future Advertising Company, a subsidiary of China Central Television, or CCTV. While the ads he sold were mostly for entertainment programming, he *did* work for the Chinese government. What truly inspired this Guangxi man?

Every friend in China expanded my understanding, each one a professor of China 101 conveying their unique perspective of this vast, diverse nation. Simply by being a foreign English speaker, I gained free tutelage on the local culture.

Yet with each conversation we had, I realised I had to brace for unpredictable insights or prickly revelations that were seemingly lurking on the tip of this middle-aged Chinese man's tongue. Calvin's candour provoked thrill and apprehension in almost equal measure, with the apprehension slightly edging it. We navigated risky terrain with no guides other than our sometimes conflicting experiences, with easy banter shadowed by the threat of swift descent into controversy. A misstep hid behind any casual chat. I marvelled at the insider's view I got while treading uneasy ground, wary of triggering tripwires.

I sensed a shift in Calvin's demeanour before he began to speak—a subtle darkening in his gaze, shoulders tensing as if bracing against a sudden weight. He had switched from the breezy, urbane companion I had known almost in an instant.

When he eventually spoke, his voice emerged low, stripped of its usual warmth. 'I need to tell you something. About where I was in 1989 ...' He drew a sharp breath, eyes boring into mine. 'I was there. At Tiananmen Square.'

I studied his face, reading what I could in eyes gone distant, in the tense lines that suddenly creased his features. Behind my measured silence, curiosity raged through me, a storm of inquiries battering relentlessly for release. Was he there? And if he was there, what did it mean? Did it imply he was an anti-communist activist hellbent on overthrowing the party? Or, as he explained, the protests weren't actually about democracy as much as they were about wanting reform. Could I get in trouble for associating with him if the government found out? Or was he testing me? Had he lied to assess my reaction?

Perhaps he intended to discern if I would express approval over his participation or observation of such a sensitive event in Chinese history. I recalled him making some comments that might have indicated dissatisfaction with the government ... but wasn't he with the government? He worked at CCTV, after all.

To my relief, he didn't demand an immediate response from me, electing instead to divert the conversation. 'I don't know what the future holds,' he said. 'I want to raise my daughter in China, but I'm also concerned about the future here. We're getting much better in China, but there is still an unsteadiness. It could go either way. We could end up like Iraq.'

'Iraq?' I repeated, more confused than ever. Comparing the two countries seemed illogical.

He explained that because of China's diversity, the country might split up into several different countries if anything catastrophic happened and conflicts rose to unmanageable levels. 'Wouldn't that be awful? Imagine all of that history just vanishing,' he lamented, a sour look on his face.

In the years that would follow, the Chinese government's actions in Tibet and Xinjiang made me realise that Calvin's forecasts were not farfetched. Whether described as forced integration or cultural assimilation, these were likely calculated manoeuvres to consolidate and secure unity. Destabilising ethnic factions spelled catastrophe for such avid students of history as the Chinese leadership proved to be with their high esteem for traditions.

Calvin worried far more than most, which I found quite disturbing. He was what you could call well established: an international degree, a good job, a family and many more options than the average Chinese person. If someone in his position felt so concerned about the future, was there any hope for all the young people I'd met who were still trying to find their footing and determine what direction their lives would take?

The rest of our dinner was quite enjoyable. Calvin was delightful when he put his many worries aside and it was almost shocking how quickly he could do it. 'Since I invited you, I will pay the bill. I'm the host,' he proclaimed. I often felt guilty about my Chinese friends constantly picking up the tab, but I felt less so about Calvin paying. After all, he was older than me and a successful advertising executive at that. Beyond that, he had a way of making you feel at ease and being so cool about everything.

We strolled around the lake after dinner, still engrossed in conversation. Calvin never seemed to run out of things to discuss and it astonished me how much wisdom and knowledge he had to impart. Since he'd previously lived in North America, I also got the sense that he understood me better. Between dinner and our walk around the lake, we spent almost six hours in each other's company and didn't leave Houhai until well after midnight.

'I want you to meet my family next time,' Calvin offered with a smile. With that, he flagged down a taxi for me and explained to the driver where I needed to go.

The night had been enlightening and pleasant, the kind that makes you sleep with a smile on your face, but it was followed by an unsettling dream. I jolted up, shaken from a nightmare in which all my fears became reality. Calvin was an agent of the Chinese government, trying to gauge who

I was: friend or foe. After I had woken up, I felt downright silly and a bit remorseful for having such absurd notions creep into my dreams. But despite our extensive chats, I knew next to nothing about him. Speaking to a foreigner, much less an American stranger, about such delicate matters seemed unimaginable for most Chinese people.

I had since discovered that communism in China didn't appear to resemble the Soviet model that I had grown up seeing on TV, but I also reminded myself to be cautious and to tread carefully. It was impossible to be aware of something yet unknown to me. Besides, no one ever died from being a little paranoid, at least not that I knew of.

A few days later, I emailed Calvin an article from the *New York Times* that was part of a series in 2007 about Chinese manufacturers producing tainted goods. A few more emails later, he wrote:

> 'Interestingly enough, the authors have made a few good points that China has to face seriously. However, things might not work in the same way here as they do in other nations. Think about how people, bicycles, rickshaws and cars go through a street crossing at rush hour every day; perhaps they are all in danger, yet they make it most of the time. I guess this society has its unique principles underneath the surface which keep the world rolling along. Let's look at the positive changes, do what we think is the best, and pray for it.

Sometimes when I talked with Calvin, he appeared stiff and on edge, as though balancing on a tightrope of tension.

Once when I casually mentioned wanting to browse a pirated DVD shop, he insisted we go that very instant, unable to even wait until the next day. The urgency in his voice bordered on panic. I often wondered if this was something to be wary of, but his actions never gave me any concrete cause for worry.

During another evening at dinner with his friends, our conversation touched on my previous career. 'You didn't tell me you worked for Congressman Udall,' Calvin interjected, though I had shared no specifics beyond being a former Capitol Hill staffer. I froze with my wineglass halfway to my lips as the table conversation flowed on around me. How would Calvin know which official I had served if I hadn't disclosed that tidbit? The realisation dawned—he must have researched my background. But why did he do that? I quickly shrugged off the uneasiness. Calvin loved to have information and it didn't seem too weird that he'd want to know more about a person he was spending so much time with.

Whenever I read any news about China in the international media, I began to look forward to discussing it with Calvin and inquiring into his intense convictions. His age granted him experience, which meant his opinions were quite practical and mature, and his fluency in English was a bonus that made for more extensive discourse.

The *Washington Post* published an article about riots occurring in Guangxi, Calvin's home province. It stated how government officials had travelled for a compliance check to a part of the province where the one-child policy hadn't been enforced in many years. Tragically, when the officials found families with more than one child they issued fines equivalent to several thousand US dollars. Many people in this particular town had simply ignored the policy, so mayhem was erupting.

When Calvin claimed that he didn't know about the unrest, it didn't surprise me—Chinese media had a reputation for its censorship. However, he knew all about China's restrictive one-child policy and had discussed its strictly enforced parameters with me in detail before that. In typical Calvin fashion, he'd alluded to its advantages and disadvantages and the fact that the government had arbitrarily enforced the policy in different regions of the country. Cruel tales of forced abortions would circulate in certain remote villages—but if you travelled elsewhere, you could meet plenty of families with multiple children. As with many other matters concerning China, it wasn't always black and white. I was beginning to realise that it was probably that way in most parts of the world.

It became apparent early on that our relationship would centre on conversations about Chinese culture and etiquette and issues in the news. I had a little fantasy about how I'd pick up Chinese as an extra language, but as with many of my other language exchange partners, Calvin preferred to converse in English than to teach me Chinese. One critical phrase that he did teach me, however, was how to tell a taxi driver that I was ready to alight. '*Zài zhèr tíng ba,*' words that I would go on to repeat a thousand times over. I always thought of Calvin when I did.

While it might have bothered others, I didn't mind that Calvin hadn't taught me much Chinese. He had a lot more to bring to the table and our conversations had taught me valuable lessons beyond language. The vast wisdom he shared with me was worth more than having another language tick.

One Sunday when Calvin and I met for lunch, I realised I had only scratched the surface during my previous visits to the 798 Art Zone. As we wound through the narrow alleyways, the old factory buildings loomed around us like relics from a forgotten era. Calvin brought the place to life in a way that you would only expect a tour guide to be capable of.

'This used to be Factory 798, a military manufacturing centre,' he said, hands glancing over the faded redbrick walls. 'Back then none of the state-run factories had names. Just numbers.'

I peered up at the sawtooth roofs rising steeply overhead. Calvin explained how their sharp angles let northern light flood the production floors below while blocking the harsh summer sun, maximising natural light to conserve energy.

'The Soviets helped us design them originally,' he added.

We emerged into a hidden courtyard, once perhaps filled with equipment and workers but now hosting an outdoor exhibition of abstract sculptures. I recalled reading how Factory 798 faced demolition in 2004 until public outcry helped transform it into a hub for Chinese contemporary art. The old buildings found new life as galleries and cafés rather than fading into rubble and dust. The utilitarian architecture itself became part of the allure.

As we explored 798's new incarnation, its industrial bones now intertwined with modern creativity, I was able to deeply appreciate the beauty of the history and future contained within those brick walls. And with Calvin there to decode and embellish it with his vivid narration, I saw twice as much.

After his tour, we had lunch at a Korean restaurant in the complex.

'I'd truly enjoy having you over,' Calvin confessed over bibimbap, his voice tinged with regret. 'But my father-in-law is ex-air force. They keep their compound locked up tight.'

My chopsticks froze halfway to my mouth. 'Your father-in-law is military?' I could almost feel the blood flowing away from my now half-numb knuckles.

'A general once, but don't worry, he's harmless now.' Calvin's grin reminded me of a fox baring its teeth. 'I probably shouldn't even tell you this, but some of those apartments near your place in Chongwenmen? They're filled with top brass.'

Maybe it was how casually he had said it, but it didn't take long for me to regain my composure and the blood flow to my knuckles. I wondered if he noticed how my chopsticks were moving a lot slower.

We finished eating and climbed into Calvin's government-issued car, the buildings and crowds of the art district fading behind us as we drove halfway across the sprawling city. The Summer Palace disappeared in the rearview mirror before Fragrant Hills came into view, a refreshing oasis of vibrant green. I never could have found this hidden paradise without Calvin's guidance. It was yet another beautiful experience that I owed to him.

He parked at a small café nestled under the hills. A wooden sign reading 'Sculpting In Time' hung above the door. We sat at a patio table, the hills rising around us, the air clean and crisp. Three cats soon joined us, curling up under our chairs as if we had always been friends. Time seemed to slow and the hectic downtown had been replaced by unbelievable tranquility.

Calvin told me the owners were a Taiwanese couple who had opened several branches in Beijing. 'Most people call it

SIT for short,' he said. The Western vibe brought in young Chinese customers, especially those who ordered coffee instead of tea. I pictured their other branches bustling with customers in Wudaokou and Fuxingmen. But here, it felt like time was ours to do with as we pleased. The hills stood sentinel and the cats dozed without a care as we whiled away the afternoon under the sign reading 'Sculpting In Time'.

I had mentioned to Calvin my preference for photography over painting. He remembered and when we settled into the café, pulled out his MacBook Pro emblazoned with a glowing apple.

'Let me show you some of my photos from Canada,' he said, eyes bright with enthusiasm. His laptop awake, he angled the screen towards me.

A rocky coastline emerged, evergreens dusted in snow clinging to the cliffs as icy waves crashed below. 'Newfoundland,' Calvin remarked. He clicked again. On a street in old Quebec appeared stone buildings clustered along a cobblestone road under a blanket of white. Another click revealed the expansive teal face of a glacier, tiny kayakers paddling across the rippled cerulean water.

Calvin had a bit of small talk or a series of witty stories to garnish every picture as he flipped through, his words flowing faster, his expressions more animated. He swiped through vistas of Vancouver's glass skyscrapers mirroring the mountains behind, then the thunderous roar of Niagara Falls' cascade unleashing itself over the cliff.

Though my memories of visiting Canada were faint, seeing Calvin's eyes light up as each new scene embodied his passion for the country he had called home, I couldn't help but feel a kind of affection for the place myself. The vibrant hues and thoughtful framing of each professional quality shot unveiled the depth of his connection. I could scarcely fathom how these landscapes must have appeared to him having grown up in pastoral Guangxi. His photos sang with a fondness for his adopted land. No need to tell—the images said it all. But Calvin still told and did so most beautifully and impressively.

Eventually, the informal chats ended and, as usual, we steered our conversation to heavier topics.

'Do you think the Chinese government would ever just fold and give up on the Taiwan issue?' I asked.

His answer came instantly and adamantly: 'No way.' He explained that if the government did that, it would be eternally blamed for letting Taiwan break away permanently. It was the first time I had ever considered the possibility that the Communist Party bowed to the preferences of the people, but it made sense. From my Western perspective, Taiwan seemed like such a small issue in the grand scheme of things and it gave America so much leverage in the region that just walking away seemed more strategic for China than doubling down. Calvin, however, disagreed.

'Not having control of Taiwan makes China vulnerable to attack,' Calvin remarked over his cup of coffee. 'If a foreign military planted bases there ...' He trailed off, brows knitting.

I leaned forward, drawn in by the vigour with which the historian in Calvin conjured up and dissected past conflicts. He explained that experts now recognised that the Axis powers in the Second World War ultimately failed because they overextended, draining resources by trying to span the miles between supply and demand.

Through all the hours we spent touring galleries, dining in restaurants and talking about history, he hardly spoke of his wife and daughter, except for when he mentioned that he would like me to meet them. For a culture that prized family as paramount, Calvin seemed strangely content to while away night after night hosting lavish dinners with a foreign friend rather than heading home himself.

I had stereotypically assumed that family time would be precious for Chinese men, picturing heartwarming anecdotes and proudly displayed family photos. Calvin shared no such sentimental familial attachments. His daughter never tumbled giggling into his arms upon returning home late. No doting wife tidied his collar. The bar crowds and posh restaurants held more allure than home.

When one of our appointments brought us to Gold Barn, a popular Yunnan restaurant in Sanlitun, Calvin finally began to open up about his marriage over deep-fried chicken wings that were irresistibly crispy on the outside and juicy on the inside. He spoke with some hesitation about how he and his wife had been married for twelve years; things had worked well enough until 'the child' was born seven years ago. After that, his wife stopped tending to him and seemed to care for him much less. Their lives seemed separate and his wife moved into another bedroom with their daughter, a routine that persisted even seven years later. In his words, 'She changed.'

Calvin's admission shocked me. I had come to realise that Chinese northerners were much more open, whereas southerners like Calvin rarely spoke about personal affairs. He could go on endlessly about politics, but speaking about matters of the heart came with notable difficulty.

'My wife is so controlling—she can explode at the most minor things. If I don't put my toothbrush back in the same place, or if the child messes up on her piano playing, she blows up.' He may have spoken harshly, but his expression revealed pain. I started to feel bad and I gently offered the possibility that his wife might be suffering from postpartum depression. However, he rejected my theory. She'd had the baby such a long time ago.

'That doesn't matter if it's never been treated,' I said. 'Her attempts at trying to control all those little things may be a sign of OCD as well.'

This information made him pause. 'Do you think she wants to control me?'

I would never have imagined that a Chinese family would have these kinds of issues. Again, I was naive enough to think these things only existed in Western cultures, but every interaction with Calvin made me realise how wrong I was.

Calvin inquired about what kind of treatments were available, and I told him that America had no shortage of prescription drugs on the market, but I said he shouldn't pursue anything until his wife admitted to having a problem. Back then I believed American culture was more advanced because discussions on mental health awareness popped up frequently on talk shows at the time. In America, people suffering from conditions like OCD and postpartum depression had more ways to learn about them.

Many people in China, however, suffered on their own or in silent shame. The only thing I noticed that might have been a source of aid was a newsstand magazine called *Psychologies*. It was in Chinese, so I wasn't sure of its content, but I pinned my hopes on it containing information and guidance on such issues.

Eventually, Calvin expressed how powerless he felt living under the same roof as his father-in-law. The man did nothing to calm the fierce household dynamic. Calvin's in-laws lived on the second floor of the apartment, and he, his wife and his daughter occupied two rooms on the bottom floor. Calvin had mentioned before how he wanted to quit his job at CCTV if such a choice could improve his living conditions, but he feared that his age would limit his job prospects. He feared that Chinese companies wouldn't want to hire a man over forty years old because they believed that age affected productivity.

Another option was divorce, something Calvin had considered for a long time. I was a little shocked when he mentioned it, but the amount of time he was willing to spend away from his family suddenly made sense. He didn't think that would be fair to his daughter, however, even though he believed she could sense the tension between her parents. I extended my advice, telling him that he may harm her more by keeping their family together under such stressful circumstances. But my counsel felt in vain. Divorce was so taboo in China that I suspected many families stayed together for the optics rather than genuine desire.

So I proposed a more feasible remedy; Calvin and his wife could take a trip together, alone. 'Why don't you get out of China for a while?' This seemed to pique his interest. In a slightly uplifted tone, he spoke about how they had travelled to Europe before and longed very much to return. Escaping the norm for a while could create an opportunity to have the difficult conversations that they needed to have, and I told him so. Additionally, I suggested that he designate a family night reserved for just him, his wife, and his daughter. Knowing how Calvin avoided his troubles by staying out late every night, I could only imagine that his late night habit added more strain to their relationship. I was gutted knowing that I was indirectly contributing to his marriage troubles.

Calvin seemed relieved to have all this out in the open. It certainly helped me understand what he was dealing with and why he felt trapped between his job and family. His desire to spend more time with me was partly for nostalgic reasons; I likely reminded him of his carefree days abroad. Having a foreign friend must have provided him with sanctuary because of our cultural differences as I wouldn't hold his problems to the same standard that a Chinese person might.

Calvin was a man of dual selves—the polished advertising executive burdened by his country's uncertain future; the family man drifting from domestic waters, finding truer kinship amid foreign waves. My expatriate existence was still new so there was a word I did not yet know then: repatriation. Calvin's MBA university days in Canada and adventurous exploits abroad had instilled in him an insatiable hunger, a quest for novelty. He had changed. His affinity for outsider company was born of landscapes his eyes could no longer see, fertilised by distant shores his feet could no longer tread. Life overseas had reshaped him; restored now to China, he would remain an outsider, a square peg pressured to fit again within a round hole.

SAFE

The embassy has seen more cases of minor confrontations involving American citizens escalating into serious altercations. In a few cases, arguments over as little as 10 RMB have led to injuries, property damage, police involvement and restitution. Identifying potential confrontations before they become physical and extracting yourself from the situation before blows are exchanged is the wisest course of action. If you become the target of a drunken group or individual, leave the area immediately. Do not try to talk to them, reason with them, or argue with them. Once you are targeted, staying in the same area, and 'ignoring' them normally only makes matters worse. Instead, get away from them as soon as possible.

Avoid putting others in a situation where they feel challenged and required to act. Be apologetic if the situation warrants it and do what you can to indicate that no offense was intended. Should you find yourself engaged in an altercation despite your best efforts, do your best to defuse the situation as quickly as possible and leave the area as soon as the situation allows.

If the police are called to the scene, 'fight' participants are normally taken to the local police station to determine fault or work out a settlement. If injuries are claimed, the police may require the claimant to go to a hospital to determine the severity of injuries. The severity of injuries will determine the seriousness of any crime committed.

—US Embassy consular notice

I often received emails like this from the US embassy in Beijing, warning me of rampant violence, and it perplexed me every time. Where did all these incidents occur? What was happening? Despite China's well-known media controls, the press catering to English-speaking foreigners seemed less restricted. Even *China Daily* published news about crime, but nothing I saw ever reached the level of anti-foreigner sentiment.

I don't believe the embassy sent these messages as part of a coordinated effort to make China seem dangerous. Cases must have cropped up here and there, but I never heard about them. As far as I knew, I'd never lived in a safer city than Beijing.

Images of the Tiananmen Square massacre had been cemented in the minds of Westerners of my generation; however, I knew much had changed even before I'd moved to China. I did not expect to witness violence of that sort. As for small crimes against foreigners, even that idea was difficult for me to accept. For foreigners in Beijing, the forums in the *Beijinger* were the easiest places to exchange information. You could scroll through and read different claims—almost universally unverified—about petty crime in the area. I had to suspect that most of these incidents involved alcohol, which never mixed well with visiting a country where you didn't understand the language or culture.

Most foreigners walked around assuming that the locals wanted to rip them off. Foreigners made easy targets, supposedly.

Expats often joked about the 'foreigner tax', convinced that locals subjected them to higher prices. And yes, in China's early opening-up phase in the 1980s, it was not unusual for English menus at some restaurants to feature higher prices.

But by this period such biased thinking was on its way out, especially in the big cities like Beijing. Generation X and millennials in China mostly considered foreigners as fascinating people from whom they could get a fresh perspective or discuss topics they wouldn't dare broach with their compatriots.

Most of the time, if foreigners did get ripped off it was usually only for a small amount. An extra kuai here or there. Some locals took advantage of foreigners' inability to speak the language—the occasional taxi driver or scheming waitress, for instance. But most Chinese people approached all dealings with foreigners with straightforward honesty and respect. The way they saw it, having a foreigner frequent their business or ride in their taxi gave them an invaluable boost in prestige as well as a rare opportunity to highlight Chinese hospitality. As foreigners, we got the red carpet treatment from locals—a heightened level of care that I couldn't imagine Chinese visitors receiving in Western countries.

Interestingly, despite the safety I felt as a foreigner, apparently many Chinese citizens didn't feel that safe. The irony was almost comical. One of my language exchange partners told me that as Chinese teens prepared to leave their hometowns to study in other cities, their parents had stern conversations with them, warning about the dangers of society and cautioning them to be wary of others.

The Chinese had learned not to see or hear evil on the bus or subway, instead turning inward, into themselves, as the pickpockets plied their trade in the most audacious daylight. But who can fault them for following the code of self-preservation above all else? Keep your head down and mind your own business. Sometimes, they kindly informed the victim after the perpetrator had left. Whenever I told Chinese people that Americans might try to stop the thief, they were incredulous and asked, 'But what if they have a weapon?' They just couldn't understand that a sense of justice would make people try to defend the defenceless—even at the risk of one's own life. Frankly, I found it rather funny that they always used the 'weapons' argument on me, given that guns were illegal in their country.

Big cities like Beijing and Shanghai were safer, but crime still emerged here and there. Videos occasionally popped up on YouTube showing motorcycle gangs in South China snatching bags from pedestrians on the streets. While a few of my friends later told me that 'a new mayor' had solved the problem, many Chinese people attributed Guangzhou's relaxed relocation policy as a bigger factor. Though no longer the cramp on mobility it had once been, China's household registration system, or *hùkǒu*, still posed an impediment for millions of citizens.

Introduced in the 1950s to keep rural residents from flooding into the cities, the system required citizens to obtain legal permission to live and work outside their home province. By 2007, reforms had chipped away at once rigid enforcement. But vestiges remained firmer in the likes of Beijing and Shanghai, whereas factory-dominated Guangzhou kept its gates more ajar. The Pearl River Delta continued its long tradition as an industrial vortex sucking in low-skilled labour from less prosperous interior provinces, *hùkǒu* permits be damned.

I'd only lived in China for a few weeks when a mass shooting at Virginia Tech occurred in the US, leaving thirty-two dead. A South Korean native studying at the American college had carried out the attack. Almost all my new Chinese friends wanted to discuss the incident, most of them questioning me about America's relationship with firearms. I realised then that I had grown so numb to these types of shootings in America that their questions startled me. I had never considered how horrific these incidents—commonplace in the United States—looked to the rest of the world. And yes, I felt ashamed for my country and at a loss for words.

One thing I loved about the character of the Chinese people was how they placed so much weight on practicality and pragmatism rather than focusing on lofty ideals. The issue of guns was always a hot topic for the Chinese, since the weapons were banned there. A couple of years after the Virginia Tech shooting, a friend invited me to his apartment during Chinese New Year. We started talking about gun ownership in America and he said, 'Do you know why guns are banned in China? Because if we had them, we'd have even more shootings than America does.'

It was one of those moments that made me reconsider so many of the debates about these types of issues. It wasn't that the Chinese placed themselves on some higher moral ground; they just had a more realistic view of how the world operated. For all the stressors that came with living in bustling Beijing, having to worry about guns was not one of them.

KEN SMITH

Even just a few months into my China escapade, I couldn't believe the roster of VIPs with whom I now rubbed elbows—ministers and moguls, princelings and power brokers. That didn't mean I always got to talk to them—the language barrier was brutal—but I still hadn't expected to get wheeled out in front of all these important people. It wasn't lost on me that few Chinese people would have experienced such access in the US. The scope of AITA's business model between officials in China and those in Australia and New Zealand meant that I was mingling with important people right away.

One of the highest-level visits AITA organised was with Ken Smith, a member of the Victorian Legislative Assembly. Smith was an old friend of Michael's who'd visited China occasionally. Despite his exposure to China, Smith's sheer ignorance about how to work with the Chinese galled me. Normally our company briefed visiting officials on the dos and don'ts, but I guess Michael assumed Smith would know better.

The driver sped along Beijing's Second Ring Road, carrying us to our appointment at the Beijing People's Congress Standing Committee. Wordlessly I sat in the leather passenger seat, studying Michael and our visitor sitting in the backseat via the rearview mirror.

Michael tapped his fingers impatiently on his briefcase, sneaking glances at the 'Honourable' title preceding Ken Smith's name in the dossier on his lap. The distinguished

Australian official sat calmly gazing out the window as shadows flickered over his face.

At sixty-two, Smith exuded energy and vigour. His full head of hair, grey at the temples, was neatly parted and combed. He had a strong jawline that lent his square face a masculine appeal. He was very much a man's man. His admiration for China also ran deep.

Smith turned to Michael, 'Is this near that delightful pub from my last visit, Maggie's?'

Michael nodded, surprised and impressed by Smith's sharp memory. 'Yes, it's just down the road.'

With a genial smile, Smith said, 'Perhaps I'll stop in for a pint when our business here has concluded.'

I studied the older man, astonished. Despite the crucial iron ore exports and trade imbalance issues on today's agenda Smith seemed perfectly at ease, concerned only with ending his day with a drink. Clearly here sat a man who truly understood life's priorities.

The meeting room felt imperial, with platinum-white curtains and glistening crystalline windows. The spotless perfection felt all the more stunning given how many dust clouds the city's ceaseless construction kicked up.

We were meeting Jin Shengguan, the vice director of the National People's Congress. I had sat through enough meetings by now that I'd started to get the drill. Each side would sit in chairs opposite each other. Then, servers would bring each attendee a lidded cup of green tea with loose tea leaves, a bottle of water and a hot towel to wipe their hands or face. An ample supply of fresh fruit always sat in a basket nearby. The casual American tradition of asking attendees, 'Want a Diet Coke or some coffee?' must have seemed uncouth to the Chinese, I thought.

An interpreter usually sat behind the Chinese official, speaking into a microphone so foreigners like me wouldn't feel so lost; the young man who served as the interpreter on that hot August day seamlessly navigated English and Mandarin without ever looking flummoxed. As I would come to learn, interpreting for a government official was a job reserved for the truly talented. The Chinese side monitored us with an unblinking exactitude throughout the talks, searching our every fidget and blink for revelations we dared not voice aloud. Aware of this, I kept myself painfully stiff, alert and conscious.

Chinese officials often dressed like Western businessmen, their suits tailored and impeccable. But I always noticed their shoes and socks. The design seemed too simple, too gauche, even cheap-looking in contrast to their suits. I rarely ever saw black socks. They usually chose a colour that contrasted too loudly with the suits they wore. And the biggest faux pas of all was that the socks didn't go high enough up the ankle, leaving a sliver of exposed skin between sock and trouser leg. While Westerners like me would consider this a serious wardrobe malfunction, it was all by design in China. Like many aspects of Chinese society that made it so appealing to me, a general 'fuck it' attitude was ever-present.

That evening, we'd arranged a dinner with a member of China's Supreme People's Court. I got a bad feeling from the 'justice' who attended the dinner. I had no evidence the judge was compromised. However, I was sceptical of anyone closely affiliated with Michael's business dealings.

A few minutes into the meal, Ken started talking about his

first trip to China twenty years earlier. 'I expected to arrive in some backwater village and instead I landed in China's most beautiful and advanced city: Shanghai.' I immediately recoiled. If there was one thing people in Beijing could agree on, it was their mutual hatred of Shanghai. The city had a troubled past and the Chinese were well aware that most foreigners put Shanghai on a pedestal only for its brash, glitzy vibes that seemed so un-Chinese. Many of these aspects foreigners fawned over weren't Chinese elements, which only added to the rub. Many living in Shanghai tended to view the rest of the country—including Beijingers—as 'rural folk'. As Smith continued to sing Shanghai's praises, no one at the table looked amused.

The second—and the worst—mistake was when Smith criticised the Chinese government for allowing smoking advertisements on television. He blurted out this particular gripe after two members of our table had excused themselves to have a cigarette downstairs. Smith boasted that Australia and other 'advanced' countries had long ago banned TV commercials for tobacco, even bragging that some countries had debated banning smoking in one's own car. My mouth dropped at this. My instincts as a former aide to a government official told me to rescue him from this mess, but he was in too deep now.

Smoking was, at the time, a way of life. Government statistics showed that nearly sixty-one per cent of men smoked. Nearly sixty per cent of male physicians smoked too. As a whole, China consumed about one-third of the world's tobacco at the time. Needless to say, smoking had become an important part of tax revenue—and a lot of tobacco-related companies included state-owned firms.

I waited with bated breath to see how the judge would take such direct criticism. Using an interpreter, he delivered a rebuttal that made him sound like he agreed with Smith, but I could feel the tension in his tone. The judge explained the history of cigarettes in China, crediting the United States with introducing the modern cigarette to the country in the early twentieth century. He called it a better product than opium, which the British had first thrust upon the country. China eventually woke up to the dangers of opium and outlawed it, ultimately switching to tobacco as a safer alternative. Smith nodded smugly, blind to the lecture he was being given.

The judge continued speaking of tobacco and cigarettes for nearly twenty minutes. He extolled their development, place in the economy, use in pop culture, and social benefits. Then he revealed himself to be a smoker, saying that now, at age sixty-one, he had no health problems. 'Deng Xiaoping, one of our greatest party leaders, died when he was ninety-three and he'd been smoking since he was a boy,' the judge concluded. I couldn't tell from Smith's face whether he realised he'd been smacked down.

The justice also criticised other countries—namely America—for opposing China's one-child policy. He said that if Americans lived in China, they would understand the need for it. Like everything, issues between China and America—the West in general, really—were so complex. Reproductive planning in America was less about healthcare and more about winning elections. Chinese dissidents told of forced abortions, huge fines and other stories that made China's early use of the one-child policy sound barbaric at best. And yet how often had I crammed myself onto a crowded bus at rush hour and thought, *Thank God they took steps to manage their population*. Although China eventually cancelled this policy, demographic analysts later showed that the country should have ended it much earlier. This would have helped mitigate an underpopulation crisis in China caused by not having enough younger people to sustain its rapidly ageing population.

At the end of our dinner, Smith invited the justice to Australia for a 'big barbeque'. He said that it would be an elaborate affair and they could even take a dip in the swimming pool. The justice smiled curtly and thanked him for the invitation. 'I wish I could invite you to my apartment, but it's much too small to accommodate a guest, especially an important foreign one like you,' he responded.

Afterwards, in the lobby, Smith shot me a toothy grin and asked, 'Do you think that went well?'

MAY HOLIDAY

I received an unexpected week off when China's Labour Day *wǔ yī* (May 1) arrived. At that point, I had been in Beijing for seven weeks. Suddenly I found myself with empty days to fill, not yet aware this 'Golden Week' in May would be the last. Coming changes to China's holiday calendar in 2008 meant this vacation marked the end of an era.

I spotted an ad in *City Weekend* for Chinese classes at a school called Frontiers and eagerly enrolled in a language boot camp over the holiday. When I mentioned my plans to register in person, my coworker, Nick, insisted on joining me, though his raised eyebrow betrayed scepticism.

Nick demanded we take the bus instead of the subway since it was cheaper—0.40 jiao versus 3 kuai. I rolled my eyes. Apparently, the concept 'time is money' didn't exist here. We walked to an unfamiliar bus stop linking a tangled mess of bus routes. It was the fullest bus I had ever ridden. I didn't have one inch of open space to myself. It was so cramped I could barely breathe—and the people crowded around me stomped on my feet more times than I could count. And the bus took a full hour to arrive. Nick's focus on saving money? He whipped out his military ID and got on free. I still had to pay. I kept thinking about that air-conditioned, efficient subway. But I did save 2.60 kuai!

We found the Frontiers school a short walk from the bus stop, tucked inside a pleasant office building. Dongzhimen felt on the cusp of commercialisation, not yet a bustling centre like other subway hubs. But construction crews working on a new airport express line ahead of the 2008 Olympics hinted at the area's impending boom.

I entered Frontiers wary that many language training centres were money mills, quality depending largely on instructors and curriculum. But as my first ever Chinese course, Frontiers' holiday schedule—six hours of daily classes—seemed a wise investment for fast progress. Other options were more expensive or less intensive.

As we got in the elevator, I could see sweat on Nick's brow. Nervously laughing, he said he 'wasn't sure' about this school. I squinted my eyes. *Odd*, I thought.

The third floor opened into a lounge where international students relaxed over coffee, welcoming us with inviting scents and smiles. A man strummed a guitar, sporting an Abercrombie & Fitch tee. A young Indian woman glanced up from her notebook, beaming as I passed. Their presence lent the school legitimacy.

'I'd like to enrol in the holiday camp,' I said swiftly to the receptionist, relieved when she smiled and passed me a clipboard holding forms in English.

Nick paced as I filled out the paperwork. 'Aren't you going to ask questions?'

I shook my head, having already read the website's description. My true test would come when sitting in the first class.

Nick roamed the language centre, opening doors and peering inside, searching for something unknown. He returned to the front desk and began questioning the woman in Chinese, his voice rising as he leaned towards her. She argued back and they went back and forth, their words forming an indecipherable cacophony that I tuned out, unable to understand. I chuckled under my breath, focusing on the form in front of me and hoping no one would connect me with the man causing the commotion.

The woman presented Nick with a textbook from behind the counter and he flipped through it, checking the content. He walked over to me and insisted that I look at it too.

I shrugged, 'Looks good to me.'

'Walk with me,' he said. So, we set off and looked inside the different classrooms. They looked like—well—classrooms, complete with tables, chairs and whiteboards.

Apparently Nick's presence had complicated my registration, requiring special negotiation to defer the tuition payment. No foreigners had likely brought local companions to inspect the school before. The administrators probably resented his extra scrutiny. I offered an apologetic smile as we left.

In the elevator, Nick reiterated a lukewarm 'so-so' assessment. I asked if the 825 kuai fee seemed excessive. 'Probably not to an American,' came his oblique reply. His own monthly rent hovered around that amount. For my 5000 kuai salary, investing in intensive language lessons could pay dividends.

As we walked out of the building I told him that enrolling was a gamble, but it was a calculated gamble. Frontiers was not a fly-by-night school, this much I knew for sure. The more we discussed it, I figured out where Nick's concern lay. He thought that I believed the school would make me fluent after only a week.

I laughed. 'I know a short Chinese course won't make me fluent. But it's a start.' With Scarlet leaving, I had no foreign friends left. Joining this class could help me meet people who understood my experience. As the only non-Chinese person at my company, I often felt disconnected. Explaining my life here to family and friends back home required too much context. I needed someone going through the same thing, someone to commiserate with.

Classes began on Tuesday, 1 May at 9:30 am.

Mandarin poses notorious challenges for English speakers. As a tonal language saturated with unfamiliar sounds, it joins Arabic atop the list of most difficult languages to master, demanding extensive dedication. Even highly motivated American personnel at the prestigious Defense Language Institute reach only modest fluency in twenty-five weeks for French or Spanish, forty-seven weeks for Czech or Russian. Their beginner Arabic and Mandarin courses require a daunting sixty-three weeks. I had one.

Being American posed another challenge. In the US, foreign languages stir controversy. Many people judge those who don't speak fluent English. I assumed similar attitudes must exist in China towards foreigners' Chinese language skills. However, most Chinese people I met understood Mandarin's difficulty for nonnatives. They expected mistakes as part of the learning process. Still, there is a gap between logical understanding and emotional reactions. Even if people acknowledge language acquisition takes time, hearing inaccurate tones and misused words may still grate.

Even native Chinese speakers must dedicate effort, often growing up conversing in regional dialects before formal Mandarin schooling. While some dialects resemble standardised Mandarin, others like Shanghainese bear no similarity. Most begin *pǔtōnghuà* instruction focusing on accurate tones, then progress to written characters. I occasionally overheard Chinese praising each other's precise pronunciation, underscoring that mastery takes conscious work rather than passive osmosis.

I boarded a strangely vacant subway on May 1 amid morning rush hour, finding seats readily available. The holiday exodus from Beijing granted rare breathing room aboard public transit. With many residents escaping the city or sleeping in, I relished the gift of personal space during my ride to Dongzhimen.

I arrived at Frontiers early. Opening my notebook, I started to nibble a pastry I had picked up at a nearby convenience store. More students trickled in. Our beginner-level class would have seven students.

A blonde woman entered in sunglasses and a straw hat, uttering a British 'good morning' in greeting. Professional photographer Helen Couchman had lived in Beijing only a few months like me, documenting the extraordinary pre-Olympics transformation. Her striking photos revealed the migrant workers powering this change, capturing their hidden dormitory lives spent earning meagre wages on perilous construction sites, families left behind in rural villages. Beyond the glitzy 'Bird's Nest' stadium headlines, thousands of these men endured squalor and separation to erect the soaring Olympic spectacle. Despite minimal Chinese skills, Helen fearlessly immersed herself with subjects.

'What is that?' a Frenchman asked, eyeing her food quizzically.

Helen chuckled. 'Haven't a clue. There's a man outside my flat hawking them.'

'*CōngYǒuBǐng*,' a Chinese woman standing at the front of the class said.

'*Cōng....Yǒu...Bǐng*,' she repeated as we stared, confused. She must have been our teacher.

'Scallion oily pancake,' the woman proclaimed with excitement as Helen quickly put the rest of her breakfast into a small bag.

'*Wǒ jiào FēiFēi*,' the teacher said, 'My name is FeiFei.'

Most of the class responded with the perfunctory '*Nǐ hǎo*' but some of the more advanced students used the formal '*Zǎo shàng hǎo*' for good morning.

Speaking slowly and with lots of body language, FeiFei, whose English name was Sunny, gave a brief overview of our accompanying textbook. Pulling the whiteboard behind her, she started drawing a banana on the board.

'*Xiāng jiāo*,' she said as slowly as she could.

We repeated the words as she walked behind each of us, put her face close to our mouths and corrected our pronunciation. Because this word was comprised of two characters, the stress would land on the second character, *jiāo*.

'*Xiāng jiāoooooooooooooooo*,' she seemed to be saying as we struggled to keep up. Clearly lesson one would focus on food.

My gut sank realising my classmates had all studied in China for months, even years, yet were still at this basic level.

'Seriously, you're still at this level?' I blurted out, dumbfounded. They laughed knowingly—Mandarin offered no hacks.

We sat packed inside that stifling room for six hours a day, freed only briefly for a one-hour lunch and two ten-minute breaks. It proved too intense. The other school's gentler pace of three daily hours now seemed wiser to absorb the lessons, especially with spring's perfect weather beckoning outside. Was I squandering my precious vacation like this?

Two of my classmates were American. The man was from Chicago and the woman from New Jersey. Somewhere in their mid-thirties, they'd enrolled in a Rutgers University MBA program in China, and had arrived last autumn. They seemed cold.

'We need to buy notebooks,' the woman whispered to the man as she eyed mine. He nodded in a bored fashion.

'Would you like some paper?' I said, trying to be friendly.

The woman's thin lips pursed into a straight line as she snatched the paper from my outstretched hand. She gave it a curt nod without glancing up. I stood rooted in place, stammering the beginnings of sentences she clearly had no interest in hearing. Not once did her eyes meet mine.

Frankly, they could at least have been civil. Rutgers flew their faculty to China to deliver the classes with a two-week break in between. It sounded like a great program to me, but they seemed grumpy about it.

I asked the woman what she did when class wasn't in session.

'I fly back to New Jersey,' she said.

I did not know what to say to that. For several months, she'd flown to America and back again every two weeks. It didn't make any sense. Forget the exorbitant costs; I couldn't even imagine the toll on her body. She told me she did it simply because she disliked Chinese food. I guess she used those trips to export American treats back to China—maybe that's why she seemed so unhappy.

I prided myself on really having immersed myself in China.

Studying the language made the country a lot easier to live in and too many foreigners didn't do it. Beyond that, though, understanding Chinese people was just as important. So many of these foreigners had come to dip a toe in for a bullet point on their résumé.

Alper Alpay, an alcohol exporter from Turkey, and Philippe Andreoulis, a *journaliste* working at China Radio International's (CRI's) French broadcast service, became my buddies throughout the class, navigating our intensive Mandarin lessons by day and Beijing's dizzying hutong nightlife by evening. One particularly memorable escapade unfolded at the Passby Bar, a wonderfully eclectic watering hole nestled in the Nanluoguxiang alleyways. Weathered maps, RetroChrome photos and Tibetan prayer flags slathered the walls, vestiges of the owner's cycling odysseys across China.

Unlike the largely homogeneous Chinese populace surrounding my apartment in Chongwenmen, Passby Bar swirled with a mix of local and foreign patrons chatting enthusiastically. My eyes settled on one man who appeared American, likely in his late twenties, sitting alone on the patio. Bobbing his head to music piping from his iPod, he jotted Chinese characters onto scrap paper.

When the waitress cheerily approached for his order, he effortlessly rattled off a string of fluent Mandarin that made Alper, Philippe and I gawk in awe. As she giggled in response, he grinned back calmly, betraying no hint of the language anxiety the three of us suffered. I fumbled to mimic even simple vocabulary like 'apple', feeling utterly dwarfed listening to this linguistic dance flowing casually beside me.

Yet observing someone so at ease conversing in the native tongue gave us a glimmer of hope that we too could reach understandable Chinese.

That evening evolved into a jovial affair, though admittedly my global IQ paled in comparison among such worldly travellers. My attempts to dissect affairs like Myanmar-North Korea diplomatic relations or protests in Turkey against an Islamist presidential candidate fell flat. Alper and Philippe possessed a nuanced grasp of international dynamics that exposed my comparatively parochial perspective.

When friendly banter turned to probing why the French remain so notoriously terse abroad, Philippe bristled in defence of his compatriots. Yet he swiftly regained composure and playfully noted my American peers' aloofness in class that day—not a single smile cracked across their tired faces. The New Jersey woman even jaunted back to the States biweekly, Philippe reminded me, as Chinese fare proved too daring for her delicate palate. Touché.

We tucked into Passby Bar's signature lamb kebab pizza, and it was an absolute treat. The cumin had a lovely tang that danced on my tongue, and the bright red chillies gave each bite of that tender lamb a proper kick. Our English-fluent waitress explained that the crust gained its crispness from an eggs-and-flour-only base without adding water, achieving the perfect balance of structure and yield.

She elaborated on the five-hour marathon marinade bathing each loin received before a brief roast to medium rare. Thin slices then adorned the bare crust, their juices melding with melty imported Italian cheese during a final blistering in the wood-fired oven. Never had lamb seduced my unsophisticated palate so utterly. The Old World and New collided nightly at Passby Bar in exotic fashion.

My friends erupted in laughter over a viral YouTube clip showing Americans failing to locate basic countries on a map.

'What foreign languages do American children learn in primary school?' asked Philippe. His eyes were wide with curiosity.

I hesitated, bracing myself for the reaction. 'None, actually. We don't start languages until high school and even then it's usually pretty basic.'

He froze for a moment before managing an incredulous scoff.

I shifted in my seat. 'I mean we take a language like Spanish or French, but not that seriously. More like a fun elective.'

With narrowed eyes, Philippe wrinkled his nose as if catching a foul scent. He leaned back slowly and took a long swig of wine, maintaining eye contact. An awkward silence hung in the air.

China had been an escape, a dream, and then it had become a reality. I had come to Beijing to lose myself in another culture, to imagine my own life far beyond the boundaries of home. Putting yourself in a foreign context is one of the best ways to see yourself without a filter. I was different from them. My friends were worldly and sophisticated, and I simply wasn't. That day, seeing them fit in, I discovered the kind of person I wanted to become here in Beijing.

The morning after our escapade demanded discipline to drag myself back to the boot camp. Residual lagers still echoed in my pounding temples, protesting the early rise. During the lunch break, I accompanied Sun-Young Kim, a

Korean-German deputy director with state development bank KfW, to a nearby noodle shop. She embodied the archetype of laser-focused corporate dynamo, having enrolled in rigorous training in Frankfurt before her China secondment.

Sun-Young attacked phrasebooks with vigour between bites, while I self-consciously nursed my throbbing hangover. The contrast left me equal parts envious of her penetration as a new Mandarin student and mildly intimidated by her naked professional ambition. The woman seemed incapable of idle chatter while opportunity to polish verbal skills beckoned. Watching her will a working vocabulary into being through sheer diligent effort rekindled my motivation, even as I craved a nap more than additional study at that moment.

'I'm struggling today,' I said. 'Why can't we have part of the class outside? It's so beautiful and warm and we have to sit inside for six hours.'

'That's how they do it in China,' she snapped. I shrunk back.

Grimacing, she told me that she'd come to Frontiers planning to become fluent as fast as possible. Akin to Scarlet, she was a foreigner with an Asian face. She wouldn't get as much slack as an obvious foreigner like me. Losing grip, she dropped her chopsticks on the floor.

'How do you say chopsticks?' she said.

'*Kuàizi.*' After eating most of my meals with locals, I had become intimately familiar with Chinese food. What I lacked in vocabulary and confidence in the language, I made up for with total immersion into local life.

We asked the waitress for another pair of chopsticks, which she didn't even understand after we repeated the word three times. In desperation, I held up my pair of chopsticks as a surrender and she finally understood.

'I can't believe my company transferred me to Beijing,' Sun-Young said. 'They told me I'd be in Shanghai. God, I wanted Shanghai.'

'Why?'

'Are you kidding? Shanghai is sophisticated. If we were at a restaurant in Shanghai, the waitress would speak enough English to at least know the word for chopsticks.'

I'd never been, so I wouldn't know. Still, I'd never heard anyone put Beijing down like that. I was probably more of a Beijing person than a Shanghai person anyway.

'We better get going. Three more hours of class,' I grumbled, checking my Nokia phone.

'It's hard for you, isn't it?' she shot back. I guess my vulnerability made her stronger.

As our boot camp drew to a close, a collective sigh of fatigue and satisfaction rippled through us. My weathered notebook, stuffed with new phrases and vocabulary, would continue guiding my odyssey to fluency. In our week together, my classmates had revealed to me yet another angle of Beijing life.

We retraced our steps to Passby Bar. It was only fitting that we celebrate our multicultural journey together at a bar that brought the flavours of the world to one little corner of Beijing. We insisted that FeiFei sample a brew from each of our countries—Erdinger, Kronenbourg 1664, Newcastle Brown Ale, Gara Guzu, Miller Lite—as we raised glass after glass toasting FeiFei, who by equal parts strict instruction and good-natured camaraderie equipped us for the road ahead.

Then Helen, with mischief glinting in her smile, reached

into her bag, concealing a surprise. It was a collection of photos she'd taken of the construction labourers at the Olympics site, the Bird's Nest. Men gazed from the frames, faces creased from days of gruelling labour. By stepping inside cordoned fences, Helen had documented the unsung craftsmen erecting China's glistening return to the global stage. Many were far-travelled migrants, unnamed and uncredited in the structure's larger story. Yet Helen's portraits immortalised them as individuals—more than transient ghosts, she recorded their names, hometowns and signatures with a print for each to keep. Through her lens, the workers transcended anonymity, leaving an imprint that would endure. You need not have met these rugged builders to feel their enduring spirit fused within each iron beam.

As our celebration drew to a close, I surveyed the faces around me, foreigners drawn from distant lands: Britain, France, Germany, Turkey, the US. Beijing bound us, seekers united by curiosity. New friends raising glasses amid lamb pizza in the smoky warmth of Passby Bar. In that happy swirl it struck me then that we had forged something together here, not just phrases and grammar but a kinship our future selves might look back on one day with a fond shake of the head and whisper *'hǎo xiàng'*—sweet memory.

JUDY

I hugged my coat close against my chest as I hurried to work, the concrete grey and cold under my slipping steps. Judy was up ahead, seeming to drift along the sidewalk. A smile stretched wide as a sunrise, eyes gleaming as if drunk on a dream. She looked right through me when we nearly collided, mumbling something I couldn't grasp. High on life was my guess, or high on something. What had seized her with such joy?

Judy's eyes glimmered with nostalgia. 'I stumbled on a rerun of an old favourite show the other day. It followed a secretary, somehow managing to make her boss fall in love with her,' she said, a smile playing on her lips. 'Preposterous plot, of course, but oh I was obsessed at the time.' She gave a small chuckle, shaking her head.

I had always suspected that she harboured a crush on our boss, Michael. When he entered our office, her body language shifted—she became nervous and almost giggly. I knew most of the girls in the office took a liking to Michael. His wealth and air of authority inevitably stirred admiration from the Chinese employees.

I surmised that she was referencing some American television series. Judy went on and on about it, describing another episode in which the secretary rescued someone from drowning. Apparently, that episode encouraged her to learn how to swim. For a while, I thought she was obsessed, losing her mind to an imaginary world. Eventually, though, I realised these fantasies created a compelling distraction that not only helped her face the monotony of our everyday work but made it feel adventurous as well.

Although only twenty-eight, she stressed about her age every day. She sent me the occasional text message fretting over her image. She'd say, 'The wrinkles around my eyes are more and more apparent. I want to die.' And when we sat in the office, alone and idle, she always brought up how old she looked. 'Glen, I'm getting wrinkles from staring at this computer all day,' she fussed before directing her attention towards me. 'How old are you?'

When I revealed that I was thirty-one, she shrieked. 'You look much younger.' She quickly pulled closer to study me with suspicion. 'But you have wrinkles near your eyes.' When I explained that those lines were called crow's feet, she asked me to write the term on a piece of paper. For the next few minutes, I watched her study this new morsel of vocabulary.

Judy grew up in China's northernmost province, the remote border region of Heilongjiang. The only peculiar thing about her outwardly unassuming self was the way she spoke openly about her parents' separation. In China, divorce was not only rare but almost taboo to mention. Few people admitted to living through such circumstances. As time progressed, Judy and her mother had grown increasingly distant from her father. She'd ventured to Australia in pursuit of an MBA and upon returning to her hometown had discovered her father had died during her absence. Nobody had sent word to her, but she told me many times she'd already considered him dead—emotionally, at least. Nonetheless his death came as more than merely an afterthought.

'It was weird finding out like that,' she told me a few times.

Judy worked closely with me at AITA where much of my everyday duties involved improving the emails my Chinese colleagues wrote. I remember the first time I received a draft of something that Judy was working on and, although I understood the overall intention and meaning of her email, it was in no way professional enough to send to a prospective client.

I corrected some bits of her writing and then pulled up my chair beside her computer before explaining what changes I had made and why I considered them necessary. Afterwards, I did my best to reassure her, saying, 'All in all, you did pretty well.'

That simple gesture of encouragement caused her face to light up, and she smiled. 'I wish you were my manager,' she said. Perhaps no one had ever complimented her work before. I discovered too late the thin line between supporting others and hindering their growth—my desire to help often landed as condescension.

A few days later, Judy and I started working on another project that required a significant amount of writing. Knowing that I would have to review and correct her anyway, I proposed that I'd write it myself and be done with it. My American mind valued efficiency. However, the Chinese mind valued process. Thus, Judy insisted on completing the first draft and then having me 'perfect' it, leaving me a bit frustrated about my unnecessarily multiplied workload.

After four long days, she sent me her version. To her credit, it was nowhere near as bad as I had anticipated. and the only standout problem was the unrefined format. There was no room for error, however, and the piece needed to embody nothing short of absolute professionalism as it was a backgrounder for Australian government officials. My red pen hovered over the pages, hesitating, though her writing shone with a keen intellect. Still, the rigid formatting strictures of Michael's assignment bristled in my mind. I tidied the margins and delicately reorganised arguments already convincing in substance. In a small script, I applauded her efforts despite all formatting constraints, hoping to motivate and encourage her. Unfortunately, Judy wasn't convinced.

It was impossible for her to overlook how I had discarded her efforts. This resulted in a stiff atmosphere between us for several days before I realised that my actions had demoralised her. That was the last thing I'd ever intended to do. It simply made sense to write the document from scratch in native English for efficiency's sake, but Judy was proud of her position and wanted to perform her own job. After all, what had she been hired for? I also didn't understand that a big reason Chinese firms employed foreigners was less about checking boxes and more about being a mentor, a teacher.

I made a mental note to refrain from extensively editing her work even though I also didn't want to placate her. It proved difficult to find the balance between reinforcing quality work and still allowing someone to maintain their sense of pride. After a week, Judy reconciled our budding friendship with a jar of homemade peanut brittle. She approached me at my desk and I accepted the peace offering. At the very least, Judy and I seemed to like each other as people. How challenging would it be to work with her if we didn't?

As Judy's trust in me grew, so too did her dependence. I recall one particularly slow morning when I'd come in twenty minutes late, resulting in her sending a flurry of distressed text messages: Glen, are you all right? Are you coming into work today? Will you be on your computer later if I need help?

I soon noticed that she switched between two distinct outfits every month. Half the time, she dressed in a pair of blue jeans with a pink stripe down the side, and for the following two weeks she opted for blue sweatpants sporting a white line. She declared Reese Witherspoon her idol, but I couldn't quite place who or what exactly inspired her fashion sense. Even though her taste in clothing seemed questionable, Judy was self-conscious about her appearance. She refused to go on the company trip to the Great Wall because she didn't want our colleagues to see her in a bathing suit, which was fair enough.

I often caught Judy intensely studying her own reflection in the mirror while sitting at her desk, pretending to work. When she wasn't doing that, she set her empty gaze on something outside the window, vividly daydreaming or taking small naps. Her frequent detachment from her surroundings led me to assume she had a rich interior life. After a while, she told me something odd was happening to her. She said she felt exhausted at work and needed frequent breaks, yet she had boundless energy upon leaving. When she said doctors couldn't find a reason, I counselled, 'The work you're doing here isn't inspiring you,' to which she slowly nodded in recognition. It seemed she hadn't yet learned that work wasn't everything.

One evening we left the office together and casually conversed while passing the police station beside our office building. We paused in front of the station and it seemed menacing enough to unnerve me. To make matters worse, Judy kept loudly broadcasting her distaste of living in China after spending so long abroad. Her time in Australia, she said, made her feel that these were completely different worlds. Even though I hadn't lived in China long, I could relate to this sense of disconnection. But it was another commonality that made us grow ever closer.

'Chinese officials use our money for their own benefits, like travelling,' she harshly lashed out and my heart raced with tension. I was painfully aware of the police station steps behind her and I frantically darted my gaze between her and the station doors. I wondered if speaking out like this in public was considered unlawful. Judy raged on regardless, claiming that the foremost problem in her country was the lack of accountability. That broke the dam and I finally dared to inquire about a subject I had long meant to ask a Chinese person but had never felt bold enough to raise: 'Did you know about Tiananmen Square?'

In 1989, the massacre seemed impossible to forget and even more absurd to simply sweep under the rug. But Judy said although she knew about the protest there, she had never seen any photos or video footage. It wasn't a topic anyone brought up. I expressed to her that, as a foreigner in her country, it seemed that things were improving and reforms could likely occur with her generation moving up into leadership. She shrugged off the possibility and we parted ways.

Back at my apartment, I pondered on our conversation. Very few young Chinese people cared for politics or the governing system in their own country, which was understandable. From my perspective, China wasn't as communist as I'd expected to find it. The open market, albeit not fully open, was making ripples of change. For people like Judy, it was better not to dwell too much on what you couldn't change and instead focus more on things you could. The Chinese were deadset on thinking forward like that.

Judy was unlike the others in the office. She possessed a certain youthful candour—at times almost childlike in her blunt sincerity, yet worldly and outspoken in a way that caught me off guard. I never envisioned finding such delight in her company, what with our contrasting manners of work. But this other Judy intrigued me and I felt eager to unravel her character's multifaceted layers. Perhaps there was much left to learn in unexpected places.

DAVIS

One chance encounter led to a new friendship. I was at the Tree, a concealed courtyard site complete with, as one would expect, a large tree sprouting from the centre of the restaurant. Though intimate in scope, the Tree's modest menu dazzled with wood-fired pizzas boasting blistered crusts that gave way to zesty tomato sauce alongside salads popping with fresh produce and toothsome sandwiches oozing with flavourful, molten cheeses kissed by the open flames.

In the warmer months, people knocked back Belgian beer while sitting in the courtyard. On chilly nights, sitting beside the pizza oven was a godsend. As I sat with the menu in hand, I couldn't help but smile. Moving to Beijing opened my eyes to a global world beyond anything I could ever have expected. I knew experiencing China firsthand would lead to cultural discoveries, but I wasn't prepared for the incredible diversity and international character of the city itself. Every day reminded me of how ignorant and unsophisticated I was. I often felt like a poseur because my young Chinese friends put me on such a pedestal. They thought I was more worldly than I was.

I was browsing the menu when a young man, no more than twenty-four by the look of him, broke away from his group of friends. He pulled out the stool next to mine and took a seat, a sly half-smile forming on his face. He was attractive—and he was several inches taller than me, even though I was six one. It was impossible not to notice him.

'Davis,' he said, holding out his hand.

'Hi ... I'm Glen.' I was caught off guard—most Chinese people wouldn't have come straight up to me like that. As I shook his hand, I caught a whiff of beer on his breath and realised that part of his forwardness might have been thanks to liquid courage. His face and neck were lobster red from 'Asian flush', which occurs in some Chinese people who lack an enzyme to process alcohol. Almost defiantly, Davis maintained his smile despite the fire raging under his skin.

His story spilled out. Originally from Henan Province, he had majored in business English at Tianjin Foreign Studies University and had been working in Beijing for the past three months as a salesman for the Rockwood Group, a logistics company. His role included managing the airfreight delivery team, selling cargo space during a time of booming exports from China. The demand for air cargo kept him busy finding space on planes heading abroad as Chinese manufacturers rushed products to overseas markets. Davis had bounded over to me with designs on making a new foreign friend.

With more than 1.3 billion people, China was then the most populous country in the world. The intense competition for resources and opportunities put tremendous pressure on citizens to succeed. Coming from Henan Province, where nearly one hundred million jostled for space and opportunity, Davis battled assumptions. Some figured he must have resorted to lies or cheating to break away from the pack. Saying that you were from Henan to another Chinese person could shut down a conversation—but foreigners didn't share this bigotry. I wasn't immune to such prejudice either; when meeting fellow Americans abroad I would at times catch myself subconsciously typecasting them based on their hometown or university. Expatriate living presented a prime chance at reinvention for many. I could thus relate to Davis's interest in me—in his eyes, I represented a similar blank canvas on which to project his renewed sense of self.

'Which beer should we get?' Davis asked. We surveyed the large range of Belgian beers, none of which we had heard of, much less tried. They had selections like De Koninck, Duvel Moortgat, Gouden Carolus Blusser, Hoegaarden Westmalle and Chimay Blonde—I had no idea what I was looking at so picked one at random and moved on.

'Do you miss your family?' I asked.

Davis waved his hand without missing a beat. 'Not really. I need to focus on my career now.'

Career first, everything else later, which seemed to be the modern China story. As he stood up to catch the bartender's attention, I was reminded again of the fact that he was as tall as my six feet one. 'Did you drink a lot of milk growing up?' I asked, wondering if that had contributed to his lofty stature.

'No, my family couldn't afford it. I think I grew so fast because I played a lot of sports when I was little. I played NBA.'

'NBA? Like—basketball, you mean?'

'Yes. You should play sometime.'

I flushed. 'I'm not exactly an athlete, not even when I was a kid. I'm a bit more comfortable in a library than on a basketball court.'

'Ah,' he snapped his fingers, 'I'll get you to play one day.'

Despite his youth, Davis struck me as serious and wise. I asked him if he had become a party member during his college years. 'Yeah, I did,' he replied.

Party membership was conferred only on top tier students, so he had clearly done well. I could've guessed that from his flawless English. Still, he wasn't shy about sharing his anxiety for China's future. Pollution, overpopulation and scarcity kept him up at night. Stories covering these issues stood in sharp contrast to the news about China's 'inevitable rise' back home. Most Chinese people were not nearly as confident about their country as the rest of the world seemed to be.

'I would like to get an MBA from America—I think an American education would help me a lot,' he said. 'I took English in college but I'm leaning towards international business and, frankly, China is different from most other countries. English might get me in the door but I think I need a bit more education to get over the culture shock.'

Davis chuckled as he recalled struggling through Mandarin class in college. The Henan dialect he spoke at home bore little resemblance to the official tongues taught in school. Over the centuries, China's vast landscape had created a blossoming diversity of regional languages. But priorities changed as the country modernised under a communist mandate. Binding citizens together now meant pushing *pǔtōnghuà*, the common national speech centred on Beijing vernacular. So for Davis, English language skills would need to wait. Mandarin came first while English proficiency lingered on the periphery of his academic duties.

'But your English is so natural.'

He grinned, a little proudly. 'American movies. We watched them secretly late at night in the dorms. Everything from action flicks to'—he leaned in conspiratorially—*'American Pie'*.

His Americanised speech finally clicked into place. I couldn't restrain a shocked burst of laughter at this mild-mannered young man who regularly sprinkled 'bullshit!' into our conversation. He grinned sheepishly as I raised my eyebrows in surprise.

He regaled me with tales of bingeing vulgar American comedies with his college dorm mates, picking up 'rad' slang and brash mannerisms they thought epitomised the carefree American spirit. They envisioned the US as a tantalising promised land where people lived freely, spoke fearlessly, and acted brazenly without judgment. A stark counterpoint to the societal constraints back home.

'We dreamed that maybe in America, some nobody from Henan could completely start over and do big things,' Davis confided in me, his face open and hopeful. His gaze held mine, two minds meeting in empathy across the table.

'Americans seem so open and there are endless opportunities there. I want to run a business in the US.'

'What kind?'

A sly smile crept across his face. 'Whatever kind will make me rich,' he exclaimed with a wink. I couldn't help but laugh at his audacity, clinking our glasses of Hoegaarden together in amusement. We took long swigs, two eager migrants dreaming of fortunes yet to be built in Beijing.

Like many of my young Chinese friends, Davis expressed clear desires when he spoke about his dreams. There was an intensity to his generation. From a young age, Chinese citizens were thrown into cutthroat competition at every stage of life. There were too many people and someone else could always replace you. That anxiety and competitive spirit pushed the people forward, forward, forward. In contrast, Americans seemed complacent.

*

We kept in touch after that first night, primarily via email. He posed questions about English or business norms. 'I want to try Western food,' he wrote one day. So I took him to TGI Fridays.

As we settled into the red leather booth, Davis peered at his menu, perplexed by the options. I gently pushed the house specialty—baby back ribs glazed in Fridays' smoky, sweet barbecue sauce. Their rich aroma instantly wafted upward, hints of tender pork and caramelised sugars mingling into a mouthwatering perfume despite the half-rack portion.

'You should experience these the classic way, with your hands,' I urged. Yet Davis baulked, insisting knife and fork allowed him to 'eat like a gentleman.' I hid my smile behind a napkin as he sawed doggedly through the ribs. He eventually capitulated with an almost palpable sense of relief about midway into the meal and dug in fully with bare fingers.

That enduring mix of determination and naivety resurfaced as Davis recounted his endless back-and-forth with a fictional Nigerian prince, hunched eagerly as he offered aid. Picturing him nearly walking to the bank before uncovering the fraud brought laughter bubbling up. Tears sprang to my eyes envisioning the shame and confusion that flooded him. Davis ruefully shook his head as I gasped out giggling apologies at his credulity. But such sincerity and yearning to help was quintessentially Davis. With sauce on his fingers and blotching his cheeks, he remained perfectly himself—and I wouldn't change that for the world.

As we lounged in our booth, Davis told me about his girlfriend who lived back in their hometown. They had dated since high school and he was eager to marry her but needed a foundation first. Her parents wouldn't let her marry him until he could provide an apartment and have more career security. I knew the story all too well by now. Young men needed prospects to gain approval from their future in-laws.

'I hope I get a chance to meet your girlfriend one day,' I said.

A light bulb must've gone off in his head. 'My girlfriend is flying to Beijing. We should all go to Tianjin together. You can see where I went to college.'

When we met at the train station the following weekend, Davis seemed genuinely surprised that the whole train was already sold out. No problem. We decided to stand the whole way. Tianjin was about an hour and a half outside of Beijing during those pre-high-speed train days and more and more people kept crowding on.

'Do they limit the number of people who can stand?' I asked.

'No, they think the more, the better.'

Davis said that during the Chinese New Year, people would lie under the seats on the train.

'Once I had no personal space left,' Davis glumly told me. 'This is China.'

It certainly was.

After about fifteen minutes of getting crammed and elbowed in the corner, Davis had a brilliant idea. We could eat lunch in the dining car. I was so happy he thought of it. Sure enough, there was an empty table. Getting to sit was already worth every penny we spent on the surprisingly satisfying meal.

Davis's girlfriend, Yang Yu, sat beside him. She had a

quiet vulnerability that made me like her immediately—she wasn't shy as much as pensive. She didn't speak English, which made things a bit awkward. Davis was thrust into the role of interpreter while I silently blamed myself for not knowing more Chinese. I also wondered if she thought I judged her for not speaking English, then considered a liability for good career prospects. Maybe she feared I would criticise her to Davis. I couldn't help cringing at the thought of spoiling her vacation by tagging along. Inevitably someone had to get left out and, on this trip, it was her.

As Yang Yu ordered our lunch, Davis gazed out the window, a reverent smile playing on his lips. 'I graduated from Tianjin Foreign Studies University,' he mused. 'That neighbourhood still holds so much old-world charm—home to some of the most authentic European architecture remaining in China.'

I blinked in surprise. 'Wait—European architecture in China?'

I pestered him with more questions. He smiled indulgently, explaining how this port had become a patchwork of European cultures. Back in 1858, the Treaties of Tianjin had forced China to open Tianjin to British and French trade. And by the 1890s, settlements from six other European nations had also sprouted up.

It was hard to imagine what that blending of worlds had looked like. These foreign powers each had staked their claim, building up mini cities within a city. Prisons and barracks had appeared, emblazoned with Italian crests or Russian onion domes. German schoolhouses had welcomed expatriate children. Austro-Hungarian hospitals had cared for the colonial sick and injured.

Yet the most striking features today are the residences that remain—oh, those villas. Veritable palaces in the French rococo style, British Georgian terraces, Saint Petersburg inspired manors ... thousands of fanciful buildings had lined the streets. With ironwork gates and pruned rose bushes, it was no surprise Tianjin had once earned the moniker of the Paris of the East, an exotic fusion of cultures all vying to leave their stamp in bricks and mortar. I couldn't wait to experience it myself.

As Davis and I chattered on, Yang Yu slipped away, only to emerge minutes later bearing a platter of Tianjin's iconic specialty, *mǎ huā*. The golden churro-like dough sticks had been fried in fragrant peanut oil to achieve a perfectly crispy texture. As I took one crunching bite, the dried-out dough bloomed inside. As I offered my praise of '*tǐng hǎo chī*' (delicious), Yang Yu leaned forward, eyes glimmering expectantly. I realised that, as an outsider, my words held surprising influence—the power to elevate or diminish. I saw clearly a shy hope to impress. And seeing Yang Yu's reaction, I guessed she wished dearly for me to later tell Davis, 'What a treasure your girlfriend is.'

Davis leaned in, his voice lowered. 'I haven't told Yang Yu this. My family ... it's complicated.' He went on haltingly to explain how his parents gave him up to be raised by his aunt at only five years old. Meanwhile his older brother was sent to live with another uncle entirely.

Davis always suspected money troubles played a part, though the details were hazy. 'My aunt was only twelve years older than me. Still a kid herself. But she'd lived in the big cities like Shanghai and Guangzhou before moving home,' he said. 'I guess my parents thought she seemed worldly, that she could give me opportunities. But taking in a child?' He shook his head. 'She wasn't ready for that.'

I nodded, surprised as he outlined his formative years shuffled between relatives. He looked down, confessing it was still his aunt he felt closest to, the one he even called 'Mum' now. At thirteen, when housing with his aunt collapsed, Davis rejoined his actual parents. 'Things were never the same again. That closeness was ... gone.' He gave a resigned shrug—painful history not easily reconciled.

I considered how freely Chinese people opened themselves to me. Was it my foreignness? My manner? These intimacies were willingly given, no matter the reason. I knew this unburdening of deep secrets was something never to be taken for granted.

As the train slid into Tianjin, I glanced over at Davis, his face lit up with a kid's excitement. In a blink, he'd gone from random guy at a bar to the person who understood me the most right now. Funny how that happens if you put yourself out there and open up. Two souls hoping this big, messy China might embrace the seeds of us that had not bloomed yet. No matter how far you wander, belonging is about finding not a place but your people. Davis was good people. This was a day I would remember. Right time, right place, right friend.

THE BOOKWORM

When my dinner plans fell through one evening, I decided to see if Judy wanted to join me instead. Upon asking what she was up to, she told me her typical routine—eat some fruit and then off to bed. I sensed Judy led a rather solitary life, her nights lacking excitement or company. She sounded pleasantly surprised when I invited her out. Though deeply fascinated by Western culture from her time in Australia, circumstances now confined her to more modest daily activities. Yet Judy possessed such a vibrant, worldly outlook that I sensed that, deep down, her adventurous spirit longed for new experiences and connections. A spark keen to be rekindled.

En route, Judy started opening up. Quite a few of the conversations she initiated with me concentrated around the burden of marriage. She informed me that she had dated a fellow Chinese student while she attended college in Australia, but he refused to marry her. From what she told me, many Chinese students living abroad didn't venture far from their compatriots. Sometimes this made practical sense—they could cover personal expenses for each other—and other times it was simply because of the awkwardness of making local friends. Coming from different cultures only added to that difficulty, so even the Chinese people who spent a considerable amount of time overseas still didn't have the chance to fully comprehend the culture in which they lived. Judy often spoke of her time in Australia in vague terms with most of her comments relating to her Chinese classmates. 'Glen, almost no one could understand the professors. The accent was so different from what we grew up learning,' she said.

I asked Judy to tell me about the dating scene here. She explained generally men still made the first move though, being an extrovert, she had no qualms about taking the lead when necessary. But even in modern China, unspoken codes govern courtship's delicate dance. No edicts are engraved in stone yet every son and daughter intuitively knows the steps by heart.

'I hate going on a date with Chinese men,' Judy exclaimed. 'It's not a date like you see in American movies—it's like an interview. They ask you questions about your background: hometown, parents, college, health, salary. It's so unromantic.' Taken aback, I told her how in America a suitor would never question his romantic interest on their wages. After I explained the 'breadwinner' concept, she looked genuinely surprised. Something so mundane to me seemed almost far-fetched to her.

I had heard great things about the Beijing Bookworm, a popular café started by Alex Pearson, the daughter of a former British diplomat. Originally created to house Alex's extensive English language library, it had become a beloved gathering place for Beijing's international and globally-minded locals. Located in the Sanlitun neighbourhood, it served as an oasis for expats and Chinese returnees alike—well-travelled souls eager to connect.

The Beijing Bookworm not only offered an immense English library but served as a renowned location for regular events like author talks and poetry readings. There was a colourful bar and café stocked with all kinds of Western foods, but for a long while I had hesitated about visiting the place. I felt like

I almost didn't belong there as a newcomer. I worried that foreigners who had lived in China for much longer than I had wouldn't welcome my presence. The particularly intimidating ones were those who worked at embassies, served as foreign correspondents, or spoke Mandarin fluently. I, admittedly, had Chinese impostor syndrome.

I thought the Beijing Bookworm would be the perfect place to take Judy—a chance to indulge her nostalgia for Western culture. The concrete steps leading up to the café were brilliantly painted with colourful stacks of books. Red velvet lanterns cast a cozy glow about the space. Lining the walls were shelves filled with row upon row of English books—a true treasure to come across in Beijing.

The café's three large rooms and rooftop terrace were more of a vibrant cultural venue than a restaurant. While the kitchen served classic Western fare like pasta and sandwiches, what made it special were the books, free Wi-Fi and comfortable couches that transformed it into a relaxed, lounge-like hangout. Some visitors tapped away on laptops, others ate and more still curled up contentedly reading in corners. Despite being in the heart of Beijing, there was a transporting quality—with its bustling yet laid-back vibe, it could have been a chic literary café in London or New York.

As we settled in, a server materialised with complimentary bread and butter—a gesture foreign to Judy's experience. After briefly querying the waiter, Judy turned to me with an expression of relief and wonder. 'It's free,' she remarked. It was endearing to witness her introduction to this Western custom through fresh eyes.

Though Judy professed a love for cheesecake, many Western

flavours still awaited discovery so I gladly accepted her request to order on her behalf. The prices did give us pause, with entrées averaging a steep 80 kuai—nearly ten times a typical work lunch. The imported books also came at Western costs, likely reflecting substantial shipping fees. Still, in a heavily censored media landscape, the Beijing Bookworm felt like a singular oasis, its shelves reflecting true intellectual freedom. All literary genres were represented, even historical analyses of taboo topics and China's political legacy. The candour was striking given constraints facing Chinese publishers, yet it seemed tolerated because the patrons were mainly expatriates or foreign-educated locals.

I suggested the tuna pasta, thinking Judy would enjoy it. My hunch was right—she happily finished every last bite. I ordered beef, vegetables and fries but found my own meal rather bland, even if the fries were hot and crisp. However, the draw of the Bookworm clearly wasn't exquisite cuisine—it was the lively, cultured atmosphere.

'What kind of guys do you like?' I asked out of sincere curiosity. Judy was unpredictable and for that reason I didn't think she would want a man who was confined within a specific type. After brief consideration, she answered, 'Tom Cruise and Bill Clinton are very handsome.' She asked me on more than one occasion to send her photos of eligible bachelors in America, the only criteria being 'wealthy and handsome'.

We decided to splurge on chocolate mousse for dessert. It was overpriced, but the look of joy on Judy's face as she savoured each rich bite made it worthwhile. Unlike those too polite or self-conscious to show enthusiasm, Judy ate with relish, unabashedly relishing the moment. Her authenticity was refreshing and charming. More than the food or ambiance, her company was the best part of the evening for me. With Judy, there was no pretence or airs, simply honest, openhearted connection.

Most Chinese back then regarded a woman older than thirty to be an undesirable old maid. Part of what drew older Chinese women to foreigners was the realisation that many outsiders didn't share those beliefs and wouldn't mind dating an 'older' woman. Americans often were cast as 'broadminded'— essentially code for having loose morals. Pop culture was widely to blame for this perspective; movies like *American Pie* and TV shows like *Sex and the City* only further pushed the narrative of Americans having no inhibitions.

Many years later, I dated a wealthy Chinese businessman who was a partner in a German manufacturing company and divided his time between his homes in Beijing and London, giving him a cosmopolitan air.

'Do you know why everyone in the world thinks Americans are so slutty?' he asked me. 'Because you guys do things the rest of the world doesn't do. Smile and casually converse with strangers—most of the world isn't like that, but the casual approach of Americans makes everyone believe that you want to sleep with them.'

Americans fostered an idealistic notion of discovering one's 'soulmate', ensuring a fairytale ending—a concept many Chinese admired in contrast to their own pragmatism. Here, people could date for entertainment and exploration, but many saw marriage as largely transactional. It was vital that you found the right person to build a life with, and compatibility and shared interests were considered a bonus.

Judy's generation occupied a complex middle ground—enjoying unprecedented freedoms, yet still bound by enduring cultural expectations. Unlike her parents' arranged marriage, Judy could exercise greater choice in a partner. China seemed to be going through a national coming of age, questioning timeworn relationship conventions as part of its breakneck metamorphosis.

I knew that this generation wasn't allowed to date in high school, because their parents would strictly forbid anything that would distract them from the paramount importance of their studies. That attitude had begun to wane in the big cities like Beijing where it was increasingly common to see high school students in matching uniforms holding hands. However, most Chinese people still had their first sexual experiences in college, far away from the steely judgment of mum and dad.

Given the gender imbalance favouring males, I suggested Chinese women seemed to hold considerable power in dating leverage. But Judy swiftly dismissed that notion, shaking her head as if my crude cost-benefit analysis had missed some key concept. As is often the case for an outsider here, economic laws failed to capture deeper cultural complexities and equities.

'But you even have an MBA. And from Australia,' I protested. She waved it off almost bitterly, saying foreign credentials often get dismissed as reflecting poorer domestic performance. *If you were truly exceptional, you wouldn't need to go abroad* was the unspoken verdict. With China's top-tier universities being extremely selective, studying overseas implied you simply couldn't make the cut at home.

Regarding dating, Nick later told me that as soon as Judy

and Phoenix hit the office in the morning, the first thing they did was rush to log on to a dating website. In addition to the societal pressure of getting married, Chinese parents also pushed their children to settle down. It was routine for employers to ask candidates about their marriage and child-rearing plans. For Judy, it was increasingly urgent; turning thirty was like a clock striking midnight. The sooner a Chinese woman got married, the faster she could start a family. For many women who grew up in Chinese culture, domesticity was widely preferable to career work. Meanwhile, Judy's situation wasn't ideal. In 2007, the single folk living in the big cities like Beijing were getting married much later than their countryside compatriots.

Judy was honestly unique in her own way. She was relentlessly brazen and I couldn't imagine her conforming to the demands of her uncompromising culture.

As the evening wore down, I remembered that part of the reason I had invited Judy to dinner was because she sent me an email asking for American gardening tips. There were some websites I could recommend, not to mention magazines like *Martha Stewart*, *Sunset* and *Home and Garden*. More than anything, she'd piqued my curiosity with this specific request and when I questioned her about it she flushed red.

She shyly revealed she had met a Shanghai suitor online, a gardener coming to Beijing that very weekend. Anxious to impress, she now sought a crash course on soils and bloom cycles—conversational fertiliser for their imminent first date. I gently reminded Judy that every day in America, perfect strangers match and meet with online swipes, no longer leaving such things to fate or meddling aunts.

Judy described the lively conversations with her Shanghai suitor, until she finally sent him some photos and his responses slowed. I suspected perhaps by Chinese beauty standards, Judy's curvier figure now gave him pause. Still, I encouraged her—if appearance alone could sway this man despite their connection, then he was unworthy of her time. As their meeting neared, I gently advised taking safety precautions, including initially meeting in a public space rather than going straight to his hotel. Judy nodded gratefully for the advice.

The bill came, delivered by a waiter who looked like he'd be more at home on the streets of Detroit. Strange, since most eateries here put locals in those jobs. I flashed my UnionPay card and asked if it was acceptable. 'Usually,' he sneered, in a tone that implied today might not be one of those usual days. Suddenly all my old feelings of not belonging came flooding back, stark reminders of my outsider status. This Beijing Bookworm, with its expatriate vibe, no longer felt like my scene. Instead, it spurred memories of why I preferred the company of the Chinese in my time here, their warmth and generosity of spirit acting as the perfect antidote to encounters like this one.

We shared a taxi home, making small talk during the short ride to our neighbouring apartments. Sensing Judy's lingering unease over her impending date, I sought a pleasant distraction. Glancing up at the night sky, I remarked lightheartedly how unusual it was to see the moon tinged brown amid the haze. Judy looked puzzled by this, so I explained it was just the smog playing tricks, lending its muddy veil to the heavens.

'What colour is the moon in America?'

I speculated aloud if Beijing's heavy pollution could create a prism effect, altering the usual white colour of the moon. Judy furrowed her brow, insisting the moon had always shone brown in China's night skies—an immutable fixture referenced since ancient times in Chinese literature.

After seeing Judy home, the driver dropped me off. Yet waking next morning, a distressed text awaited—her suitor had abruptly postponed his trip, claiming an eleventh-hour work conflict. Sensing an ulterior motive behind the cancellation, Judy's self-confidence had clearly taken a bruising blow. *Glen, tell me, am I truly so ugly?*

POWER

My company apartment was a plus, no question, but it came at a hidden cost—the knowledge that Michael could access my home anytime he desired. Sure, he had never actually used the key tucked in his pocket to materialise unannounced. Still, the threat of it needled my thoughts as I tossed restlessly in the darkness. I'd jolt awake, pulse hammering, remnants of the same nightmare fading—Michael bursting into my bedroom, backing me against the wall to dress me down over some unspecified failure.

Awake, I recognised the scenario as irrational. Asleep, my mind perceived something more sinister. My job, visa and apartment could all vanish on Michael's whim. And Michael's whims tended to flare without warning. I tried to assure myself that he wouldn't appear unannounced and certainly wouldn't threaten me in my own home. In the muted glow of lights through my bedroom window, the apartment felt like a jail cell. I knew that no matter how long I worked in China, I would never allow myself to be in this predicament again, with my housing tied to my job. Peace of mind was paramount.

As the days marched on, I found myself increasingly torn about my work at AITA. I felt I was, at best, misleading people and, at worst, caught up in something far more troubling. Operating in China demanded a high threshold for ambiguity, but Michael's leadership brought this to an extreme. Would we end up embroiled in something that would spur Chinese authorities to raid our offices? We were living on the edge. If not for my infatuation with Beijing and the thrills it provided, quitting and heading home would have been an easy choice. However, I kept reminding myself my contract was for only twelve months; I could withstand anything for a single year. I had to test myself.

I never quite grew comfortable with the power dynamics at AITA. The privileges associated with 'leadership' here were entirely different; choices American companies might judge harshly hardly even mattered in China. Certain things were simply expected in the game of life. Established hierarchies meant you knew where you stood in the pecking order and what you were entitled to.

One notable example was the relationship between men and women. I had heard that most Chinese people found it amusing that Americans reacted with outrage over President Clinton's womanising, culminating in his impeachment for the Lewinsky affair.

'Punished for getting a blowjob? He's the president of the United States. He's a leader, one of the biggest there is. Of course he's entitled to play around.' Chinese people wouldn't bat an eye if they heard similar stories about one of their leaders, whether in the government or the private sphere.

In our office, Michael worked with his wife, Vicky, a woman who approached her career with meekness. A great deal of her time was spent appeasing disgruntled clients after Michael's blunt and tactless dealings. She constantly found herself softening harsh truths he had delivered, hoping to mitigate the fallout from his undiplomatic approach. However, she was more than just a peacemaker. She often had a look in her eyes as if to silently convey, *I know this is absurd, but …*

Vicky occupied a private office, apart from the rest of us. The door, perpetually closed, created an invisible barrier that separated her from the bustling activity of the office. In that seclusion, she dedicated her days to a whole host of enigmatic tasks. While I couldn't fathom the precise nature of her work, it seemed to revolve around the intricate curation of itineraries for Chinese delegations heading to Australia and New Zealand. The gravity of these responsibilities left no room for error.

One thing I presumed was that Vicky excelled in the realm of motherhood. Amid one of Michael's explosive outbursts, he took it upon himself to disable the internal chat software used by employees for business purposes, irritated that so many of them used it for personal conversations. The consequences were immediate and far-reaching as if he had shoved a stick in the company's gears. Burdened by her husband's impulsive decision, Vicky released a weary sigh before assuring us that she would rectify the situation, albeit at her own pace. Enduring life with Michael was merely an occupational hazard—as long as the perks outweighed the headaches.

Vicky slid silently into her office each day. Her shoulders curved inward ever so slightly as she settled in, like a marionette with its strings faintly slackened. What intricate dance did she perform each day, steeling herself against the sacrifices the coming hours would demand from her?

Michael and Vicky had two children together, yet Vicky rarely joined us for after-work outings, which puzzled me until one evening when Michael asked me to join him for dinner.

The ambiance of SOHO, the trendy Japanese restaurant in Jianwai, enveloped us in a low hum of conversation. Here, in this classic Japanese minimalist setting, the table before me was simply set—crisp linen draping cleanly over earthy wood. A constellation of pendant lights dangled elegantly overhead. The gentle glow of the lights wrapped around us, reminiscent of starlight in a midnight sky.

Leaning in across from me, Michael's eyes shimmered with anticipation. He longed to unveil his hidden world, to ensnare me in the tangled drama of his affairs. Cherry, one of his current lovers, joined us for dinner. Like a wannabe princess holding court, Cherry glided across the dining room, her posture unyielding. Everything from her Chanel suit to her alligator pumps rang of new money.

When Cherry spied Michael, an intimate smile curved her lips, hinting at secrets only she was privy to. She alone understood the nature of their connection, a thrilling temporal passion as ephemeral as her latest Chanel outfit. For now, she would revel in Michael's attention and all the doors it opened, never daring to hope for more. After all, girls like her knew better than to grasp at fairytales. Curiosity gnawed at me, urging me to uncover the story behind their meeting, to unlock the secrets between them.

I couldn't deny that Cherry emitted an aura of genuine happiness. Her radiant smile reached the corners of her eyes. Perhaps, if I had set aside my preconceived notions, I could have engaged her in conversation and discovered more about the person she truly was.

Nevertheless, this encounter proved one of the most uncomfortable moments I had experienced in a long time. Although Michael's wife and I weren't close, this situation felt like a betrayal, a breach of trust that left a bitter taste in my mouth.

Speculation coursed through my mind about Vicky's awareness of Michael's unfaithfulness. I couldn't imagine that she remained oblivious to the betrayal—Michael's brazenness told me that much. Yet the depth of her emotions regarding the matter remained a mystery. Her stoic facade provided no clues, leaving me to ponder whether she even cared. Ultimately, that kept me at a distance, unaware of her origins or background. My knowledge about her was shrouded in ambiguity, leaving me in the dark about the choices she had made along the way to this point in her life.

Unlike their South Korean counterparts, most Chinese women refrained from using excessive cosmetics, but Cherry had embraced dolled-up glamour. Even though she could speak English, she chose not to in my presence. Waves of discomfort washed over me. How could Michael flaunt his mistress so publicly when his wife sat mere miles away? My lips pressed into a tight line as I stared back boldly. An understanding seemed to pass between us in those tense seconds—my disapproval was not lost on her.

Seated next to Cherry, Michael's face radiated with pride. He smiled as he gazed at his prized possession. In his eyes, she wasn't just a lover but a trophy—a symbol of his success. The dinner party expanded to include Michael's trusted driver and Mr Zhao, one of Michael's main deputies, further underscoring the occasion's significance. Having Cherry by his side was a statement, a proclamation that he had ascended to a new echelon of power. Michael had become a big boss, a *dà lǎobǎn*.

I couldn't help but feel a hint of appreciation for Michael's trust, allowing me a glimpse into this world. However, there had to be more to the story. Michael didn't feel any shame in his actions; on the contrary, he revelled in them, flaunting his elevated status. His eagerness to divulge intimate details extended even to Cherry's living arrangements—an opulent apartment he owned at Jianwai SOHO, another testament to his status. Not only had he managed to captivate such an alluring woman, but he possessed multiple properties—clear evidence of his wealth.

As the evening progressed, it started to feel never-ending. But by this point in my journey, I had become an expert at wearing a mask-like smile. I listened to Michael's stories with feigned interest and relaxed when the conversation shifted to Mandarin, allowing them to laugh while I indulged in more sashimi. These glimpses into Michael's world, these cultural lessons he forced upon me, were not what I desired. A curtain had been lifted, exposing facets of life here that I would have preferred to remain hidden.

Michael wasn't the only one sneaking around after hours. Mr Zhao would often stay late at the office, usually accompanied by Mei, the intern with honey blonde hair and crimson lips. She stood out in her bold red lipstick—a daring statement in a culture that valued subtlety and conformity in beauty. While the other young women floated along with the tide of expectation, Mei swam against the current with her glamorous, rebellious style. Her refusal to be restrained by tradition suited Mr Zhao. When they emerged from his office, smoothing their clothes and patting down dishevelled hair, their secret was open yet hidden in plain sight.

Since Mei didn't speak English, I never got to know her

personally. However, she would always trail Mr Zhao into meetings and through the hallways. I always wondered about the nature of their relationship. Of course, I never dared to ask my colleagues about it. But one day, my suspicions were confirmed. I witnessed the girl and Michael entering the conference room together, an unusual sight considering she reported to Mr Zhao. What could Michael have wanted to discuss with her? After about ten minutes, she emerged, mascara running down her face. It was the last time I ever saw her.

It turned out that Mr Zhao's wife had discovered the affair, so Mei had to go. In Chinese companies, there are no secrets. Somehow, everyone knows what's going on. Mr Zhao didn't show up at the office for several days, presumably attempting to reconcile with his wife. I don't know if Michael paid her to leave. There was no shouting. Part of me assumed this naive girl likely accepted her fate in the hierarchy. It was a sad sight and I couldn't help but sympathise with her.

That ill-fated dinner with Michael and Cherry was, I must confess, a rather graceless affair on my part. I retreated into my foreigner's refuge of playing the fool, nodding vacantly to conversations I could hardly grasp, an outsider peering through the closed doors of a world operating by rules I resented. However, as time passed and I reflected on that evening, its significance unfolded before me like a revelation. It dawned on me that Michael's invitation carried a deeper meaning—a gesture of trust and an indication of his desire for openness. I had unknowingly passed a test in ways I hadn't fully grasped at the time. I had proved myself worthy of his inclusion.

In retrospect, I have to speculate that Michael's intentions hinged on a genuine curiosity about me—my sexuality, my intentions and my dreams. He sought to unravel who I was. It hit me that he'd invited me to that dinner with a mission, showing me what I could achieve if I worked hard enough and stayed dedicated.

That bewildering dinner peeled back my naive assumptions, revealing how little I grasped the intricate realities swirling beneath the surface. In comparison to the intricacies and layers of that evening, American life seemed straightforward. It was also a reminder that our countries were on completely different trajectories. Comparisons between China and the United States in any arena were almost meaningless given the differences in history and culture.

Mao Zedong, the founder of the People's Republic of China, famously stated, 'Women hold up half the sky.' This statement emphasised the importance and equality of women in Chinese society. Mao's declaration had profound effects on Chinese culture. It encouraged women to participate in the workforce and join the revolution. That proclamation helped lay the foundation for the ongoing struggle for gender equality in China. It created a framework for acknowledging women's contributions and advocating for their rights, leading to long-lasting effects on the country's perception of women and their roles.

I little comprehended the refined manners governing relations between the sexes. Only later did I come to grasp the relatively elevated status Chinese women held over their sisters suffering under more repressive regimes in neighbouring lands. Yet subtler customs still weighed down even the strongest of female souls here.

My crude understanding was illustrated by two men, Michael

and Mr Zhao, purveyors of hard truths. Vicky impressed me with fortitude no less potent than her fiery husband's. And Ms Xu, our lone female leader, demonstrated a work ethic exceeding that of even the most diligent man.

A woman's virtue provides no shield against double standards. Vicky endured her husband's brazen affairs with a stoic grace that I greatly admired yet knew no man would have been expected to tolerate. Ms Xu likewise worked under intense scrutiny that her male peers escaped, holding herself to high standards merely to be viewed as adequate.

The resilience of these women in the face of such injustice pulled at me. I could provide no easy solutions. Progress is slow—but not impossible.

DESPERATE HOUSEWIVES AND SHANGHAI MEN

As my friendship with Judy continued to flourish, we started hanging out on a regular basis. We were the perfect duo; Judy needed someone to lament to about her life and I got to absorb as much as I could about modern life in China. During our next dinner date, I found out that the Shanghai man had taken the initiative and called Judy every night. Perhaps he'd cancelled his trip due to business matters after all. He was working on a major landscaping project in Shaanxi Province, which bound him on site for three months. He then intended to at last make the journey to Beijing where a highly anticipated rendezvous with her awaited.

'We do seem to get along, but he's not handsome,' Judy complained, somehow missing the irony. I thought it was the opportune time to teach her a proverb: beggars can't be choosers. It took a second for the meaning to register before she jokingly slapped herself in the face and chuckled, 'You think I'm a beggar?' She laughed until tears streamed down her cheeks.

Judy was candid about her desires and shamelessly proclaimed her love of money, even though I advised that it may be best to conceal that one in front of suitors. Despite how she might have come across to everyone else in light of such an admission, I knew Judy wasn't a gold-digger. I didn't want her to ruin any potential relationships by making a false first impression. My advice prompted her to coyly ask, 'Do you think I'm a material girl?' as she batted her eyelashes. I believed she was and told her as much, but I also knew that many of her generation were similar. The country's growth had created all sorts of new anxieties and the Chinese were discovering that keeping up came at the cost of immense stress.

Although I had numerous friends, I had grown particularly fond of Judy. Hers was the first number I called whenever anything interesting happened and that felt mutual for the most part. One night, I came home to find that a plumbing leak had left my kitchen floor completely flooded and I didn't think twice about whom to contact. Soon enough, Judy had helped me arrange for a maintenance man to visit my apartment.

Desperate Housewives emerged as one of Judy's obsessions, so much so that she insisted on dissecting the entire program on one of our outings. It had convinced her that all men eventually became fed up or bored with their partners and resorted to cheating. Furthermore, she believed that all American women stayed at home and didn't bother to work. Bree was her least favourite character on the show.

'She's terrible. She doesn't listen to other people's opinions and her own children rebelled against her. This must mean she's a bad woman.' She scrutinised each of their fictional personas with such intensity, getting hung up on attributes she disagreed with.

When Judy started to realise how much time we were spending together, she asked if I ever invited any of our other coworkers to dinner. I told her that I didn't and seemed genuinely surprised that I liked her. 'You're funny and intelligent. Why would I not hang out with you?' I asked, trying to put her at ease. Whenever I sent diary entries to friends back home, they always thought she sounded colourful.

Hearing that had her overjoyed. 'Glen, you must write a book about all of this. Take your notes and write a book. Then it will be turned into a movie and I can play myself. Please, Glen, I want to be an actress and move to America.' I laughed in response and told her that she'd be too old to play herself by the time this story went to print, let alone made it to the big screen.

Sex and the City, which many young women in China watched and loved, also graced Judy's lineup. Her choice character was Carrie because Judy was inspired by the way the actor, Sarah Jessica Parker, got the lead role while being—in Judy's words—'not so attractive.' I vouched that many American women appreciated her natural and approachable appearance. Judy took a liking to Samantha as well, of course. 'She doesn't hide who she is,' she said. 'She puts it out there.'

It was apparent that all the celebrities Judy adored shared similar traits—traits she herself yearned to embrace. In contrast to these fictional characters, she saw her coworkers being puppets playing to the strings of the boss and putting forth false personalities.

'I can't do that, Glen. If I don't like someone, I can't pretend that I do.'

The man from Shanghai later invited Judy to spend the October holiday with him in Shaanxi. Naturally, she was nervous about the meeting because he had made it apparent that looks were of paramount importance. Over and over, she posed the question—how to respond should he spurn her interest? My answer remained unchanged: 'If he is shallow, then he isn't worth it.' With her radiant personality, Judy felt different from most of the women I had previously met and I truly wanted her to find the right match.

Knowing how hooked she was on American entertainment, I invited Judy to my apartment one weekend to unwind and watch an online series that had found an audience with expats in China. *Sexy Beijing* was hosted by Anna Sophie Loewenberg, better known by her Chinese name, Su Fei. Originally from Los Angeles, she was a Jewish woman who spoke fluent Mandarin and could thus create the type of YouTube content that one wouldn't find on Chinese TV programming, which was stuffier and more risk averse. *Sexy Beijing* largely focused on love, dating and relationships in China, and it detailed common stereotypes to give Westerners a better understanding of modern-day Chinese courtship. Even though each episode was only five minutes long, they were remarkably captivating.

I opened a bottle of Great Wall red wine for us to indulge in while enjoying the show. As darkness fell and the alcohol gave rise to a new frame of mind, one thing led to another and we shed our clothes. Judy was intoxicating and, unlike most women, she didn't shave under her arms, but I found the simplicity arousing.

The October holiday came about and Judy travelled to Shaanxi for the anticipated meeting. Their utter lack of chemistry came as no surprise. She hated how he tried to negotiate over every little thing, even attempting to barter a train ticket at a lower rate—a fool's errand during sold-out national holidays. I later discovered that Shanghainese men were notoriously tight with their money and many women avoided them for this reason. In addition to his already unflattering temperament, he also informed Judy that while she had a pretty face, her body resembled that of a forty-year-old. She vowed not to get married after that and instead focused on pursuing her own entrepreneurial dreams.

'I am done with this game of love. Now, I will make my own money,' she said.

VISA

If foreigners in China knew one thing back then, it was that having a visa was essential. Americans often took visas for granted in 2007. I mean, a lot of Americans didn't have passports. Why travel abroad when the US had enough to explore already? Considering America had some of the least generous vacation policies and national holidays in the world, few could justify leaving anyway. For those Americans who did have passports, visas often came as an afterthought given how many countries welcomed us visa-free. Only those wishing to move abroad or stay an extended time needed to navigate the maze of visa applications.

But visas—and the barriers they represented—were something every foreigner experienced in China. Closed borders had been a reality here for so long that having the ability to even visit the Middle Kingdom was not to be taken for granted. During the Mao Zedong era of 1949–1978, foreigners practically didn't exist, and the few who made it in usually arrived from those countries the fledgling People's Republic of China had good relations with, like the Soviet Union or other communist states.

By 2007, citizens of almost every nationality required a visa to enter China, even for short-term travel. Novices usually viewed this as part of China's sprawling security apparatus. One could imagine a visa officer doing a deep dive into an applicant's background to assess if they represented even a tiny threat. However, as my time in China wore on, I took a more cynical view: the government didn't care that much, it simply wanted to profit an extra kuai or two.

All the red tape delayed my initial departure date to China a few times. Much like the slog through Thanksgiving, Christmas and New Year's in America, things slowed down in the weeks leading up to the Chinese New Year. The holiday could land in either January or February. And if you needed a visa or a renewal during this period, it was usually a nail-biter. I had an epiphany. This endless lag was preparation, not punishment; a crash course in cultivating Chinese-style patience. Navigating inscrutable government bureaucracies was merely the gateway ritual. No one valued transparency, the process mattered above all else and we were all subjects of the Chinese state. If you raised too much of a ruckus, you might not get a visa at all. Those unwilling to embrace the uncertainty rarely lasted long in China.

Upon receiving the visa invitation letter, I was filled with a sense of good fortune. Without delay I gathered my documents and passport and dispatched them to the consulate in Chicago where I knew officials would carry out their process on Beijing's timeline, not my own. When my passport was returned, now bearing the all-important visa, I felt as content as any Olympic medallist who sees his hard work validated by the weight of gold newly placed around his neck. That highlighted the fact that you couldn't take anything for granted. Want to visit or live in China? It's for the privileged few. China well understood the illusion of scarcity made the ordinary seem extraordinary.

Part of the reason I paid an employment agency to help me get a job in China was to get assistance navigating the complex visa process. There was so much conflicting information on the internet. I knew I didn't qualify for a work visa—the coveted Z visa—because I hadn't received my university degree yet. It seemed clear that a degree was required for the Z visa, yet some job advertisements promised one even without a degree. Sometimes this meant something improper was happening; other times it meant that a government department had secured a special arrangement. In reality, the process was so confusing that many Chinese HR departments simply didn't understand it either.

Having told the employment agency I didn't have a degree, I decided to let them handle it. The less I knew, the better. My path to China would follow the F visa, or business visa. This was technically a short-term visa for business purposes, like assessing exploratory opportunities or visiting a company branch office in China. In 2007, the F business visa was a blessing for many foreigners. Other visa types like the employment visa had additional requirements, such as presenting university transcripts or proof of good health. The F visa avoided those requirements; you had to circumvent the law only slightly. And the most obvious perk of working illegally? Not paying income taxes.

I didn't linger much on the topic of visas once I got past the immigration office. But one day, Tan Lu, our office manager approached my desk.

'Tomorrow the driver will take you to the PSB. Take your passport.' Her voice suggested this was a serious affair. More importantly, what was the PSB?

The driver tapped me on the shoulder the next afternoon. I smiled. Although he didn't speak English, he knew the word 'passport' and wanted to make sure I had mine with me. I did. We drove about fifteen minutes, skirting close to Lama Temple in the Andingmen area before an imposing building came into view—the exit and entry administration office of Beijing Municipal Public Security Bureau, known by everyone as the PSB. Its architectural style focused more on utilitarian design than aesthetics. A combination of off-white and grey shades coloured the building. This was about as close as most foreigners would get to Chinese officialdom during their stay, so the building didn't need to be imposing—you already felt the magnitude.

As I stood before the door, a knot formed in my stomach. Had the powers that be discovered our arrangement? Would they levy a fine? Throw me in jail? Banish me from the country? The existence I had painstakingly nurtured in Beijing teetered precariously on the edge. And the fact that the driver was tongue-tied in English only ratcheted up my angst. What exactly was awaiting me on the other side of that threshold? The driver motioned me to enter. I wiped my damp palms on my trousers and stepped inside, my pulse thundering in my ears. There was no going back, only going through. I steeled myself and crossed into the unknown.

Chinese people lined up to make photocopies, ask questions of officers, get new photos for their applications, apply for passports and bustle about in that hectic way that came with living here. The driver led me to an escalator and we rode in silence to the second floor.

A Communist Party seal dominated the back wall, glinting in the fluorescent lighting. Beneath it bold Chinese characters proclaimed the office's formal designation. Behind the counter, uniformed officers with badges emblazoned on their jackets sat ramrod straight, stone-faced as they processed a mountain of paperwork with mechanical efficiency. Not a hint of a smile cracked their all-business facades. The approaching Beijing Olympics had clearly deluged this department with extra duties and bureaucratic procedures. As the expressionless staffers raced against the clock to clear application after application, one could only imagine the unprecedented workloads and pressures placed on them in preparation for the global spectacle that was to come.

The waiting room was crammed with other foreigners shifting nervously on wooden benches. Some glanced up with knowing looks as I entered, while their Chinese companions stared straight ahead. One gangly blonde tipped his chair back, long legs splayed as he yawned. His eyes glazed over the peeling white walls, half bored to tears, half wound up tight as a spring. I squeezed onto the bench beside two women murmuring quietly in what sounded like French, their fingertips worried raw from chewing. Had they also slipped some cash under the table for their papers? We all jumped when the PA squawked out a visa number, breaths held, praying each time it was our turn to get it over with.

The driver guided me to a standing desk. He took out some paperwork and I saw my visa application photos. He stepped away for what seemed like an eternity. When he came back, he handed me his mobile phone. It was Tan Lu. She whispered, 'Do not tell the officers that you are here working. Do you understand?'

I swallowed hard while the driver's eyes drilled into mine, searching for any sign I'd misunderstood her instructions. We both knew failure here was not an option. Caught in the deception, I'd be consumed whole by Chinese justice, my naivety no excuse. I glanced at the driver's stony profile, feeling the weight of his future balanced with my own.

'Oh, okay ...' was all I could mutter.

I'd stepped into some invisible trap. The driver snatched up his phone, the urgent Mandarin heightening the tension as Tan Lu assured him of my understanding and cooperation. I could feel cold trickles of sweat as I meekly tailed him to the counter. There, two uniformed officers awaited, one bored junior staring into space, no doubt still under training. The other scrutinised me with flinty eyes, then scanned my passport with ominous deliberation. He studied my visa renewal form impassively which could signify anything. I felt small standing there, two passport photos in hand while the agent flicked through my documents.

'Sign here,' he ordered curtly. The driver's relief was palpable as he mopped his brow.

Then a miracle—the officer's face softened into a smile. 'Just making sure all's in order,' he said lightly. 'So which state are you from?' Beside me the driver's shoulders relaxed as he read the signs, knowing we had passed some test. But his eyes betrayed caution still. Time we moved along—no need to jeopardise this lucky break. My papers had raised no alarms today. But our ruse might not hold up to prolonged scrutiny.

Had the officers guessed that I was working illegally at the driver's company? Probably. But China had bigger fish to fry.

For a few minutes, the officers bantered with the driver, then they handed him a receipt. It was done.

We'd been spared, somehow. Don't look back, the driver's

fast pace warned. The senior officer's smiling gaze followed me out, prickling my neck.

Unknown to me, this was the sunset hour for the storied F visa. In the frenzied preparations for the 2008 Olympics and the consequential Communist Party congress to select new leaders, these permits would undergo scrutiny, leading to progressive tightening of the rules. My brush with authority had alerted me to the precariousness of expat life here. I soon became consumed with the subject of visas—and found myself hardly alone in my obsession. Save for diplomatic credentials, all foreign residents remained subject to the whims of officials who could cancel the right of residency on the slightest pretext. Even those few possessing the coveted permanent residence cards found nominal protection at best, with renewal required every decade. The authorities held all the cards in this game, reshuffling regulations according to their designs, while foreigners vainly sought to divine meaning behind each new policy shuffle. As *lǎowài*, foreigners could never be certain which way the political winds would blow.

Perusal of the English-language *China Daily* indicated the state's growing unease. Frequent notices referenced ever-tightening border defences against dangerous 'elements'.

Anxieties reached a fever pitch as the Olympics approached. Grim-faced officials invoked plots to damage China's long-awaited return to the global limelight. Enemies were gathering beyond the borders—an invisible army of agents, malcontents, saboteurs prepared to infiltrate and ruin the paramount event. Every visa application now represented a potential breach of security. China had suffered a century of humiliation; no one would be allowed to embarrass the homeland with billions watching. The Olympics had to unfold flawlessly on cue. Consequently rejection rates for visa applicants suddenly soared. My growing obsession with deciphering each regulatory change gradually immersed me in the intricacies of immigration policy—fine preparation for my later career in Chinese human resources. I came to know the Public Security Bureau well, even counting some officers as friends. But in those tense months I remained another foreigner attempting to interpret the opaque rules to find my tenuous place in China.

Days later, Tan Lu poked her head into my office, grinning smugly. I raised my eyebrows in surprise as she handed me my passport. Flipping through the pages, I noticed a new visa adhered inside, complete with place of issuance as Beijing.

I leaned back, wearing a thin smile, feeling strangely proud as I slid the passport into my bag. Technically I still wasn't working 100 per cent legally but scoring this visa made me feel oddly important. Maybe I'd picked up a loophole trick or two from hanging around companies like AITA. It definitely gave me insight I would have missed as some expat stuck in a cushy corporate office all day, sealed off in a bubble. No exposure to the griminess of how bureaucracy actually functioned in China.

But there I was, navigating back channels, learning Mandarin phrases probably excluded from the Rosetta Stone language learning software, getting handles on the little nuances that greased the wheels or jammed the gears. The ins and outs expats didn't deign to ponder.

My employment terms remained murky, but I sensed I'd

started unlocking the secrets. I was cracking codes. I was gaining access to the real China beyond anything a guided tour could show.

THE TEAHOUSE SCAM

I used to think that everyone in China was out to pull a fast one on me. It was a stereotype I carried with me before setting foot in the country. But here's the twist: the first time I fell for a scam, it wasn't by a local but by a Brit living it up in Shanghai. But that's not the tale I'm about to share.

For outsiders, one of the most surprising aspects of living in China was the general sense of security, a rare comfort, especially compared to crime back in the US. And the capital, Beijing, was regarded as the country's safest city although danger still lurked near tourist hotspots. As foreigners flooded sites such as Wangfujing—their version of New York's Times Square—crime followed. Tourist-savvy grifters multiplied, becoming ever more creative with schemes designed to line their pockets.

After I finished my Mandarin lessons for the day, I hurried towards Wangfujing's bustling shops and restaurants. The pedestrian avenue fused modern malls with narrow lanes unchanged for centuries. I skirted the intersections lined with display cases proffering fried scorpions, centipedes and grubs roasting on skewers. Vendors enthusiastically waved the creepy-crawlies at passing tourists while wary locals averted their eyes.

But on this August evening few were interested in dining. Instead, excited crowds pressed towards a gleaming display window—the Nike flagship store throwing open its doors for the very first time.

I joined the crowds flooding the multi-storey glass building opposite the country's first McDonald's. Once a quaint hutong district dotted with street-food stalls and mahjong-playing retirees, Wangfujing was now a neon-lit canyon lined with international chains and luxury boutiques.

As Nike's 13,000-square-foot flagship beckoned, I wondered what changes might come to this ever-evolving corridor. Would even glitzier malls muscle out these early pioneers? Would the fried scorpions hissing in sidewalk pans vanish? Ambling through Nike's pristine interior, I glanced back at the familiar red McDonald's sign with newfound appreciation, a relic of humble beginnings.

Nike aimed to merge local culture with its trademark flair. Promotional banners featured hottie track star Liu Xiang, while store employees sold limited edition hurdles shoes bearing his autograph. The clean industrial decor juxtaposed oddly with Wangfujing's chaotic energy. Racks bursting with jerseys and sneakers beckoned people drawn more to Western fashion than fried scorpions. Wangfujing had become characterised by the new edging out the old. However, Nike made a clever promise to reverse this trend—to provide a uniquely Chinese experience that fused global sportswear authority with national athletic heroes. This was its vision for the future.

I felt a tap on my shoulder as I left the Nike store. Turning, I was met by kind eyes. 'Hello. Where are you from?' The greeting burst forth enthusiastically from the young woman appearing suddenly at my elbow. She clasped my arm with unexpected familiarity, her smile bright and infectious.

'I'm Kathy,' she said in accented but rapid English, her words tumbling over themselves. She gestured theatrically to the clutch of giggling girls beside her. 'We are university students, practicing our English.' The girls waved eagerly as Kathy introduced each one, stumbling over their unfamiliar English names.

I studied her face, striking and open. With porcelain skin and braided hair, she had the disarming beauty of a modern twenty-something Chinese woman, dimples dancing as she embraced the future while clinging to the comforts of home.

'Free tonight?' Kathy purred, her doe eyes peering up at me with such faux innocence that, though recalling the cautionary tales of people like her, I still hoped her intent could be as pure as she seemed. The smiling cohort didn't seem threatening.

I gently pulled myself from her eager grip, thoughts swirling. 'Oh, I'm so busy with class,' I hedged. 'But sure, message me.' I rattled off my number, expecting that to be the last I heard from her.

Wangfujing was supposedly an epicentre for a so-called 'teahouse scam' that expats online sensationalised. As I scrolled through forums in the *Beijinger*, I read horror stories from green foreigners new to China's complex culture clash.

The tales featured innocent sightseers whom sweet-talking students lured into touristy teahouses along Wangfujing's shopping streets. Hours later, the shaken sightseers would emerge, wallets empty. The scam worked as follows: An outrageously inflated tab, sometimes absurdly rumoured to exceed $500, would mysteriously appear when it came time to pay. If the shocked tourist dared protest, the waiters justified the total, claiming rare teas had been served. The local companion would smoothly back this up, hinting that in Chinese culture, questioning the bill was inappropriate.

The tourists that fell for the teahouse scam weren't all fools. Lacking Chinese language skills, cell phones or awareness of cultural norms, many visitors likely paid their inflated bills and left quietly, knowing they'd been swindled but feeling powerless. In particular, solo travellers seeking 'authentic' interactions may have been prime targets, desperately hoping to connect with welcoming locals despite the language barrier. An eager new 'friend' conversing fluently in their native language over tea in a charming teahouse setting seemed for some an offer too tempting to pass up. Yet the cruel deception lurking beneath this fabricated cultural encounter ensured a sobering reckoning awaited these naive wayfarers. Indeed, with no recourse and perhaps shamed by their own lapse in judgment, these hapless marks had little choice but to grudgingly settle the tab and shuffle home, lacking even the travellers' tales they had envisioned recounting.

As Kathy waved goodbye her grin never wavered, but with a few months in China under my belt, I considered myself seasoned now, not a newbie. How dare a scammer try to target me. I guessed from those *Beijinger* rumours that she wouldn't waste time pursuing someone already wary of the ruse. These schemers sought naive prey, not veterans like me.

I couldn't help but raise an eyebrow. It all felt a bit too dramatic, too perfectly aligning with those online rumours. Would any wide-eyed tourist really swallow a $500 tea bill without so much as a peep? Something wasn't adding up. Would any teahouse genuinely risk such a brazen swindle under the police's watchful patrol? Surely most Wangfujing locals and vendors were good-natured people intent on making an honest living from the crowds. Still, drifting into one of the area's ornate backstreet teahouses with Kathy did strike me as imprudent, given the neighbourhood's shady reputation. Best not totally ignore those nagging internet rumours and find out the hard way. If nothing else, the stories made for a colourful urban legend more than probable reality.

Kathy's friendly yet oddly ominous text message caught me off guard the next morning: 'I like foreign friends,' she wrote. After the previous day's odd encounter, doubts still swirled about her intentions.

By Sunday, I contemplated bailing on our meetup to escape the baking summer streets and melt into my bed, but resignation soon took over—I needed to pass through Wangfujing for afternoon class regardless. With a sigh, I grabbed my sunglasses and braced for Kathy's next round of friendly ambush.

We were to meet at the Crowne Plaza Hotel near Dengshikou. Kathy suggested the leafy side avenues nearby, shielded from Wangfujing's chaotic waves of tourists—and perhaps prying eyes.

Crossing the intersection, I scanned for Kathy's smile and there she was. A different pony-tailed young woman in a yellow sundress waved eagerly as I approached the hotel. At her side came Kathy herself, beaming widely as she burst through the revolving doors. The pair eyed me with an intense gaze, seeming to size me up.

Then came the line that erased all doubts about Kathy's intentions: 'Hello, where are you from?' Word for word her scripted line from our first encounter. As adrenaline spiked, fight-or-flight wrestled within me—I could storm off, or I could humour her ploy a while longer to unravel more threads of her scam-artist web.

Apprehension flooded me as I imagined leaving here shaken and $500 poorer, fodder for yet another cautionary tale in the *Beijinger*. Yet part of me itched to peek inside this world and discover how far the charade went. So I met Kathy's gaze, managed a hesitant wave and stepped forward to greet her, a wary half-smile creeping onto my face

I was a bit perplexed by how stupid Kathy was in pursuing me for this scam. I waved a number of red flags meant to deter her scam:

'Yeah, I know Wangfujing well. I hang out here for my class at least three times a week.'

'I have so many Chinese friends. They've all told me that I only need to call them if I run into any kind of problem. Isn't that cool?'

'I don't drink tea and I'm not hungry.'

Kathy got lost in her own story. The first evening we met, she told me she was a Beijing Language and Culture University student. As we walked this time, I asked her where she went to university.

Pause.

'I already told you.'

'I know, but I forgot.'

'Peking University.'

Kathy said she was from Shanghai and had many foreign friends there, but she had none in Beijing and wanted to make some. Right ...

We passed a tea shop on the street and she said we would visit one, 'but not that one.' *Yes, because they don't pay you to lure in targets*, I thought. She decided to cut through the Oriental Plaza shopping mall to get to the teahouse she had in mind—a clever trick. This, I'm sure, is because she was worried someone would recognise her and tell me that it was a scam. Shopkeepers paused their sales pitches to frown at her passing form. A trio of policemen broke off their conversation to track her with narrowed eyes. A grandmother clutching her grandchild's hand suddenly switched sides, tugging the little boy closer to the buildings and away from Kathy's stride. My gaze bounced from person to person as we walked, taking in these subtle cues. While the locals rarely intervened directly, their body language spoke volumes—pursing lips, wary side-eyes, shaking heads. I noted people's reactions, reading the unspoken signs. They knew this university girl, knew her scam artist ways.

As we hurried through Oriental Plaza, her fingers danced across her phone's screen for the briefest moment, tapping out a text. Of course—she was alerting the next link in the chain, passing word of the mark she had hooked. I pictured the teahouse receiving her dispatch, anonymous hands reaching for the pot, preparing the leaves, the trap laid in plain sight. Our brisk heels clicked along the polished floors as we slipped towards some ambiguous reckoning.

We arrived at the teahouse and went upstairs. It was deserted except for a security guard at the door and two employees. The interior had the gaudy aura of a Chinese restaurant in America, decked out with exaggerated oriental tropes to convey exotic authenticity. Paper lanterns dotted the ceiling, casting a crimson glow over intricate Chinese lion sculptures and decorative screens painted with sages wandering misty mountains. Vases and jade figurines crowded every surface. The space evoked a Westerner's idealised fantasy of ancient China rather than the Wangfujing reality of globalised commercial bustle just outside its doors. To a fresh-faced tourist, this heavy-handed decor would heighten the impression of a genuine cultural experience. To me, it screamed tourist trap, complete with mandatory souvenir shop crammed with kung fu novels and panda plushies. In 2007 Beijing, locals were more apt to visit Starbucks. This kind of decor simply wasn't cool. College-age kids thought teahouses were for their grandparents. Teahouses were for quaint Chengdu, not surging Beijing.

When the server appeared silently beside our table, Kathy feigned surprise before burying her nose in the menu without glancing at him. It was hard to know how much the prices were inflated. Some pots on the menu said 200 kuai, but I knew from reading about the experiences of other victims that these cheaper teas were usually sold out. She asked me which one we should get. I told her I didn't want any tea—after all, it was hot outside. I wanted water. She insisted that I should pick the tea since I had 'invited her'. I shot her a venomous look and said, 'What?'

She didn't respond, instead quietly ordering tea while I had water. We sat in tense silence until she picked up a menu, asking about dinner. I declined. She insisted I had invited her.

'What are you talking about?' I said, to which she yelled, 'You invited me here.'

I'd had enough. Abruptly, I said, 'I'm leaving now,' and stood up.

Kathy's eyes went wide with surprise as I stood to leave—clearly few people uncovered her ruse so early. Her formerly fluent English suddenly failed her, mouth agape before she stammered weakly, 'Just ... a moment ago.' I wasted no time grabbing my bag and heading downstairs, dignity intact.

In the hallway I brushed past two men, clearly teahouse employees, frozen in bewilderment at my abrupt exit. Jaws slack, they stared uncomprehending as I strode briskly onward, pride swelling in my chest at having narrowly dodged Kathy's trap.

When I got back onto Wangfujing Street, I started breathing heavily. I felt like I had done something wrong, even though I was the victim. Why did I give Kathy my number in the first place? I considered calling one of my friends, informing them, asking them to alert the Crowne Plaza about the scam to make sure fewer people would run into it. I harboured some shame for getting involved in this. I wasn't a tourist. I had already been living in Beijing awhile.

As I left, Kathy texted 'You invited me to dinner. Why did you leave? You need to come back and pay for your water.'

I didn't respond, refusing to be drawn back in. I never heard from her again after that desperate last grasp failed.

In June 2007, the US State Department added a note on the teahouse scam to their China crime page, anticipating a surge in tourists for the coming Olympics. Months later, *China Daily* reported on Shanghai authorities dismantling a teahouse ring. I'm certain the teahouse scam had inside help—possibly corrupt cops—given its brazen operation in Wangfujing. Over time, the scam's infamy led to fewer reported incidents each year.

Scams shadowed the footsteps of travellers worldwide—China hardly claimed a monopoly. Tales from Southeast Asia in particular conjured schemes of unmatched ingenuity born from hardship. Yet the teahouse ruse seemed an anomaly in China, a nation briskly rising, threaded with glistening opportunity. Factory jobs abounded; white-collar careers called. The scam struck a dissonant chord in a country positioned for greatness.

And what became of Kathy, immersed in China's relentless transformation? This quick-witted girl, brimming with audacious pluck? Did the tide turn within her too? Did she watch her country soar yet leave her grounded, simmering with resentment? Or was it greed, simply another transaction completed with cold precision?

Kathy was undoubtedly an expert at reeling in unsuspecting marks, yet I pictured a shadowy boss figure in the background, claiming the lion's share while she carried out the dirty work.

I imagined Kathy glimpsing the glittering new shopping malls and sleek towers erupting overnight, the billboards screaming wealth for the taking. Maybe she witnessed classmates landing cushy jobs or buying flashy cars through family connections. As Wangfujing transformed at a bewildering pace, did Kathy feel desperation that she too must find an angle and hustle hard for her seat at the table before opportunities evaporated?

JUDY'S PLAN

I nodded along as Judy chattered, picking at the remnants of our dinner. Her monologues always followed the same script—she would unload her latest drama without stopping for a breath, not noticing my failed attempts to interject.

'You really are so easy to talk to,' she'd proclaim when the bill came as I mustered a polite smile. I never felt used, even if our friendship felt one-sided.

Judy summoned the courage to leave AITA, sneaking off to interviews on her lunch breaks. She'd return flushed with optimism after charming some young male hiring manager.

'I really think this is it,' she'd whisper with a conspiratorial grin. But I knew the odds were stacked against her in round two.

Sure enough, she sulked back the next day, fuming about the middle-aged female HR rep who looked her up and down with pursed lips. 'She took one look at me and sent me packing. Told me to try the competition,' Judy spat.

I nodded sympathetically while she ranted about how those women were just jealous. In her mind, the only reason they rejected someone as smart and competent as her had to be her youth and beauty.

I sighed inwardly, wishing I could make Judy see her potential. Instead, I smiled blandly as she geared up for the next interview, determined to beat what she perceived as discrimination against pretty young women.

'So many people, so much money flowing into this city,'

she murmured. Her red-lacquered nails tapped an impatient rhythm on her knockoff handbag.

I nodded, feeling the pulsing drive and restless energy that permeated the city. Everyone was on the move, chasing deals, connections, a sliver of advantage.

'I need one solid opportunity,' Judy said, turning to me with a fierce glint in her eye.

An article in *China Daily* that year emphasised the employment dilemma by reviewing a recruitment ad for body scrubbers, foot massage therapists and general customer service 'facilitators'. The post received more than five thousand applications, some of which included graduates from prestigious institutions such as Beihang University, Beijing International Studies University and Nankai University. A recent graduate from Tsinghua University with a master's degree even applied for a doorman position and said he would undergo an unpaid trial to compete for the job. People desperately needed opportunities that didn't exist. According to the National Bureau of Statistics, nearly 60 per cent of Beijing's new graduates were unemployed in 2006, and half of the graduates who had jobs weren't satisfied with their salaries.

I leaned forward, recalling our late-night brainstorming sessions, scheming about the future over beers after numbing workdays. We had both sworn we wouldn't stay at AITA forever.

'What if that opportunity is us?' I asked. Judy raised a sharp eyebrow, intrigued.

The Judy I knew lived off the next challenge, addicted to the adrenaline rush of round-the-clock negotiations, always wanting more. I pictured her up at 2 am, poring through business books, perfecting her English accent with language tapes, and consuming any information that could launch her next conquest in this endlessly competitive environment.

'If anyone can make it, we can,' I said. Judy's red lips slowly curved into a smile that said the race was on.

With the adrenaline pumping throughout the Chinese economy, I pictured limitless opportunities for us in China. Judy and I got along splendidly, we shared a great dynamic and I knew we could make a success out of any project. I was optimistic about our potential and started keeping a notebook with ideas. We met one weekend at the Sculpting In Time café to ponder some of my notions. Over a plate of French fries and weak iced coffees, we spent the next several hours brainstorming.

My first concept was wholly American: Chinese people worked long hours and nearly every family had a baby, so I figured a babysitting service would thrive. I suggested that we could provide a platform that connected families to the right caretakers and we could manage all the recruiting. I watched Judy mull over this idea for some time. After she inquired a bit more and asked me to clarify what exactly I meant, she delivered her verdict. 'Chinese people won't accept this.' I merely glared at her, somewhat bitter at having my first proposal crossed off the list so effortlessly.

Apparently, families in China wouldn't allow strangers to care for their children; instead, it was typically the job of elders to look after their grandchildren and take care of basic household duties like grocery shopping and making dinner. Sure, elite families regularly hired foreigners to work as nannies for the benefit of their language skills, but the average Chinese family wouldn't allow just anyone to supervise their kid.

Flummoxed, I moved on to my next blockbuster idea:

introducing the concept of fruit smoothies to busy college students. It made perfect sense to me. With fruit stands, *shuǐguǒtān*, stationed around nearly every corner of Beijing, it was no secret that Chinese people adored fruit. Area parks sold candied fruits on sticks, and an elderly man regularly sold watermelons right at the gates of my apartment building in the summer. Having an on-the-go meal in the form of a fruit smoothie could help busy city dwellers, and I knew that the Chinese were always open to new ideas, especially those originating from the West.

The gyms were never empty, vitamins were glorified and other types of supplements were already growing in popularity. The way Chinese people already embraced healthier lifestyles, in contrast to most Americans, further underscored my conviction that this was a winner. I wanted us to target college students as they were usually short on time, and getting them hooked on our new product at the start of their adult lives could pay dividends in the future. Judy eagerly agreed that the scheme had potential. 'I'll go to Tsinghua University next week and see about renting space in their school food court.'

We both left our meeting feeling enthusiastic, but when Judy returned a few days later, the news came with a sharp downside. The rent would slam us, costing more than 4000 kuai a month. We computed numbers and took the most essential fees into consideration, reflecting on products like fresh fruit inventory, cups, straws and utensils. Even with Judy working there full-time to save us the cost of labour, the math didn't add up. Profit was viable only if we charged 40 kuai a smoothie.

'Too expensive,' Judy said.

I argued that a Starbucks coffee almost mirrored the price, but Judy was quick to force reason. 'Glen, these are college students. They don't have a salary; they don't work. They won't spend 40 kuai on a drink when they can eat in the school canteen for practically nothing.' It was another culture shock to me, so I accepted defeat and suggested we could simply move the concept to another demographic. Gyms were few and far between, but most of them sat in upscale areas like Guomao and there was no way we could find cheaper rent out there.

Judy blurted out a better idea. 'Glen, you should become an English teacher and use the scripts from *Sex and the City* and *Prison Break* as the textbooks. When we learn English in school, it is so boring. It would be very popular.'

A wry smile crossed my face before I could stop it—not because she'd said something dumb. Nah, it was actually a pretty sharp suggestion. I respected that kind of out-of-the-box thinking, the urge to push boundaries and make learning fun instead of a drag. That was my Judy.

In that moment, seeing Judy so elevated and engulfed in her idea, I realised that I loved her. Despite everything, I always looked forward to seeing her. She made me laugh and the time we shared together never felt wasted. Did that not permit enough motive for me to love her? She was remarkable, unapologetically herself and brilliantly understood her own brand. Like me, she was a dreamer, and for that reason I never once felt ashamed about sharing the ideas I had with her—even those that most people would have condemned.

The only trouble was that I knew myself too well. I could picture us setting up a relationship, a partnership, but I knew that I wouldn't be content without my own carnal privileges.

COMRADES

Every Sunday, I flipped open my laptop, pondering what to include in this week's update. My inbox overflowed with replies to 'Dispatches from the East', my chronicle of Beijing life that zipped electronically across the ocean each week.

'You made us feel like we were tasting the food ourselves,' Heather, my sister, always wrote. Ex-colleague Donda particularly enjoyed the descriptions of fashion and pop culture. I pictured mum printing out copies to pass around the neighbourhood. Even people I hadn't met were following my adventures, which baffled yet delighted me.

As I typed, I aimed to transport my readers continents away with sensory details: the cacophony of Beijing taxi horns underscoring the hushes inside Longtan Park's intricate rock gardens; the burn of fiery hot pot numbing the lips in counterpoint to the balm of *suān méi tāng*, a sour plum drink poured from Thermoses engraved with coiling dragons; young Chinese children practicing English idioms contrasting with foreigners fumbling through beginner Mandarin textbooks, every interaction revealing gulfs still requiring bridging.

Most Americans only knew China as a foggy stereotype and my experiences showed a different side of this complex country to the people back home. Maybe China wasn't such a big, scary, communist monolith after all.

I didn't include everything I did in the final edit of those dispatches. I often snipped out the most riveting aspects—namely, my burgeoning sex life.

Commercially, it was clear that a dramatic new China was unfolding. Yet Chairman Mao's portrait still gazed out over Tiananmen Square and the Forbidden City, commanding respect from many who lined up at his mausoleum to pay respects and the taxi drivers who kept a trinket with his image in their cars. Even as the nation embraced a new prosperity, hints of Mao's era persisted, clashing with the tide of change washing over China's values.

Male homosexuals in China had adopted a sly bit of insider slang to refer to their community—the word *tóngzhì*, meaning 'comrade'. This term was laden with winking irony, as 'comrade' echoed back to China's more ardently communist past. The use of *tóngzhì* thus functioned as a defiant raised middle finger to China's former socially conservative era, which had oppressed sexual minorities. After all, that stern communist precedent felt like ancient history given China's breakneck emergence as an economic powerhouse in the twenty-first century. Many optimistic voices predicted it would only be a matter of time before same-sex relationships and LGBTQIA+ culture came out of the closet across China's vast landscape. The old guard and their ways were fading, just like the collectivist values buried in rhetorical holdovers like 'comrade'. A proudly defiant and increasingly visible gay culture was poised to flourish in their wake.

China had a rich heritage of same-sex relationships dating back to ancient dynasties, though I'd been ignorant of this lineage before my arrival. I had presumed the country had upheld conservative views with little space for such affairs to unfold. For sexual minorities, dating and fooling around might be tolerated, but truly adopting an LGBTQIA+ identity remained fraught with risk. Immense personal and professional sacrifices awaited those Chinese who found the courage to be true to themselves. The reality was that people who identified outside traditional norms endured discrimination across large swathes of the nation simply for living their truth.

I was deeply curious about the country's gay scene but approached it cautiously. Having my first encounter with a Chinese man seemed essential—like something I almost needed to get over with. Not a bucket-list item per se, but something that I had to try. Otherwise it would have been like visiting China and not trying the Peking duck. It didn't matter if I was actually attracted to them or not; it just had to be done.

I had little exposure to Asians when growing up and thus no real feelings, positive or negative, towards them other than the obnoxious stereotypes I'd seen on TV. Once I arrived in Beijing, those American stereotypes immediately shattered.

Chinese men in Beijing were tall—often taller than me—and more masculine than I'd expected. I found it sensual the way northern Chinese men spoke Mandarin. Although I didn't really understand the words or meaning, I wrote in my dispatches that their voices sounded like well-tuned cellos. I was smitten. In my later China years, a core part of my identity would centre around my status as a 'rice queen': a white man exclusively attracted to Asian men. But having recently arrived in China, I had only started learning and experimenting.

In those pre-smartphone days, dating apps had not even been conceptualised. I relied on meeting men the way I would back in the States: Craigslist. Since arriving in China, I'd scanned the personals section to get a flavour of what was out there. There was one young Chinese guy who posted a photo of himself holding a camera over his face, which frightened me. Did he plan to photograph me during our encounter?

Eventually, after much trepidation, I worked up the nerve to post an ad myself. As a foreigner still struggling to find my footing in fast-changing Beijing, approaching its vibrant but little-understood gay circle felt intimidating. Yet my longing for connection emboldened me. I pressed submit. I don't remember what I wrote, but from what I recall, I listed my limits in excruciating detail. I didn't want to disappoint anyone. Although I was thirty-one, I had no confidence and while I thought I had a healthy amount of sexual experience, I had little idea of how vanilla I was. My liaisons in America mostly revolved around me giving guys blowjobs and maybe an occasional roll in the hay. Wasn't that all gay sex was?

When the first email dropped in my Hotmail account, I had a feeling that this was the guy. He was direct, included photos of his package, and was obviously eager. He lived in Chongwenmen too, so we would have plenty of chances to meet on a regular basis. His words held no pretence and his forthrightness was refreshing.

Still, I kept hesitating, wondering whether same-sex trysts were even legal here. What if it was a trap? A sting? Maybe he would blackmail me. I was already paranoid about China's state security apparatus, but this opened more dangerous—and somewhat stimulating—possibilities.

When he arrived at my tiny flat, I flushed with embarrassment noting how he gazed about the cramped, outdated space I called home. My room could barely contain the enormous king bed incongruously situated inside. But if he noticed the clashing style, he was too polite to mention it. I studied him as he told me about his work arranging overseas deals that obligated him to frequent exotic locales and gourmet restaurants. He was shorter than me by a few inches, his frame carrying evidence of one-too-many banquets.

In America, I would have gotten down to business right away, but I wanted to talk to him first. For all the aspects of Chinese life I'd examined with my friends here, I'd never dared broach the gay topic with any of them.

'Look,' he said, staring me in the eyes. 'I'm going to tell you something about China. You just got here, and you're going to meet lots of young Chinese guys. They are going to tell you that China is becoming just like America, that they don't care what their family thinks, they won't get married, and they plan to be gay. Don't believe them,' he said.

Then he told me his secret: he was a newlywed.

'Here, it's not the pressure from your family that's the problem. If you aren't married, it can kill your career. Your bosses will start asking about it. You eventually have to do it.'

He explained that the pressure to get married was less intense from his family than it was from his professional circle. Perhaps not being tethered down meant that an employee had too many choices. It could have also been good old-fashioned advice on how to lead a happy, stable life in the People's Republic of China.

My lover had more experience than me, and while I had been expecting—hoping, really—that I would be his first foreigner, I was sadly mistaken. His travels meant that he'd had a variety of encounters. He regaled me with stories about gay bathhouses in Germany and Turkey where men started copulating in front of each other in groups. I was shocked. The modicum of information made me realise there was a much larger gay world out there. What else had I missed?

The thing about Chinese northerners is that they didn't want to fuck around. He lied to his wife and told her he was doing overtime at the office, so time was of the essence. When I suggested that I didn't want to take off my clothes, it was like an affront. We were here to have fun, after all.

'Get naked.'

I responded well to his authority and confidence. He was a playful lover and wanted to test my limits. While the so-called secrets of Asian sexuality had been a trope in the West for years, I must confess that I did things with him I had never done before. And I loved it. Intimacy with him felt equal and natural and, for the first time, I felt I had nothing to be ashamed of. I was someone for him to mould into a more active, daring partner, and his sexual experience—and even his time spent overseas—made me feel that I had a lot to learn from him.

From then on, our encounters followed a predictable routine. When he was nearby and in the mood, a text message would ping on my phone. Was I home or not?

'We can have sex in front of other people. People can watch. There are places right here in Chongwenmen, like the bathhouses overseas, where this happens,' he said.

That floored me on a couple of fronts. I could never imagine having sex in front of strangers. And my seemingly dull Beijing neighbourhood had sex clubs nearby? For gay people? It was a lot to absorb.

While I enjoyed our time together, eventually I stopped responding. I'd grown as a lover but I was still too closed off for him. He found me confounding and frustrating and I found him too daring for my tastes.

Having checked off 'have sex with a Chinese man' on my to-do list, I felt freer to pursue something more substantial. Perusing online personals again in search of a real date, I eventually met a young man from rural Shaanxi Province who worked in Beijing. Unlike my first urbane lover, this newcomer had been raised in an impoverished village far outside Beijing. His country upbringing had rendered him skittish and uncertain about big city dating rituals. We had to exchange numerous emails before he built up enough trust to share his phone number with me.

We met outside the Chongwenmen subway station. Though I had neither seen a photo nor met him previously, I recognised him immediately; it was an innate sense of familiarity. He looked sheepish and scared, as if our mere presence together for dinner would lead to consequences. He also had a request of me.

'When we get on the subway, let's not talk till we get off,' he said.

We rode in silence to our destination, looking at the floor of the subway and avoiding the gaze of our fellow commuters. In truth, I got a lot of attention using the subway as a foreigner. If we both spoke English, we would attract even more eyes. As someone deeply closeted and coming into his own, that must have been a nightmare for my partner.

We arrived at the Jianguomen neighbourhood and walked to a small Western restaurant, typically empty at this hour—a prerequisite he felt necessary. The empty dining room assured privacy.

He was only twenty. He had lived in Beijing for a few months and, although a college dropout, he had a studious air about him. When he spoke, he adjusted his glasses in a professor-like way but once we sat at our corner table in the dead restaurant, he started to loosen up.

'When did you realise you were gay?' I asked.

'I had these feelings ... for guys,' he said, looking off. 'I'd had them ever since I was a child, but I didn't know what they were or what they meant. Nobody talked about stuff like that. Eventually, I started searching the internet and putting my thoughts out there. That's when I learned that gay people existed.'

His description gave me chills. I couldn't fathom what it must be like to walk around having these urges without even knowing the words to describe them. Back in America I got teased growing up—kids called me a 'fag'—which meant that I had a label before I even knew myself. And while America didn't have great gay representation in media other than an effeminate 'best friend' character here or there, it did have some space—something that a questioning person could hang on to and learn from. But China in the modern era? There wasn't going to be a *Will & Grace* reboot on CCTV anytime soon. Youths, especially those from the countryside, were largely on their own.

We spoke for hours, riveted by our vastly disparate lives. He hailed from a tight-knit village, his existence bounded by local customs and agrarian rhythms. Meanwhile, an improbable destiny had borne me, a rather uncool gay American, halfway across the globe to land on his doorstep—an unlikely emissary dispatched by Craigslist. Our single dinner was a one-time affair that resulted in only further emails. Nonetheless, I apparently ranked as resident expert on matters of LGBTQIA+ sexuality in the Western world. I offered what knowledge I could. I was the best window he had.

And so I moved on to another lover of convenience. Not a lover in the romantic sense, but a hook-up buddy. I mean, we never even had dinner together.

That was Mike, a Chinese Canadian expat. Communication didn't present a problem—at least, not in terms of the words we spoke—but other barriers existed. Mike was well-paid and lived in the upscale expat enclave Lido, not too far from Beijing Capital Airport and was far from my digs in Chongwenmen. However, Mike's well-paid expat status meant that he had a personal driver, so coming to my neighbourhood didn't bother him unless he got caught in the city's epic rush-hour traffic jams. I guess he felt I was worth it.

Although he came from Chinese heritage, Mike didn't speak Mandarin, nor did he seem too interested in picking it up or studying the culture *at all*. He was in his forties, and he had once been an expat in Japan, so when I explained my difficulties in getting around the city, he had a tip for me.

'You know what I did in Tokyo? You just call a luxury hotel. All the staff are bilingual. Pretend to be a guest, tell them where you want to go or what you want to do and then hand the phone over to the taxi driver or whoever,' he said.

My sexual experiences with Mike were okay but not as exciting as with my first lover. Part of the problem was that he never wanted to leave. Not to say that I was accustomed to the *wham-bam-thank-you-ma'am* style, but I valued my time. Encounters with Mike dragged on and on. I originally assumed he needed a lot of stimulation to get off, but then it dawned on me that he was lonely. Desperately lonely.

I knew that our experience in China was unequal. As a white foreigner I had privilege that he didn't have. As someone with a Chinese surname, locals would judge Mike extra harshly for his ignorance of the language and culture. As an American, I became an object of affection for Mike and a safe harbour from the outside world. But we differed greatly. I craved to learn as much as I could about China, as fast as possible; for him it felt uninteresting and stifling. He was a textbook example of an expat living abroad for a pay cheque. While there was nothing wrong with that, we had little in common other than being two lost souls in this mega-city.

While Craigslist had proven bountiful in getting me laid, I wondered if there was more out there. I turned once again to the *Beijinger*'s classifieds section. I'd heard the 'Language Partners' tab was often a sly avenue for people looking for another type of partnership, and this was the result. I chose Mexican Wave as the site of my date with Lawrence Xiu. The restaurant was located across the street from the Silk Market. Mexican Wave was one of the first Western-style restaurants to open outside a hotel and was under American ownership and management, making it even rarer. With nearly two decades in business, Mexican Wave was a survivor.

Lawrence was different. First, he showed up wearing a black suit. He seemed well-groomed, polished and spoke English with a distinct but cute British accent. Native Mandarin speakers often pursed their lips when they enunciated whereas native English speakers loosened their lips and throats. When Lawrence spoke, his English sounded slightly guttural but endearing. What made him all the more impressive was that he was only twenty-four.

I chose Mexican Wave because it gave me the upper hand. Not only was this foreign food, but it was also Mexican cuisine, and margaritas were my specialty. Growing up in New Mexico, my exposure to fajitas, green-chilli stew and sopapillas was limitless and Lawrence was keen to discover my knowledge.

He eyed his glass, the pale liquid catching glints from the strings of coloured bulbs dangling overhead. 'What type of liquor makes up this concoction?'

'Tequila's the foundation,' I said, 'made from the agave plant.'

'Te-kill-ah.' He sounded out the foreign word deliberately, etching each syllable onto his tongue. A flush was already spreading up his neck after the first sip—his Asian glow making its standard appearance. Yet he drank deeply again and signalled for another round before our food arrived. The band began a new tune, horns mixing with the faint buzz as Lawrence drained his third glass.

Sitting in Mexican Wave, we could have been anywhere. There were foreigners all about—many having shopped for knockoff goods at the Silk Market—and with all the energy of locals and foreigners dining together, I was back in Washington.

Dinner started with a duo of house-made salsas—a pleasantly herbaceous tomatillo and smoky chipotle—paired with crisp corn tortilla chips. A rich *queso fundido* followed, proving an irresistible table-side companion. Our journey continued with a selection of tacos showcasing various proteins, each prepared with a finesse that displayed the quality of ingredients. Delicate seasoning highlighted the prime characteristics of each selection. The *carne asada* sang with the juice and light char expected from a premium marinated skirt steak. Next arrived a quesadilla filled with melted Chihuahua cheese enveloping tender shreds of marinated *pollo asado*. And of course, even more margaritas accompanied this culinary detour to Mexico.

At some point in the night I realised that I had no desire to sleep with Lawrence. It wasn't that he was unattractive; he just wasn't my type. Lawrence was someone I wanted to be friends with, not a fuck buddy. Emboldened by the margaritas and the bar's 2 am closing, Lawrence insisted that we take a taxi back to my place. *Uh-oh*, I thought.

Lawrence was one of those Chinese who had a thing for foreigners and got handsy in the back seat. Having grown up in Hebei Province, interactions with foreigners were rare for him, imbuing them with an air of intrigue and openness that appealed to his aspirations as a gay man constrained by traditional norms.

When we walked into my small bedroom he flopped on the bed. He was ready. I, on the other hand, turned on my Sony Vaio laptop and accessed iTunes for background music while making small talk. 'And this is the book I'm reading right now …' I said.

Finally, I saw the look on his face. 'Are we going to have sex?' he asked.

I looked down and shook my head. I could feel his disappointment. We had had a great evening. Nothing sets up a first date quite like salsa and margaritas.

'Give me a massage,' he said as a means of compromise. I decided that it was the least I could do. He continued to try to seduce me but I was more sober than I'd realised.

In the years that followed, Lawrence and I crossed paths

now and then as fate would have it. He had transformed into a strikingly muscular figure, his once lanky frame now taut and brimming with confidence. Yet during each chance encounter—whether amid the chaotic rush of commuters at the subway station or under the colourful lights of Beijing's pulsating Destination gay club—an air of wistfulness lingered, echoes of our intimate history. I had fully embraced my affinity for Asian men since then. But wide-eyed Lawrence was the one I had let slip away in those dizzying early days. His enduring charm aside, I realised the folly was mine in failing to grasp something special standing right before me at the time.

MANAGEMENT WITH CHINESE CHARACTERISTICS

U*h-oh*, I thought as soon as I sneezed.

Silence.

I stifled another sneeze into my elbow as I reviewed the coming New Zealand delegation's schedule at my desk. The muted 'achoo' barely cut through the click-clacking of keyboards and low murmur of my coworkers' phone conversations. Lifting my gaze, I scanned the office. Phoenix frowned at her computer screen as she typed furiously. Sally highlighted passages in a report, head down. Judy laughed at something on her phone. Nick sipped his hot water, staring blankly out the window.

My nose tingled again and I grabbed a tissue in time to catch another sneeze. I waited for a reflexive blessing from one of my office mates that never came. Donning a tissue did little to hide the sound in the small space we shared. I wadded it up slowly, glancing around. No one met my gaze or paused in their activity. They kept on as if nothing had happened.

Back home, a sneeze inevitably triggered a courtesy response. Its absence made me hyper aware of the clicking keyboards, the photocopier's whirr, the sigh of the ventilation system. I leaned back in my chair. Could they not hear me? Did they simply not care? The consistent stream of working noises said otherwise. A tense energy pervaded the office and I couldn't figure out why. What transpired in the hour I was out to make the mood so stark? I rubbed my palms on my pants, pushing back the creeping feeling I'd somehow angered them.

There were no easy answers. I did some Googling and read somewhere that sometimes when a person sneezed, the Chinese would respond with '*Bǎisuì*', meaning 'may you live a hundred years.' But it seemed no one said that anymore. As time went on, I noticed that whenever somebody sneezed, no one even cared. *Phew!* It had nothing to do with me. Chinese people just didn't acknowledge sneezes, apparently.

I'd had no trouble accepting that people did things differently in China, because so much was different on the surface. In the West, a glowing tan was the badge of rest, relaxation and affluence. In China? Tanned skin marked you as a peasant or labourer. Porcelain complexions were prized. But what I hadn't expected—and what captivated me to no end—was the country's rebellious spirit. Chinese people didn't view what they did as rebelling, of course. They did what they wanted. But even that was rebellion in and of itself. Their distinct fashion choices, like wearing a shirt with a random English word on it, felt like a big middle finger to the rest of the world. I envied their national confidence, which highlighted how much unnecessary stress the rest of the world put on things that didn't matter.

The era of American entertainment had shown China's younger generation what the West valued, but many of them didn't subscribe to these notions. It made me realise that because you watched *Friends* or drank Coca-Cola or even had a burger at McDonald's, you didn't universally bow down to American values. Instead, the Chinese focused on living their best lives—pursuing higher education, securing high-paying jobs and achieving their personal goals.

Typecasting is inevitable. I often made snap judgments about people with merely a glance—speaks English, doesn't speak English, rich, poor, gay, educated, and all the rest. When I went out with my Chinese friends and made a passing comment on what I thought about someone—'He looks like a farmer'— they all stared at me. My friends didn't put much stock in my uninformed opinions, probably because I was often wrong. Quite regularly, in fact.

*

Rolling power outages plagued the city that summer. The electricity went out at work for two hours one afternoon. I initially passed the time by texting friends on the phone. Eventually, three men from another department strode into my office. I had exchanged smiles with them in passing but assumed they did not speak English. Their plain sartorial choices also made me think we wouldn't have much to talk about. People from different worlds, I assumed. Once again I was utterly wrong.

'What was the name of Nixon's national security advisor in 1972?' one of the men quizzed me. As that happened well before my time, I had to take an educated guess: Henry Kissinger? For perhaps the first time since I got to China, I was right. Richard Nixon was popular in China for establishing relations between countries and, by extension, so was Kissinger. One of the men recounted an anecdote that Kissinger had shared in an interview in China, explaining that because he hadn't been born in the United States, he could never become president but could work for the president. The men found this amusing.

Seeing a chance to learn more, I leaned in and asked in a low voice, 'Are you all party members?'

The three men exchanged quick glances before shaking their heads.

'No, we do not participate in politics,' the eldest replied, stroking his beard.

'But may I ask why you wish to know?' another added, studying me curiously.

I looked at the floor, choosing my words carefully. 'Well, coming from America, politics is often a common topic of discussion.'

The bearded man chuckled. 'Yes, I have heard Americans value speaking openly of these matters. But here things are different.'

The third man nodded in agreement. 'For most Chinese people, there is no point dwelling on politics. Whether one supports or opposes the party, there is little we can do to change anything.'

'So better to focus on improving our own lives—our work, our families, the things within our control,' the second man said.

The bearded man patted my shoulder with a smile. 'You understand now, my friend? Here, it is not our way to fixate on power we cannot change.'

I was ambivalent. Americans spent so much of their lives tangled up in or complaining about the government that they often got tired of it. Many stopped voting or labelled all politicians as do-nothings. For China, I worried that the people's lack of engagement gave the government unfettered power, ripe for abuse. It represented two different trains of thought, and I struggled when I wrestled over which one was 'right'. I often wondered how politics impacted on other areas of Chinese life, like the office.

Working in an office with Chinese colleagues quickly shattered the notion that China intended to adopt Western practices wholesale. I sat nervously at the conference table, remembering my conversation with the men the day before. My colleagues had asked for my help in formatting a meeting with an Australian government delegation and I was eager to impress. I was a former congressional staffer brimming with ideas. Polishing English for most of the day didn't exactly excite me but I understood government relations. And at the time, a huge priority for the Australians was to increase imports of wine to the burgeoning Chinese market.

'So, I think we should start with some formal introductions,' I began, trying to sound confident. 'Then, I suggest we have a PowerPoint presentation of the market potential for increased Aussie imports in the market, followed by a Q&A session.'

My colleagues nodded politely, but as soon as I finished speaking, they began chattering in Mandarin. I couldn't follow, but their animated gestures suggested they were arguing. All I could do was gawk.

After a few minutes of heated discussion, one of my colleagues turned to me and said, 'Thank you for your suggestions, Glen, but we have decided to structure the meeting in a more typical Chinese style.' I tried to hide my disappointment, but the way my face fell probably betrayed how crestfallen I felt. As the meeting approached, I couldn't help but worry that my colleagues were making a mistake by not following my Western-style suggestions. When the day of the meeting arrived, I watched nervously as the Australian delegation filed into the conference room. Paper cups of lukewarm water were situated at each seat at the long table.

Our guests looked uncomfortable from the start, as the hosts offered no formal introductions and jumped right into the presentation without explanation.

I cringed as our team went on and on without pause, never once stopping for questions or feedback. It was clear that the Australians were getting restless, and one of them finally spoke up. 'Excuse me, can we have a moment to discuss what we've heard so far?' she asked.

The Chinese hosts looked surprised but agreed to take a short break. As soon as they left the room, the Australians began speaking rapidly among themselves.

'What was that?' one of them exclaimed. 'They didn't even give us a chance to ask questions.'

I tried to intervene, but it was too late. The damage had been done. Despite my best advice, traditional values had won out and the meeting had been a disaster.

As the delegation left the conference room, my team turned to me with a look of disappointment but no comment. I couldn't help but smile at the irony of it all. It wasn't that something was getting lost in translation—it was that the company refused to adapt. I realised that everything needed adaptation. This need extended beyond office protocols to every facet of Chinese life, whether it be in the field of economics, society or business.

The phrase '... with Chinese characteristics' appeared quite often in mass media and political analysis when commentators dissected modern China. 'Diplomacy with Chinese characteristics' was a favourite example. While I didn't know it at the time, linguists had coined a term for this indigenisation—*běntǔhuà*. As a rule, China adopted ideas from other countries and then adapted and transformed them. While eagerly accepting Western advice, the Chinese clung steadfastly to their own cultural traditions. Despite a few hiccups here and there, I came to appreciate this in many ways. It meant that the country would never become a carbon copy of the West. China would always be China. I found that reassuring. Even though McDonald's and Starbucks franchises kept popping up everywhere it didn't mean that the Chinese would become Americanised anytime soon.

Still, I was far from being an expert on China. I relied on my knowledge and intuition to make judgments. However, I had formed opinions on the Chinese work ethic and how that could affect the country's future. Many of my colleagues at AITA arrived early, stayed late and worked weekends. How much they were accomplishing I didn't know, but optics meant a lot to them. They put incredible focus on their work and refused to spend hours surfing the internet or chatting with coworkers at the water cooler. I guessed the only 'weakness' Americans would find in their work habits was the tendency to nap at lunchtime.

I pondered often, were they ready to displace the US and take the global mantle of power? My coworkers struck me as dedicated, good people, yet their reasoning gave me pause about China's capabilities to dominate globally. Once, after a meeting proposing inefficient new procedures, I caught Phoenix's eye and found my own doubts reflected there. But when I asked if anyone objected, the room's placid silence unnerved me. Back in America, griping was sport but here challenges to authority were not even contemplated.

I withheld my scepticism. Who was I to doubt these intelligent, educated professionals? My role was to integrate quietly, helping guide gradual transformation. Progress takes patience. I swore to bide my time, though a small, cynical voice whispered, *Are they ready?*

Indeed, many of my opinions about China's workforce were skewed by where I lived. Places like Shanghai and Guangzhou relied on markets and commerce. Beijing, on the other hand, was a government town, so things worked differently. Beijing's character felt as distinct from other major cities as Washington DC's unique vibe sets it apart from the bustling streets of Manhattan or the tech campuses of San Francisco. I set out to learn as much as possible about the professional world in China. Blogs were a lifeline of information and I eventually found a blog written by a Finn who had worked in Beijing for a few years:

Talent available?
Yes, but the Confucian education system suppresses innovation.

Innovation in China?
Chinese are latecomers and have serious confidence problems. Good at refining existing.

Personal responsibility?
Avoided with ifs, buts, excuses and conditions. Group responsibility.

Problem-solving ability?
Not bad, but no systematic approach or preventive planning.

Proactive or reactive?
Reactivity rules. Proactive attitudes driven by rewards. No confidence in their own ideas.

Chinese hard working?
Often yes. But the culture and system prevent efficiency.

Readiness for teamwork?
Every Chinese is expected to be a head taller than others. Trust and sharing are difficult.

Projects in China?
Personal action points and deadlines are not wanted. No systematic approach. No project management.

Using English?
Chinese use of 'Chinglish' may result in confusing emails and reports.

Gamblers by nature?
Chinese are born gamblers and have a gambling mentality.

Out of all the things that made me want to pull my hair out at work, the lack of planning took the cake. It was like management enjoyed throwing a dart at a board covered in Post-it notes to make decisions. And of course, they never bothered to involve the right people, so everyone was left in the dark. It was enough to make me scream into my pillow at night.

But I had to admit the Chinese approach to flexibility was impressive. They had a 'why not?' attitude and thought outside the box, which explained why their economy was growing at a speed that put countries like America on edge. I couldn't help but snort when I heard that my colleagues had invited faraway VIPs and potential clients to a dinner reception in Beijing with only one day's notice. And they had to pay for their own flights! I'd be insulted if someone invited me to a fancy event at the last minute like that.

The next night at the hotel banquet the AITA banner hung over a room packed with people from all over China who had flown in solely for this seemingly mundane event: the signing of a memorandum of understanding between an Australian official and a Chinese company. It was chaotic and stressful, yet I couldn't help but admire their rebellious approach. Maybe my past life as a congressional staffer had made me too uptight. Perhaps I didn't appreciate the entrepreneurial DNA that my Chinese colleagues had in spades.

*

As a foreigner I got a free pass in most matters. Ignorance is bliss, after all. English words would flicker between Mandarin phrases enough that I had some sense of what was happening whether it be conference room, contract, conference call or meeting. But most of the time I waited for instructions, which left me despondent. I knew how to plan and organise such functions, but it wasn't going to happen for the most part. Go with the flow, as they say.

That didn't prevent me from despising the management

styles that were so pervasive in Chinese companies. Where do I even begin? Management styles at AITA felt like nails on a chalkboard to me. The higher-ups had a nasty habit of publicly shaming their employees as a performance tool. The awkward 'ceremonies' never failed to mortify me as they publicly announced who would receive a raise or bonus and who would suffer a pay cut. It was like a bad episode of *Survivor*, and I couldn't bear to watch it.

To make matters worse, they handed out arbitrary fines like candy at Halloween. You waste some paper? Fifty kuai down the drain. Michael would bark at Tan Lu to make sure the fines were deducted right then and there. And when business was tough, you could bet that more fines would be dished out.

I swallowed back my protests as Michael rattled off names, doling out rewards and punishments like an emperor. My colleagues nodded politely as their fates were declared, ignorant of the humiliation. Back home, we would cry foul at this public airing of private payroll. *But I'm not home*, I reminded myself. I was the foreign mouse in this maze of customs I couldn't fathom.

They couldn't understand why it got me so worked up. 'Don't they do this in America?' they would ask with confusion in their eyes. Ha! I wanted to grab them by the shoulders and scream, 'Hell no, we don't!' There were worlds within worlds here that my brash American superior self had to bend to understand. I sipped my tea, still scalding on my tongue, and watched and learned.

Employees elevated to supervisory roles often took advantage of their new status. Being a 'leader' meant delegating your work to underlings and bullying them as they did it.

Despite my concerns with AITA, I was determined to finish my twelve-month contract. Why? First, on a practical level, I wanted to prove to myself that I had the resilience to handle it. Second, I felt that the experience provided a more honest look at how Chinese companies functioned than if I had worked elsewhere. If I had worked in a big multinational corporation, it likely would have had a culture reminiscent of an American company. For all its faults, AITA offered a chance to integrate with the Chinese and immerse myself in their culture. I loved my coworkers. Even sitting in a room with people speaking Chinese all day helped me learn.

During my months there I had the pleasure of meeting some brilliant individuals. However, it was disheartening to realise that people were viewed as mere cogs in a wheel, faceless workers in a factory. It was not uncommon for employees at restaurants and massage parlours to wear numbers instead of name tags because everyone assumed they wouldn't be there for long. Individual skills and talents were not recognised or appreciated.

This was likely due, at least in part, to China's enormous population. If someone wasn't fitting in, who cared? Hire another one. Unfortunately, this was Michael's attitude at AITA and I feared that such thinking may have permeated the entire nation's psyche. There seemed to be a belief that new employees would always do a better job than their predecessors, regardless of experience or talent. Michael loved to brag to me about his new hires, and that pride led to a major blind spot throughout the whole company. It was a disheartening lack of ability or imagination to understand who people truly were and what they brought to the table. It was truly gut-wrenching for someone who values relationships and connecting with others.

Yet, for all the differences, there were commonalities. I observed some high school students on the city bus and it struck me how loud, rowdy and rambunctious they acted. Kids are kids.

Funnily enough, on that same bus, I discovered two of my coworkers had seated themselves behind me. One was a young woman with the English name 'Apple', and the other was a Chinese man in his mid-thirties who had recently joined the company. He was eager to speak with me as he had spent about a decade working overseas, mostly in the Middle East. I asked to hear his impressions about life abroad, but he seemed more curious to know my opinion of China. And so, I gave him my genuine praise. 'Everything is better here!'

I started to list different examples of what I preferred in China over the United States. I mentioned the public transportation and even the smart technology that made lights in my apartment stairwell only activate when they heard a sound. He absorbed everything I said without comment or expression. Soon after, I saw my stop coming up and bid farewell to him and Apple.

The next day, I met Apple for lunch and she had a look on her face like she had something important to tell me. 'After you got off the bus yesterday, that man said something about you,' she said, and my heart started racing. 'I don't know how to say it in English.'

I leaned in, ready to hear what the mystery man had said. And then she presented me with the screen of her digital translator.

'Naive.'

SUMMER

2007:
China's passenger car sales rose 23 per cent in May. Beijing adds more than twelve hundred cars to its streets every day.

There are already three million cars in Beijing.

China builds a new coal-fired power station every twelve days.

Beijing hit 93 degrees in early May, the hottest for that month since 1986, the city experiencing the earliest summer in thirty-five years.

My phone pinged with a message from Scarlet. She hadn't found another job after all. Instead, she had been taken in by the Korean diaspora community, staying first with Woojung and her family and later another Korean girl during those final weeks abroad. Clever Woojung managed to get Scarlet a spot on her university's 'study trip' through Peking University. I gazed at the photos of them bicycling atop the Xi'an City Wall, wandering in Buddhist temples, embarking on a thirty-hour train ride to Lhasa, frolicking with pandas in Chengdu, bamboo rafting in Yangshuo, and gaping at giant jellyfish in Beihai before ending up in Vietnam for pho-soaked nights in Hanoi.

I admit I envied their adventure, but I felt glad for Scarlet. Woojung had invited me to join them in Vietnam, but I declined upon seeing the hassles involved—the bus from China, visas and language barriers. Wider travel could wait.

We gathered for a last supper as Scarlet prepared to depart for home, entertaining the prospect of pursuing a master's degree in England. Though first desiring to reconnect with family after months abroad, her mind brimmed with ideas and aspirations kindled from her travels. At twenty-two, Scarlet remained eager to learn and grow, an adventurous spirit seeking new horizons.

In the summer of 2007, Beijing became the arena for two extremes: suffocating pollution and scorching heat. The city's air had reached its worst quality in seven years, with a perpetually grey sky and air thick with smog and dust. Severe pollutants from vehicle exhausts and farmers' fires in neighbouring provinces had plagued Beijing for weeks. Determined to improve air quality before the coming Olympics, the government embarked on a mission to clean up the air. I questioned how much difference a year could truly make.

Someone had warned me about the temperature, claiming it could reach 120 degrees Fahrenheit. Beijing had a dual nature—sometimes humid, other times dry, depending on the day and the wind's direction. On some days, it got so hot and sticky it felt like I'd gone swimming, while other days became dry and dusty.

Beijing's limited air-conditioning and lack of water fountains posed further challenges. I found myself constantly purchasing bottled water. I discovered sweet relief in icy desserts, especially the velvety textures of Viennetta ice cream and *stracciatella* gelato—my cool oasis.

As August 2007 approached, Olympic preparations intensified across Beijing, even with a year remaining until the games. Officials banned a million cars from the roads for two weeks to gauge impacts on pollution. Residents raised a ruckus about the restrictions' consequences. Would exiled drivers cram onto Beijing's already packed subways and buses? Sardined in sweltering buses during rush hour, I felt the true meaning of 'peak madness'. Jammed shoulder to shoulder with other commuters, we lurched through snarled traffic in fits and starts. At one particularly crowded stop, the only escape was to attempt squeezing out the door. I tried pushing forward to no avail. The bus conductor shouted something above the din as the bus belched exhaust. From the gesturing hands and impatient tone, I gathered his gist despite the language barrier—move faster! My faltering Mandarin failed me, though, leaving me stranded and clueless as we idled at yet another standstill.

Sitting at my desk during a lunch break, I came across a worrying article about Beijing's air quality on the *Toronto Star* website. The August 2007 piece, titled 'Breathing an Olympian Effort for Our Athletes in Beijing', highlighted the struggles athletes were facing adapting to the conditions in the city. Canadian soccer player Karina LeBlanc was quoted saying, 'Once you get over there, it's different. Breathing becomes more challenging, almost as if there's phlegm in your throat.' According to the article, Beijing's Air Quality Index score had soared as high as 210 recently. To put things in perspective, the author noted an index exceeding 50 was already considered poor air quality in Ontario. The article said some athletes who arrived in Beijing with mild asthma found themselves relying heavily on inhalers again, despite not needing them for years. As I read this investigative report on my lunch break, I grew increasingly concerned for the Olympic hopefuls—and myself.

Beijing continued to simmer with vibrancy. Life flourished alongside adversity. Locals gathered outdoors, savouring the balmy evenings. Restaurants brimmed with diners and echoing laughter. Men shed shirts, women fluttered delicate fans. I relished it all—the sizzle of cumin-crusted lamb skewers, the clink of glasses toasting. Friends averted me from dubious street stalls so I stuck to proper sit-down joints. Rumours had spread about questionable ingredients getting stuffed where they shouldn't—like dumplings packed with cardboard instead of pork. (Later proven a hoax, though it intrigued my family back home.) Even in oppressive heat under hazy skies, a vitality pulsed through the city that summer.

Nick and I rendezvoused as usual one weekend, drawn to lively conversation as much as good eats. Our meals invariably detoured into impromptu seminars musing on language, customs, and the curious dance between cultures. Over garlic eggplant, an insight struck. Textbook English puzzled Nick. 'How does one reply when Americans ask, 'How are you?'' Textbooks taught international students sterile pleasantries only.

I detailed the tribal customs—positivity regardless of how one actually felt. I shared an anecdote featuring a charismatic police officer at my old congressional office whose signature response always rang out, 'I'm FAN-tastic, Mr Loveland.' That officer would belt it out even on the worst days.

A wry smile crept across Nick's face as I outlined his options—'Living the dream', 'Another day in paradise' or even that coy classic, 'Hanging in there'. He realised nobody expected real talk when asked how they were doing. Americans were an optimistic people desperate to believe the best, even when misery marinated beneath the surface. In this way, words unfurled culture.

Nick's eyes crinkled as he listened, then cracked open, thirsty for contextual nuance. I waved maps, tracing the topography of American dialects—cadences that arched high in the south, flattening between clipped northern vowels. The waitress wandered by and we paused, two travellers poring over a map, basking in the promise of cross-cultural understanding.

Nick sought to introduce me to new and authentic dishes—his ongoing mission. He placed a plate of fried dumplings before me and described them as 'old Beijing style'.

'These are *dǎlian huǒshāo*,' he said. They resembled potstickers shaped like thin gold bars. Legend traced their origins back to the Qing dynasty's Guangxu period, specifically to Yao Chunxuan and his wife from Beijing's Shunyi neighbourhood. Sometimes folded in half, resembling satchels worn in ancient China, these delicacies were filled with ginger, green onions and pork encased in a crispy shell. They quickly became one of my favourites.

'These are absolutely amazing, Nick,' I said after the first bite.

Grinning ear to ear, Nick splashed on an ungodly amount of chilli-laced vinegar and slid my plate back with a flick of his wrist.

'Again,' he commanded.

I sank my teeth in. Those slender gold satchels ignited sparks upon my tongue like Chinese firecrackers, at once hot and thrilling. These old-school Beijing dumplings didn't just cross the finish line—they crushed it.

As we enjoyed our supper, Nick posed an unexpected question: 'Are American soldiers kind to regular people?' I assured him military men and women conducted themselves honourably overall. Furrowing his brow, Nick clarified he had meant local police. We exchanged knowing chuckles as I conveyed our complicated relationship with law enforcement—while some served communities with selfless courage, scandals around racism, brutality and overreach had strained public trust. I sought to help Nick grasp America's complex perspectives.

I learned Nick had red lines encircling certain topics—an invisible electrified fence of unease. Instinct guided me in discerning those cultural boundaries. Though brimming with curiosity about their political system, just as they were about mine, we tacitly agreed to skirt those third rails. This unspoken accord helped us avoid deeper divides.

Nick made a comment that struck me. 'If your skin wasn't white and your eyes weren't blue, you could pass for Chinese,' he observed. I gazed at him with mingled astonishment and intrigue. Placing his hand on his chest, he added meaningfully, 'You have a Chinese heart.'

His statement moved me. It was a testament to the connections I had forged, the bonds of friendship and understanding that transcended cultural and physical differences. Nick saw beyond appearances, recognising the empathy and appreciation I held for China and its people. In his eyes, I had become a part of the Chinese experience, not simply a visitor but someone who embraced the essence of their culture. Even in oppressive heat under hazy skies, connection pulsed through the city that summer.

JESS

When Jess first sauntered into the AITA offices, my confidence cratered. Another foreign consultant—with an unmistakable youthful swagger—here to charm Michael. Jess hailed from Mount Isa, Australia, which he described as 'hell on earth. The soil is red and the whole place smells of sulphur.' Surely Michael would fete his compatriot, invite Jess to high-level client meetings from which I would be excluded. While our passports were both blue in hue, Australia's Southern Cross constellation carried more weight than my Stars and Stripes at AITA.

Yet Michael didn't pit us against each other as I'd dreaded. For sure Jess received certain special invitations in those early days that I didn't, whisked off on weekend junkets and regaling me after with tales of fancy dinners and conversations with powerful people. But we were both foreigners adrift in this place, neither of us immune to Michael's whims nor AITA's opaque motives. Jess and I forged an unspoken pact, banding together to survive.

Aged twenty-three, Jess had lived in Beijing for six months in college and by the time we met, he spoke Mandarin far better than I did. He and I seemed quite similar in some of the surface-level views we subscribed to, but in other ways we were polar opposites. He dabbled in Satanism and loved reading books on global economics. Jess embraced a long, braided hairstyle that evoked imperial China's past. But striding through modern Beijing, that swooping ponytail colliding with twenty-first-century ambition, locals viewed him as an oddity at best. To them, Jess's nostalgic coif reflected how profoundly he misunderstood the national psyche, clinging to ancient ways while they raced towards the future. It was an affectation that distanced him from the ascendant Chinese elites he aimed to befriend.

Jess had an air of confidence that bordered on arrogance at times. He was always ready with a cheeky pronouncement such as, 'The trouble with me is I'm too good at what I do.' I had to stifle an eye roll whenever he bragged like that. Even he would admit that he could let his anger bubble up over time, only to suddenly explode at full force. But still, all foreigners who ended up in China for any amount of time shared some links.

I had worked at Starbucks in college, but it was Jess who opened my eyes to Australia's sophisticated café and coffee culture, bolstered by so many waves of recent immigrants. Jess brought with him an electric coffee grinder that he unpacked the first night he took over Scarlet's old room. In return, I picked up coffee beans at Starbucks for us to grind. We started each morning with a French press before heading out to work. That ritual bonded us and helped us prepare for what lay outside our apartment door.

When a new bar opened near our office, we were thrilled. It was small but cozy. The owner strove to deliver an authentic British pub vibe. We weren't sure he executed it entirely, but he got close. He had bottled beers imported from England and hung up flags of British football clubs. Jess and I usually headed down there at three-thirty to have a cappuccino. There was never anyone else besides the owner and a server at that time. We were nervous the first time we ordered one because we wondered how well the guy could make it. However, his cappuccino was not bad.

Trouble was, it took him about twenty minutes to prepare the drinks. We were already risking a fair bit by taking our work break away from the office. Michael frowned on doing much more than sneaking a smoke in the stairwell. Of course, my American mind wrangled up a plan. We explained to the bartender one day at lunch that we'd be back at three-thirty, *sān diǎn bàn*, and wanted two freshly made cappuccinos waiting for us. He agreed with a nod. So the next day, we got there at three-thirty. He smiled at us, came over and asked us what we wanted to drink. Jess and I broke into hysterical laughter.

After Scarlet moved out, I'd grown to love my independence. While I liked Jess, having another expat glued to my side didn't appeal to me.

I was wiping down the kitchen counter when Jess emerged from his room, hair dishevelled, eyes darkened from lack of sleep.

'Morning,' he mumbled, shuffling to the coffee grinder.

I inhaled the rich tobacco aroma as Jess scooped Sumatra beans into the grinder. He gave it sharp pulses like he did when he was annoyed, unleashing bitter waves into the air.

Dumping the fresh grounds into the French press, he sloshed in hot water and the brew's earthy scent filled the tense kitchen. I closed my eyes, letting the familiar sharpness prime my senses awake.

'Was thinking of checking out that new Italian spot tonight,' Jess said over the press's harsh gurgle. 'Maybe the Bookworm after? Could use some fun for once.'

I stirred cinnamon into my mug, considering. I'd grown to love my solo weekends—language exchanges, obscure neighbourhood wanders, joining the crowds that now felt like home.

'I actually have class tonight,' I said, trying not to sound petty. Jess set down his mug hard.

'Seriously? Feels like you had an excuse every weekend lately.'

I bristled at his expectation that I'd entertain him. 'I am trying to improve my Chinese. You know how hard it is …' I trailed off, avoiding the truth.

Jess nodded, but I saw the flicker of disappointment in his eyes. I knew he still felt unmoored here compared to my growing anchor. Sipping the hot coffee, I tasted my own twinge of guilt amid the swirling grounds.

I softened my tone. 'We'll hang out next weekend, I promise. Maybe we can go to Kro's Nest for pizza since you haven't been there yet.'

Jess nodded, tension easing from his face.

I'd first seen Jess as a threat; his language skills and China experience dwarfed mine. We were in such different places. He had already made his investments in the language and culture, whereas I was just starting out. An Australian studying Mandarin made career sense but China never stuck for him culturally whereas I found the language challenging but relished the rest of the experience. Feeling I had to justify my choices made me resent him. I was living in China and didn't know how long I would get to enjoy this opportunity, damn it.

But Jess always added value when he and I had meals with Chinese colleagues. My muddled mind could scarcely grasp traditional Eastern cures or the complexities of elegant Chinese script when a well-meaning Chinese person endeavoured to explain, no matter how patiently conveyed. Jess, however, born in Australia but China-schooled, cleverly bridged the gap. With scholarly delight, he interpreted mysteries and unravelled riddles for me. Through Jess, I gained enlightenment not only of medical arts and complicated *hànzì* characters but of the essence of China itself. Despite his youth, he'd studied the country and its customs for a long time.

Another perk of having Jess around was I could avoid thrusting myself into unfamiliar scenarios alone. One night Michael told us that we were going to get foot massages after work. I had never had a massage, much less a foot massage. Wouldn't it be ticklish? We all sat in the same room and the girl assigned to me gave me a back rub then washed my feet and applied different oils and lotions. It was far from heaven. A TV blared and all the massage girls talked and laughed to each other throughout the sixty-minute process. Having Jess to focus on and talk to made the experience less awkward. Afterward, I was stunned to learn that the massage had cost only 20 kuai, the price of a fast food value meal back in the States.

Whenever Scarlet and I had hit the streets of Beijing, we found that ignorance was bliss. We didn't speak Chinese and had no idea what the people all around us were saying, particularly about us. With Jess, I always knew what was happening. When Scarlet and I tootled around the city, I suspect many assumed we were a couple. People perceived Jess and me quite differently. Many of the locals saw us as two guys running around China, trying to bed as many girls as possible as quickly as possible. One morning, when we took the bus, he told me that some middle school kids were making fun of the size of his nose—and it was a bit pronounced, now that he'd pointed it out. Later, I told Nick that I'd read about how Chinese people used to refer to foreigners as 'big nose', instead of using the more contemporary term *lǎowài*. Nick blinked several times as he processed this detail and then informed me, 'In fact, Chinese people still say 'big nose' a lot. If we see a foreigner, we will just say, 'Oh, there is the big nose.''

One night, we went to dinner at a small restaurant near our apartment. It was late, about 9:30 pm, which meant the restaurant would close soon. I sat at the table facing the door. Our meal came quickly and we started eating. But I learned something that day. Whenever a restaurant shift ends, it's customary for all the kitchen staff and waiters to sit in the dining room and eat together. About five cooks and two servers came out and sat directly across from me. I became their entertainment as they watched me fumble with my chopsticks. And I was mortified.

Eavesdropping on their conversation, Jess informed me, 'They're saying you don't look comfortable.' I couldn't help but laugh that they could gauge my feelings that accurately, but I did not appreciate their intense curiosity. It made it difficult to keep eating. I was nowhere near comfortable being scrutinised the way foreigners in China regularly were in those days.

Thousands of foreigners lived in Beijing but we rarely saw them, especially as we lived and worked in Chongwenmen, one of the most native, non-touristy, non-expat neighbourhoods in the city inhabited primarily by locals. So we were often surprised when we saw other foreigners. One evening, Jess and I headed to the Beijing Bookworm for a special screening of the documentary *Crossing Over*, a film about American soldiers who had defected to North Korea during the war and never returned. Jess nudged me on the subway in shock and pointed out that some of our compatriots were there too. A group of six American women about college age. All were of Asian descent. They were talking boisterously and laughing, but I had barely registered their presence. Yet the Chinese natives on the subway seemed entranced at the sight of them. Many were leaning forward in their seats and studying the young women. Their exuberance was so foreign and yet they had Chinese faces. A couple of college-aged Chinese guys near us finally whispered to each other, *'Tāmen shì Měiguó rén'* meaning 'They're American.'

I was with Jess one Saturday evening and we planned to have dinner in the Jianguomen area. Lots of foreigners hung out there because so many embassies were located nearby. As a result, tonnes of people prowled the streets hawking pirated DVDs, which was quite popular among foreign tourists and residents alike. Buying a DVD of an American movie cost less than the movie tickets back home. But locals couldn't believe foreigners would pay for the DVDs as they downloaded the latest releases for free from websites. The DVD hawkers usually hung outside the friendship store and Starbucks. I wasn't in the market for DVDs that night, but Jess was.

A guy came over and showed us his selection. We started browsing. Then four of his partners came over with even more DVDs and some fake watches. Jess picked out about ten DVDs, and I chose two although I wasn't that interested. I would skim-read the back of one and the guy would say

'Maybe?' and place them in a special pocket in his bag. That should have been my first clue that something was up.

The man spoke limited English but did his best to market the discs. He would point to a DVD and say, 'New one.' He pointed to the disc for *Live Free or Die Hard* and declared, 'Bruce Willis very good.' Hell, who needed film reviewers Ebert and Roeper with recommendations like that?

We negotiated the price to six kuai per DVD. Then the guy asked me, 'Six?'

I said, 'Yes, six.'

'No, sex! Yellow movies?'

'Oh ... no,' I said as I realised what he meant. 'No, but thanks.'

We purchased our DVDs, thanked our hawkers and made our way to Grandma's Kitchen to feast on mozzarella sticks, pizza and milkshakes. We decided to watch a movie later that evening and had a rude surprise. All of Jess's DVD cases were stuffed with cardboard to make it seem like they held a disc. I had actual discs in mine, but all for the wrong movies. I'd never been burned buying pirated DVDs before. We made a pledge that night to buy only from people we trusted.

I found Jess brooding after a wretched week at work, indignant, too, after being duped by the scammer—the last thing he needed. My friend stewed in uncharacteristic resentment over the trifling sum lost. But I knew Jess took pride in being honourable; the principle cut deep. Inspiration struck! We would eat dinner at Outback Steakhouse at the Workers' Stadium. Outback was one of a handful of restaurants that served steak back then. Jess had never been to an Outback and was even more surprised when I told him the chain was pretty popular in America. The prices there were high for China and priced illogically in my view. My hamburger cost 54 kuai, while only a small dessert cost 66 kuai. That was crazy. We were furious when we got the bill, especially once we saw that they had added a ten per cent service charge to the bill. Tipping was an American concept, certainly not something one did in China, and the service had not even been spectacular. Our meal ended up costing about 300 kuai, which was exorbitant, especially given our monthly salaries were only 5000 kuai.

Jess had a notorious sweet tooth. I peeked in his desk drawer one day and found four Snickers, a bag of Oreos, a bag of China's own White Rabbit taffies, a bag of mini croissants, a used ice-cream wrapper and two packets of toilet tissue—the latter being a regular feature of life in China because most public restrooms weren't stocked with it. Jess had an aversion to fruit, which was a regular end-of-meal serving as dessert. By 2007, Western products such as Coca-Cola and other staples of American convenience stores had only recently begun to gain momentum. The younger generations especially loved the foreign brands.

In the lead-up to the Olympics, Snickers was making a major investment in the country. Having done enough market research to learn that Chinese consumers loved gambling, Snickers started a 'Win a Free Snickers Bar' contest in the wrappers. The drill was to buy the bar, open it and see if you'd won one for your next trip to the store. Part of our commute to work also included stopping by a small convenience store so Jess could buy a Snickers or two. The free candy bar was such a hot-ticket item that the cashiers routinely took the proactive step of pulling out someone else's winning wrapper to let customers know about the contest. As it turned out, the odds were excellent. Out of twenty Snickers Jess bought, he must've had seventeen winning wrappers. Snickers had to have invested a tonne of money in this 'everybody wins' promotion, but it made for brilliant marketing.

Jess and I knew that the sheen of our foreign faces garnered favours and curiosities. But, as we discovered, there were also limits. We went back to the same convenience store a few days later and I picked up a bottle of green tea while Jess presented yet another winning wrapper. The cashier was a middle-aged woman who did not look nearly as enthused as Jess. Taking the wrapper, she dived underneath the counter and pulled out what appeared to be a special sack of Snickers.

As she reached in to give him one, I said, 'Something tells me that those aren't the winning bars.' And they weren't. Jess seethed, annoyed that the jig was up. He vowed that we would never go back to that convenience store, and we never did. Jess fumed, explaining that the cashier likely wouldn't even understand why we didn't come back. She probably assumed we'd returned to our countries of origin.

Jess and I spent so much time together that we eventually adopted each other's vocabularies. In time, I picked up his 'bloody hell' while he swapped Australian 'rubbish' for the American 'trash'. That was even more surprising, since Jess wasn't exactly pro-American. He held quite a few negative stereotypes of Americans. They were arrogant and always looking down on everyone else in his mind. My openness and lack of machismo simply shattered Jess's stereotype of all Americans being like our president George W Bush, who had called the Australian prime minister John Howard his 'sheriff' in the Asia-Pacific region.

When I first met Jess, I felt intimidated. Here was this Australian who spoke Mandarin and knew his way around China so well. I hadn't expected to connect with someone so different from me. But in the midst of all China's inscrutable dynamism, Jess and I found common ground. He made a sometimes scary experience into a fun adventure. And I cherished the bond we forged as strangers in a strange land.

FRYING THE SQUID

Michael wasn't entirely evil. Sometimes he did more for me than I appreciated. One weekend, his driver picked me up to take me to a clothing emporium known as the Zoo Market where Michael and Vicky were waiting for me.

'You can get clothes here for cheap,' Michael said. While foreign tourists frequented the Silk Market and the Pearl Market for knockoff clothing, locals shopped at places like the Zoo Market. Vicky glided to my rescue, not only interpreting the sellers' rapid-fire patter but bartering them down in a gruelling test of wills. I emerged triumphant with an armful of breezy short-sleeved shirts and cotton shorts costing a mere 100 kuai—an extraordinary steal no foreigner would stumble upon alone.

Michael didn't do that kind of thing often. Yes, he did frequently invite me to exclusive dinners with management or top performers. However, I came to dread those outings. Having already built a strong social network in Beijing, I barely had time for my friends or Chinese classes. Without fail, Michael's invitations meant that I had to cancel something. Not only that, but also I wasn't comfortable around him. Boss-employee relationships felt different in China. Though Michael granted me more slack than most leashed subordinates, I chafed watching him crack the whip over cowering colleagues resigned to indentured servitude. I hated faking it through meals with him. As a newbie to China, I also struggled with the most basic aspects of life. If Michael ordered a noodle dish, those noodles would inevitably slip right out of my chopsticks.

One day, Michael had secured a deal where AITA would arrange a delegation to Australia on behalf of the *People's Court Daily*, a prestigious newspaper that covered China's Supreme People's Court. 'Signed and sealed,' Michael crowed. I blinked at his rare public display of elation as he slid into his office chair, steepling his fingers with hungry satisfaction. The more prestigious the client, the more doors opened for him—in China and elsewhere.

'Dinner tonight, Glen,' he said. I cringed.

'I can't. I have a Chinese class,' I blurted.

Michael's face dropped. Yet again, I'd jammed my foot in my mouth. A boss inviting their employee to dinner was an honour. You couldn't reject something like that. Any of my Chinese coworkers would have rearranged their life to accompany the boss to dinner, no matter what they had planned.

'Next time, next time,' he muttered, a sober look on his face as he walked out. With that, I realised the gravity of my mistake, but it was too late to reverse. On one hand, I did need to learn Chinese. That would make me a more valuable employee. On the other hand, strengthening your relationship with your boss was key to survival in China—much more so than your skills and achievements.

In the build-up to the Beijing Olympics, Adidas plastered the city with confident ads declaring 'Impossible Is Nothing'—a mantra Michael embodied in business. Data, facts, logic and reason didn't matter when Michael had an idea, no matter how half-baked. But I could never figure out where he'd obtained some of these notions. One thing that surprised me was how much Michael, the company's CEO, involved himself with interviewing new hires. I could imagine him interviewing senior candidates, but he even interviewed people who seemed junior. I asked Judy if this was typical behaviour in China. She shook her head. 'Most of them will not get hired. Michael does that to learn ideas about what other businesses are doing. He wants to see how we can make money.' That explained why Michael had so many ideas that seemed to come out of thin air. Every day, he basically did a deep dive with these kids about their former employers and their methods, challenges and opportunities. *Deceitful but clever.*

After spending two hours with a candidate—one who didn't get the job—Michael asked me to tackle a project exploring the feasibility of exporting titanium to Australia. China had become the world's second-largest titanium dioxide market, and this represented an opportunity for AITA. I was excited to throw myself into the research. This was a chance to do something totally different from what I had done in my career. Unfortunately, I concluded my report with bad news.

'Based on my research, there seem to be very few export opportunities for titanium to Australia. Australia is a country rich in titanium and the country reported major mining increases in the December 2006 quarter.'

More than that, China had implemented a ten per cent export tax a few months earlier to clamp down on the export of titanium. China wanted to rein in exports and increase titanium imports. I knew my findings would discourage Michael.

Replying to my conclusions the next day, he wrote, 'Thanks

for doing this, Glen. See if we can find some companies in Australia that are looking for titanium.'

I reread the message several times. Had I submitted the wrong report? Maybe I should have used charts or graphics? How did Michael not understand this was a fool's errand? An enormous waste of time that would make AITA—and me—look like idiots.

Impossible is nothing.

'Hi, Glen. What's going on with the Victoria delegation visit?' Michael asked once, appearing from out of nowhere to pace behind my chair. 'Did you find a chemical association there? The delegation is interested in Australian chemicals.' Without waiting for an answer, he pivoted on his heel and stalked through the hallways, barking orders at anyone who came into view. He would assign his off-the-cuff ideas to each of us in an urgent, need-it-by-yesterday tone. We got no time for analysis or discussion. He expected us to just get it—and get on with it.

Michael was often his own worst enemy. He insisted on being cc'd on all outgoing emails. Part of this, I suppose, was to make sure we spent all our time working. But the rest of it was about his vanity. On multiple occasions, a prospect would hit 'reply all' with something to the effect of 'I will have nothing to do with Michael Guo or AITA.' That drove Michael up the wall. Sometimes, he would even reply with an insult. The company kept no records of people they'd had sour dealings with before, so contacting organisations was like throwing darts in the dark. Had Michael been more strategic we could have cooperatively planned events spotlighting our partners rather than fuelling an obsession with personal glory.

Things got shady after a while. A few months in, Michael told me that I would start receiving small bonuses. That confused me. Why was he rewarding me specifically? Eventually, he sent me an email:

> Dear Glen,
>
> I am writing to confirm our conversation and the extra bonus last time. I want to pay you extra RMB 1500 (one thousand and five hundred RMB) per month, of which 500 RMB will be given each month; the other 1000 RMB will be given at the end of the contract. This offer starts from May 2007.
>
> I want to do this to show my appreciation of your active involvement and devotion to the work, I would really appreciate it if you could be more proactive in assisting the staff in your office to achieve our goals.
>
> Best Regards, Michael
>
> Note: Please keep this in confidential, I will give the extra separately myself.

At the time, I'd never heard of the Chinese concept of 'grey income', so this baffled me. Grey income was a salary supplement paid in cash, untaxed, and off the books. Each month when I entered Michael's office to collect the 500 kuai, my stomach was in knots. Something seemed sordid about it, but 500 kuai was 500 kuai. Honestly, I felt like Michael added the money only to incentivise me to work harder and faster—like a commission. But with so much of the money linked to the end of my contract, I think getting me to finish my contract was part of its appeal for him. End-of-contract bonuses sprang up a lot in China. They were an acknowledgment that most people would want to flee their work but would likely hang on for a few more months solely for the money—unless they were 'fried squid', or *bèi chǎo yóuyú le*. A popular phrase from Hong Kong, to become a fried squid meant that you'd been sacked.

Like a pedestrian who crosses a street without looking and gets hit by a car, I made a nearly fatal career mistake that could have cost me my job.

Many times at work, I sat there with nothing to do: no projects, no emails to reply to, just waiting for Michael to tap my shoulder. *Does he even know I'm here?* I wondered sometimes. After Scarlet's departure, I was the only foreigner in the office for months. Not only did I have job security, but the company also needed me more often than most of my coworkers, even if only for ad-hoc projects like polishing Chinglish or researching obscure business prospects abroad.

When whispers of the University of Chicago's coming MBA student delegation to China reached my ears, I knew I had to seize the opportunity. The two-week immersion program promised a tantalising glimpse into the world of international business and I was determined to be a part of it.

With a mixture of hope and trepidation, I crafted an email to Linda Darragh, the esteemed director of the Polsky Center for Entrepreneurship and Innovation. It was a long shot, but I had to try. I inquired about the possibility of attending the opening day event, my fingers trembling with anticipation as I hit send.

The lineup of speakers was a veritable who's who of the business world, a collection of luminaries I had only dreamed of encountering. Dr Zhi Tan, the visionary president of Focus Media, would be there, along with Dr Bin Qi from the China Securities Regulatory Commission. The prospect of hearing from Dr Zhu Min, vice president at Bank of China, and Miaomiao Shi, deputy director at the Ministry of Commerce, set my mind ablaze. And of course, Frank Joseph from the US Department of Commerce would be in attendance, adding an American perspective to the already impressive roster.

As I waited for a response, the decision before me was obvious. I could either seize this once-in-a-lifetime chance to rub elbows with some of the most influential businesspeople in the world, or I could resign myself to rotting away at my computer, pretending to work.

I grossly underestimated the time it would take to navigate the Monday morning rush hour traffic from my apartment to the China World Hotel in Guomao. As I sat in the back of the taxi, my eyes glued to the clock, I silently cursed myself for not factoring in the gridlock that plagued Beijing's streets.

By the time I burst into room 8A, my breath coming in short gasps, I had arrived just in time to catch the beginning of Dr Justin Yifu Lin's speech. The audience was hanging on his every word, captivated by the tale of his remarkable journey.

Born and raised in Taiwan, Lin had made a daring escape to the mainland in 1979, jumping into the sea and leaving everything he knew behind. 'I saw that the mainland was the future,' he said, his voice filled with conviction. The Communist Party had eagerly embraced him and Lin went on to earn a master's degree in economics from the prestigious Peking University.

'I received the very first private licence plate in Beijing. It was plate number one,' Lin revealed, pride in his tone. He now served as the director of the China Center for Economic Research at Peking University, a position of great influence and responsibility. Less than a year later, he would ascend to the role of chief economist at the World Bank.

As I listened to Lin's optimistic outlook on China's future, I found myself inspired by his story of resilience and success. In that moment, any lingering doubts about ditching work for this event evaporated. I knew I had made the right choice and I was determined to soak up every bit of wisdom and insight the speakers had to offer.

In my excitement, I had made a critical error: I had failed to seek Michael's permission directly. Looking back, it's clear that Michael had granted me, a foreigner, some privilege. He had been lenient in the past, allowing me the occasional day off, but I had taken his generosity for granted.

It was a foolish oversight on my part not to send him a simple email requesting the day off. I had convinced myself that I mattered only when Michael needed something from me. I had wondered if he would even notice my absence. How little I understood the true nature of our relationship, the extent to which I was considered his property.

Of course, he noticed. The moment I stepped back into the office, an unsettling chill permeated the air, a stark contrast to the sweltering heat of late August. The atmosphere was thick and I couldn't shake the feeling that something was amiss. But when the workmates who usually gave me a friendly smile suddenly found the floor or ceiling more interesting as I walked by I realised that I had become the hot topic. Were my colleagues avoiding me? Why did they avert their gazes, refusing to meet my eyes?

The moment I settled into my desk, the uneasy stillness of the office was shattered by the sudden appearance of Michael. It was as if he had been lying in wait. I realised then that he must have tasked someone with alerting him the instant I set foot in the building.

His voice was cold, devoid of any pretence of civility. 'Glen, gather your things and come with me.' It was not a request but an order, delivered with the authority of a man who held my fate in his hands.

Uh-oh ...

I picked up my bag and we walked into an empty office across the hall. I was being fired. Floored by Michael's overreaction, I started searching for answers. He thought that I had been interviewing for other jobs, I surmised.

I shifted in the metal chair. 'My deepest apologies for any misunderstanding,' I offered with a fretful grin. 'I should have called.'

Michael slammed shut the open metal drawer. 'If you don't like working here, leave.'

I flinched but pressed forward carefully. 'I've only been here a few months but I've done great at arranging schedules for the delegations. I even got a reply from the New Zealand embassy this morning. Things have been going so well.'

A meek knock broke the tension. Office manager Tan Lu peeked inside. 'Sorry to interrupt, but the team has arri—'

Michael erupted from his chair, his face contorted with a rage so intense it seemed to radiate from every pore. In a blur of motion, he lunged for the door, his hand a vice-like grip on the handle. With a force that shook the very walls, he slammed the door shut, the sound reverberating through the room like a thunderclap.

From the other side, Tan Lu's muffled yelp seeped through the cracks. My heart sank as the realisation hit me like a tonne of bricks: my ill-conceived decision to take a day off had not only put my own future in jeopardy but had now endangered the innocent staff who found themselves caught in the crossfire.

I had seen Michael in rages like this with others but never with me. My transgression had caused him to lose face. He sat back down, his face red, the veins on his neck popping. Of all the mistakes I had made in my six months in China, this was clearly the biggest breach.

'Please, I meant no ill will,' I pleaded, the false calm in my voice betrayed by trembling hands. 'I'm still learning …'

'Okay.' The word landed like a judge's gavel. 'Don't let it happen again.'

For Michael, an immature and emotional man, this was a major concession on his part. In all his career, I was the only employee who had managed to convince him not to fire them. With Jess on board, I could easily be replaced. And yet I got off lucky. I would not find out until near the end of my contract that Chinese employees were routinely fired for taking sick days, even with a doctor's note.

I mostly hated my job but I remained determined to finish the yearlong contract. AITA offered a window into a side of China that I wouldn't get elsewhere. It also provided a platform for my emerging life in China that met my needs. I refused to let anything fuck it up.

Of all the differences in work culture, however, there was one that I had never prepared for: shaming. After Michael nearly terminated me, the word spread among my colleagues about my skipping work. The Chinese workplace's grapevine, as I came to understand it, was less like Western gossip and more like internal communication. You didn't need a company newsletter when you could rely on someone else telling you the latest dirt. Chinese employees lived and breathed this kind of information, no matter how trivial. But not speaking Chinese, I was largely out of the loop on the goings-on in the offices at AITA beyond our small room. But when the colleagues who typically smiled at me averted their gaze when I walked by, I realised I had become the hot topic.

Am I imagining things? I wondered.

The water dispenser, once a hub of collegiality, became a stark reminder of my fall from grace. Once met with friendly glances, my presence now garnered diverted eyes and a palpable chill. The facts were irrelevant; by challenging the authority of our boss I had transgressed an unspoken boundary. The message was clear: toe the line or face the consequences of ostracism.

The next day, I knew for sure I was being publicly shamed when we had a group lunch with a visiting delegation. Ms Xu, the highest-ranked woman in the company, was organising the table and deciding who would sit where. These kinds of decisions in China weren't mere formalities; seat placement directly correlated with rank. It showed who was in and who was out. She initially indicated that I should take a seat by Michael—the one facing the door. Then, I saw her reconsider me with a furrowed brow. No, I would be relegated to the lowest-ranking seat: the one with my back to the door. In the old days, invaders would usually kill the person in this seat first. Ms Xu didn't speak much English, but she gave me a look to make sure I understood what had happened. I had lost face and was being demoted. I chuckled nervously.

The ostracism, though temporary, left deep wounds. My colleagues ensured that the exclusion was palpable, a feeling you would do anything to avoid experiencing again. Being a foreigner already set me apart, but the added layer of isolation, even for a short time, was excruciating. In the Chinese workplace you didn't need a formal evaluation to gauge your performance; the feedback was immediate and unmistakable.

INDECENT PROPOSAL

With my mind vaguely set and heaps of courage gathered, I met Judy on the second floor at a Starbucks in Chongwenmen. I'd spent a long time thinking about my proposal. I bought each of us an iced mocha and nervously recited the lines in my head again and again before finding my voice.

'I like you—I like spending time with you,' I began slowly. 'You know what? We get along well.'

I hesitated, the coffee suddenly bitter on my tongue. She was gazing at me with those dark eyes of hers, patient and steadfast, and I felt a swell of affection so intense it nearly winded me. How many times had we sat together like this across some small table, speaking about our childhoods, our work, our dreams for the future? She made me want to bare my soul, to be worthy of such devotion.

'I also know that you want to get married ...' The words faded even as I uttered them. I took a gulp of coffee, throat convulsing. 'I am attracted to men. We could be together, but you would need to give me space for my physical needs. Nothing emotional with them, but I need to fulfil my physical desires.' I gazed at her with true candour. I did care for her, as much as I'd ever cared for anyone. But not enough. Not in the way I should. The way she deserved.

Judy sat there at an evident loss for words, her eyes scanning me tactfully as she processed everything I said. Then, her mouth dropped open. 'Glen. I could never accept this.' She paused for a moment, considering my words again. 'My mother ... my mother could never accept this.'

I regretted not revealing my aims more incrementally rather than presenting them so bluntly, as if negotiating a contract. Living in China had transformed me into someone who got straight to the point. Alas, the words had been spoken and there was no way to take them back.

Did I cross a line? Judy always indulged my crazy plans but it seemed I'd failed to consider that everything had its limit. Still, I rallied in defence. 'Your mother wouldn't have to know. You said yourself that men always get bored with their wives and play on the side anyway. What difference does it make that I'm trying to be transparent? To have an agreement and understanding?'

She continued to process my words and I felt the air between us compress. I had naively assumed she would be charmed by my willingness to restrain baser urges in order to nurture a genuine, fulfilling relationship with her. In truth, the idea wasn't so unusual. There were gay men who did the same thing I was trying to do, but most of them didn't inform their wives and had secret liaisons. Admittedly, I'd neglected taking the time to contemplate a decision of such magnitude and I was still unsure about whether this arrangement was the right thing either. It quickly became evident from Judy's reaction that it was a mistake to think that she would be more open-minded to forging this kind of partnership with me.

I had heard about straight Chinese women who were set on exclusively marrying gay men so they could have the kind of fun together that straight guys would oppose. Revelling in leisure travels, enjoying pamper treatments and living an overall diverting lifestyle. But this was not to be our destiny.

Judy snatched up her coffee. She stood abruptly, chair legs screeching against the floor, the sound piercing the heavy air between us. 'I have to go,' she muttered, not meeting my eyes as she turned towards the stairs. A lock of black hair fell across her cheek but she left it, the strands sheltering her face.

Miserably rejected, my greatest fear was brought to light—worse still, I was about to lose one of the closest friends I'd ever had, all because of a single miscalculated proposal. I had thought I could help Judy resolve the marriage problem that seemed to gnaw at her. Instead, I only added to that mounting pressure.

The next morning, I opened an email from Judy in which she poured out her resolution in broken English. It was clear she had spent a significant amount of time writing something that would accurately convey her emotions, and they were very conflicting. The subject was titled: 'The difference between America and China'.

> Although Americans have done a lot of studies and records on all kinds of strange human behavior, they contribute a lot to modern science. Today I realise your society's moral education is very weak. Your teachers never judge students. They always encourage and respect them, but at the same time your society also indulges their behavior. In China, the situation is the opposite. Children are coached by parents and teachers. Traditionally, teachers punish students; their parents can't blame teachers, because it will make children object to discipline. Family, parents and children are very

important parts in our life. Most Chinese will sacrifice their happiness for the other's view. I don't know what kind your mates are. I guess most of them aren't a decent class in society because high-class people obey society's discipline and are more self-controlled since childhood. Every society has its advantages and disadvantages, but these days I realise I am becoming more and more in love with my country, in love with Chinese culture. I am so glad I was brought up in this environment and did not lose myself.

I stared at my computer screen, reading and rereading her message. It stung. Not only did my own morality come into question but my friends and the society in which I was raised found their own morality questioned as well. I knew there would be blowback from Judy, but not like this.

After that, our communication and meetings became sporadic. The wedge I drove between Judy and me became an everyday burden. We never fully addressed what happened between us again, but staying busy meant that I had little time to grieve.

Judy and her mother moved to Shanghai the following year, which meant that our fading friendship would die out. We still kept in touch, but mostly through email and texting. She didn't seem to adjust well in Shanghai and I was always perplexed over the chosen destination. Having grown up in northeast China, Judy found that Shanghai was a totally different world. But maybe that was the point. I always wondered if I drove Judy to leave Beijing.

Occasional glimpses of her new life depressed me. Judy

never put her talents to use, but constantly drifted between dead-end jobs. Even worse, companies couldn't identify or leverage her talents. She was another cog in the machine to them. It didn't seem to bother her much because she never spoke about needing the salary. Her mother financed her lifestyle, so working was almost like a hobby.

When she came back on a business trip, we met at the Beijing Bookworm. I was sentimental as I headed there, remembering the good times. Judy told me about her new life in Shanghai. 'Glen, it's so hard. When you walk into a government office, the first thing the officer speaks is Shanghainese to test whether you're a local. When you switch to Mandarin, they are impolite.' She said she yearned for her former life in Beijing and spending time with me. I seized the opportunity to encourage her to move back, but she shot it down without a second thought. 'No, my mother likes it there.' She didn't elaborate.

At the end of the day, Judy was still … well, very much Judy. She still unapologetically sported her belly, beamed her infectious smile and proudly expressed her wildest dreams. 'Glen, I just want a rich man to marry me,' she chuckled, prompting a smile to rise on my lips.

Despite her challenges, Judy refused to be defeated by life. She was the eternal optimist, positive and confident to no foreseeable end. A beautiful enigma, a faithful and unyielding dreamer; that was Judy.

ANOTHER DAY

The driver and I waited in silence outside the Australian embassy, a haze of cigarette smoke wafting between us. I rubbed my temples, unable to shake thoughts of Michael's latest outburst. Exhaling a long drag, the driver cocked his head, reading the lines of tension in my face. He gestured emphatically, fist over his heart. 'Michael,' he offered softly, lips pursed around the cigarette perched there. His eyes pleaded for understanding as he repeated the friendly beating of his chest. I bobbed my head in false understanding.

Flicking away the glowing embers of his spent cigarette, the driver turned his grimace towards the embassy. His face echoed my own unease.

The driver meant well in trying to humanise Michael's volatility. But having witnessed firsthand the trail of destruction these episodes left, I harboured no such generosity. The Michael I knew behind closed doors was coming spectacularly undone under the pressures. Indeed, there was no telling what chaos he might see fit to unleash inside those walls today. More and more of our visa applications were being scrutinised, and Michael wasn't happy about it. I sensed our capacity to keep smoothing it over was shrinking by the day. The damage was becoming too great.

The workdays at AITA were often unpredictable. Some weeks I would sit at my desk with minimal tasks, only for a sudden flurry of meetings to arise the next day. As someone inclined towards planning, I had to learn to be flexible and embrace the excitement of the unknown, but it took time to grasp the true nature of AITA's operations.

The company frequently arranged delegations of Chinese provincial officials to visit Australia and New Zealand and vice versa, organising meetings with government agencies or businesses for them. I wasn't privy to every detail, but I couldn't discern the true purpose of these meetings—at first.

It was not uncommon for Australian immigration officers to verify our delegations' travel schedules, occasionally calling to confirm the itinerary. While some of the official business meetings we registered on their immigration entry forms did materialise, others did not.

I vividly recall a regrettable incident when I had persuaded an Australian agency to meet our group on Christmas Day for but 'twenty minutes'. Our delegation's no-show came as a shock.

No longer able to endure the buzzing phone in my pocket, I was confronted by a flurry of furious emails from our stood-up Australian hosts who had waited for two hours in an empty conference room on Christmas Day while the delegation probably spent the day shopping and leisurely strolling along Bondi Beach, relaxed in shorts and sunglasses.

Afterwards, the atmosphere rife with tension, I approached Vicky to vent, allowing my usual mask of diplomacy to slip.

'Sorry to interrupt, but we need to talk about the Australians getting stood up today.'

Vicky glanced up from behind mounds of paperwork, letting out a dismissive chuckle. 'Oh, just a last-minute change in plans. You know how it goes.'

I bristled, jaw clenching. 'On Christmas, though? They

waited two hours in an empty conference room.'

'No matter, no matter,' she breezed, eyes back on her computer screen. 'We'll smooth things later.'

I stared Vicky down, but her eyes didn't budge. With a scoff I spun on my heel, furious.

When my rage was met with nonchalance, a stark understanding hit through the swirling indignation. We were merely an elite travel agency providing golden visa stamps for Chinese officials and the wealthy elite. We were not here to empower anyone—not entrepreneurs, not governments. AITA had one purpose only: access.

But the access we dangled to clients, while often hollow, kept the money rolling in.

Reviewing a delegation's approaching schedule, I sighed, recalling how I'd pleaded with our travel team to diversify the dining itineraries, to no avail it seemed. Would it have pained these esteemed guests so greatly to forgo Chinese restaurants for one dinner? To risk a few foreign flavours from the lands they'd flown halfway across the globe to experience.

I'd left a folder of restaurant recommendations on Vicky's desk, full of local gems I was certain no itinerary had yet seen.

Menus touting pavlova taller than the Opera House, tender John Dory fresh from the Tasmanian waters, even that curious brown spread called Vegemite.

Conversely, the Kiwi and Aussie officials visiting China were eager to immerse themselves in local food and drink, particularly the latter.

While hosts catered elaborate banquets blending regional fare, Australian guests always made an immediate beeline for the beer taps—even amid morning negotiations. Their palates seemed to crave a reliable lager as much as any unknown dish placed before them.

No one could accuse the MP Helen Shardey of false advertising. She'd sashayed in wearing an exquisitely embroidered cardigan and a glittering Star of David brooch pinned to her chest, looking every inch the dignified stateswoman. That is, until we arrived at the buffet line and her eyes, with almost feral alacrity, spotted the free drink options.

'What've you got over there, love?' she called out briskly. I indicated it was merely an array of teas, presuming a cultured woman of her stature would have little interest in imbibing at this early hour. But no sooner had I gestured politely towards the Tsingtao bottles in the corner than she was off, moving with surprising gusto to grab a bottle.

By lunch's end, three empty beer bottles stood proudly beside her plate like bowling pins at the alley. One almost expected her to throw up her arms and bellow 'Strike!' Instead, she mildly lamented these Chinese brews were no match for a crisp Victoria Bitter from back home. Still, one must applaud the efforts on both sides. Perhaps the shortest distance between two cultures isn't art or rhetoric but the simple clinking of two bottles—one Tsingtao, one Victoria Bitter.

While we used our network and contacts, the officials and politicians who collaborated with us also benefited from the perception of furthering relations between their respective countries.

I fully understood the pressures these individuals faced. Photo opportunities were vital in the political realm and China was a highly sought-after market for conducting business. Snapping a picture with a visiting delegation from a Chinese village or small city presented an opportunity for a press release, allowing officials to showcase their efforts in expanding exports or fostering cultural ties.

The acronym MOU was on everyone's lips at AITA. Though legally non-binding, these Memorandums of Understanding sparked an optimistic spirit of alliance between two bodies. However, the enthusiasm over these pacts likely outsized their practical influence, denoting more of a verbal pact than an ironclad vow to cooperate. For AITA, MOUs served as the bread and butter for advancing our interests, forming the cornerstone of partnerships even if not contractually airtight.

Their beauty lay in suiting Chinese partners who lacked authority to formally cooperate abroad without approval from Beijing authorities. Provincial delegations and even private Chinese businesses often operated within these political constraints. Hence the non-binding MOU allowed them to signal willingness to collaborate with AITA's Aussie and Kiwi clients without requiring the immediate green light from China to take effect. While more symbolic than substantive, it was a superficial tool that provided cover for everyone involved and Chinese delegations visiting Australia could return home armed with evidence that their trip had yielded tangible results rather than being perceived as a mere vacation.

Similarly, foreign counterparts could present the MOU as evidence of progress.

Another favourite term of Michael's was 'big potato'. I found this expression oddly amusing. Whenever we were sending a Chinese delegation to meet someone in Australia or New Zealand, Michael emphasised the need to secure meetings with prominent figures, officials or departments, which he called 'big potatoes'.

But the days of scheduling meetings with local chambers of commerce were fading. China's continuing crackdown on government spending, prompted by concerns over corruption, had influenced this shift.

Chinese government–affiliated organisations became reluctant to finance trips that might be misconstrued as mere holidays or something more nefarious. A meeting with a federal agency overseas was deemed a far safer bet and akin to practices even lobbyists in Washington understood. However, due to the bridges AITA had burned in the past, arranging these 'big potatoes' was proving ever more challenging, regardless of who made the request.

I also realised that Michael had his hands in plenty of ventures I didn't know about. Arriving at the office one morning, I crossed paths with one of Michael's dubious associates. The New Zealand accent was unmistakable. Middle-aged, he had a ruddy complexion, sweat bleeding through his tank top. He and the driver were on the stairwell, smoking between peals of gravelly laughter.

I felt a pang of exclusion as I lingered there, clutching my briefcase. What stories they must be swapping, I thought. If only I could access that exclusive banter instead of being linguistically confined to this outsider's realm of smiles and gestures.

As it happened, this man was one of potentially hundreds of imported teachers contracted by Michael to work in China's remote provinces. The scheme had all the trappings of a standard business opportunity, filling demand for cheap foreign English instructors. But something about the New Zealander didn't sit right. Maybe it was the yellowing of his teeth or the drunken slur infecting his words at this early hour.

I reminded myself that wilful ignorance had its advantages. The less I involved myself in Michael's machinations, the freer my conscience would remain. And freedom was in short supply around AITA. As I hurried past them into the safety of my office, the truth rang out as clear as the laughter trailing behind: bliss often blossoms best in darkness.

NÍNGBŌ

As I waited at the baggage claim at Ningbo Lishe International Airport, I noticed some rules posted:

The checked baggage should be packed correctly and locked well.

Please check in animals and alcoholics [*sic*].

Passengers may carry 2 bottle of wine and the volume of either 1 or 2 should not be more than one kilogram.

Liu Bing, the woman who would be my interpreter, greeted me at the airport. She worked as an English teacher at the Ningbo Institute of Technology at Zhejiang University. Older than me by quite a bit, she had an infectious kindness that radiated from her warm smile. She was originally from Nanjing and had lived in Ningbo for several years.

Ningbo would mark my third business trip with AITA. Michael wasn't always forthcoming with details on why we were visiting certain places or what our ultimate goals would be. But for me, it represented another chance to explore beyond Beijing. I had hesitated to go at first because we wouldn't return until September 24, a day before my birthday, and I yearned to be in Beijing for my first birthday in China. On the other hand, I wanted to see as much of the country as possible, so I didn't make a fuss.

As we climbed into the van on the way to the hotel, Liu Bing enthusiastically pointed out landmarks. It was obvious that she was intelligent, and I could visualise her brain whirling away, making links, and analysing what I said. She hung on to every word.

Although Ningbo was warmer than Beijing in the autumn, the rest of my trip was shrouded in mist and moisture. The fog played with the streets, sparking my imagination. As night fell, even the neon brilliance of the China Mobile billboard succumbed to the all-encompassing mist, fading away like a half-remembered dream. Tendrils of fog caressed the city, obscuring the landmarks. The mist muted sounds, lending an eerie quiet to the night. Shadows emerged and receded as the fog thickened and dissipated in a hypnotic dance. The city was transformed, once familiar streets now mysterious in the encompassing gloom. Imagination sprang from every obscured corner and hazy alley. As darkness enveloped Ningbo, the fog welcomed the night.

While we stood in the hotel lobby waiting for our room keys, Michael handed me a folder that revealed the purpose of our trip. We were attending the Ningbo High-Tech Symposium. The English translation of the event made it sound mechanical and uninspired: '... a platform to showcase science and tech achievements, improve technology exchange, assemble high science and tech talent, and enhance communication in the fields of science and technology.'

I awoke to sunlight streaming through the floor-to-ceiling windows of my river-view suite at the Golden Port Hotel, Ningbo's finest accommodation. Below me sprawled a convergence of three waterways, the city's skyscrapers gleaming like mirrors along the banks. Somewhere down there was Ningbo's bund—an embankment along the waterfront, like the more famous one glittering along Shanghai's Huangpu River.

Over breakfast, I asked the waiter, 'Does Ningbo's bund predate Shanghai's?'

He flashed me a proud grin. 'Ningbo's has been around much longer. Everyone knows our history is richer.'

I smiled to myself, reminded how China often felt less like a unified nation and more like a patchwork of rivalling principalities. The competition between locales over historical bragging rights was fierce—who had the oldest temples, the most renowned delicacies, the longest span of preserved wall. Though perhaps lesser known than China's more storied cities, Ningbo held its own timeless allure.

Later, when a city official boasted Ningbo was home to the 'second largest port in China', I couldn't resist needling him. 'After Shanghai's, correct?'

His eyes narrowed, but the grin remained fixed. 'Of course. But we were still first.'

Unable to resist the siren call of the bustling bund, I slipped out ahead of the welcome reception for a glimpse. Splashing fountains captivated passersby, while trendy galleries, enticing shops and lively bars vied for their attention. Among the modern establishments, its doors open and pints flowing, was a touch of the familiar—an Irish pub had joined the mix.

Rounding a corner, I nearly collided with a trio of Chinese college students. Handsome and polished, they halted in surprise before one burst out with a welcoming 'Hello!' His friends dissolved into laughter, warm and genuine. The people here gazed with open curiosity, unused to foreign visitors in their midst. Ningbo remained off the radar for most travellers, though no less captivating. As I chatted with the friendly students, their English halting but earnest, it was clear I was as much of a novelty to them as their charming city was to me.

I walked to the main shopping district, Tianyi Square. Similar to Wangfujing in Beijing, this was a bustling zone with department stores and restaurants, and was newer and more commercial than the touristy bund.

Scarves beckoned through a store's front window, a wash of jewel-toned silk. I stepped inside, fingers trailing across the racks as I browsed. A young couple approached, eager smiles lighting their faces.

'They can wear around neck, or hats,' the man offered, gesturing to demonstrate.

'Really? How interesting,' I exclaimed, feigning wide-eyed wonder. This dance was familiar by now, the steps ingrained; foreigners must remain the uninitiated pupil, ever ready to marvel at each new reveal.

I put on an air of innocent fascination, letting them educate me on the proper way to don these scarves. With gracious nods, I allowed them to bask in their cultural authority. It was a small price, making myself seem ignorant for the gift of insight it granted.

I hurried back to the hotel for the grand welcome banquet, the opening bell for the international exhibition. Cities across China hosted these global galas, clamouring for cosmopolitan cachet. Attendees hailed from the far reaches—the UK, Poland, Italy. I found myself the lone American.

Dinner unfurled in the hotel's cavernous banquet hall. I'd expected pomp, and pomp it delivered. Red carpet stretched to the entrance, massive floral displays standing guard. Ms Liu waited for me near the door, precisely on time—no surprise from this consummate professional.

Being one of a handful of foreigners had its advantages, freeing me from Michael's orbit for the evening. With the esteemed Ms Liu as my guide, I was granted a coveted seat at the vice mayor's table. Yet closeness bred new trials—round tables and shared plates meant no flinch would go unnoticed. I steeled myself as dish after mystery dish emerged, wrestling my face into an inscrutable mask. But I swallowed my grimace along with the morsels, washing all down with gulps of rice wine. The vice mayor, oblivious, regaled me with tales of Ningbo's proud history between courses.

The shores of Ningbo teemed with the fruits of the sea, so I jumped at the chance to indulge in the local specialty—crab. My naive palate was unprepared for the primal ritual of cracking through the creature's formidable shell to expose the sweet meat within. As I wrestled with its spindly legs and scrabbled to extricate tidbits of flesh, I understood the true cost of this meal. This was no neat and tidy affair; this was a battle that left its victim in pieces. Yet any guilt I felt towards the sacrificial crustacean was overshadowed by my disappointment in its lacklustre flavour. For all the effort required in consuming it, the payoff proved anticlimactic. Though I ate my fill, it was clear that crab and I would never be proper tablemates.

I switched to my side dish and started eating something that vaguely resembled bacon. It was chewier than I expected.

'What is this?' I asked Ms Liu.

'It is duck's tongue. Very delicious.'

Uh-huh.

After we'd finished, the waiter laid two packs of cigarettes on the table.

'Glen, do you smoke?' Ms Liu asked.

'Occasionally.'

'Oh, you must try these. The tobacco was grown here in Ningbo. It's very soft and delicate.' She also insisted that I take the second unopened packet with me as a 'souvenir' which I could tell angered a man at the table who wanted them.

For all the prepping Ms Liu gave me for the dinner, I still managed to make a major mistake. I decided that I would give the vice mayor a compliment, but it ended up backfiring.

I tapped Ms Liu on the shoulder. 'Tell him this is my first time to Ningbo, and I love it. I think foreigners would love this city. People are friendly and the design is amazing. You should do tourism campaigns that target foreigners to travel here. No one has heard of Ningbo before,' I said.

As Ms Liu started her dutiful interpretation, I watched as the vice mayor's expression shifted. It went from a smile to a grim look. He curtly responded and Ms Liu told me, 'He said that they already do tourism advertising.' Then I realised that my compliment had made it sound like he and the city weren't doing enough. I cringed and stared at the floor.

After that blunder, Ms Liu seemed to feel responsible for me and monitored me closely. Another interpreter who was about my age sat down next to me. We started chatting as the dinner waned and the smoking moved to the hallway.

I could see out of the corner of my eye that Ms Liu was furious. I suppose I belonged to *her*. Still, I wasn't about to let her stop me from socialising. The interpreter's name was

Byron. He was cocky—totally my cup of tea. He had the same playful eyes that I had come to love from so many Chinese men. He looked like he knew the punchline to a great joke he wasn't going to tell. Strong without being overly muscular, he wore a blue suit that gave him instant authority. Funnily enough, he taught at the same university Ms Liu did. He was married to a fellow professor and they had a six-year-old son. I told him that we should visit the bund together after the evening's festivities adjourned, and he agreed.

After dinner, Ms Liu walked me out to the elevator and asked me what my plans were for the rest of the evening.

'I'm pretty tired. Just gonna go up to my room.' I knew enough at this stage that she was escorting me. China had hidden rules that I needed to keep. Telling her I wanted to explore with someone closer to my age would have hurt her. So I didn't tell her.

She waved goodbye and said that she would see me for breakfast.

Byron told me to meet him in the lobby about ten minutes later. He wanted to drop his bag off at his room and inform his supervisor that he planned to accompany me to the bund.

While I waited in the lobby, a familiar face appeared. Ms Liu passed right in front of me, far enough away that she hadn't detected me but close enough that she would if she directly looked my way. I instantly felt like I had done something horribly wrong by lying. She was clearly looking for someone. She then went over and dialled one of the hotel phones. About the same time, Byron emerged from the elevator.

I stood up to meet him and had hoped to get out of the lobby without Ms Liu spotting us. Nope.

'Glen, there you are! I tried calling your room. Come now, I will show you something beautiful.' She grabbed my hand and we started toward the bund.

'Okay,' I said. 'But he's coming too.' I pointed to Byron.

Ms Liu seemed suspicious. They started speaking in Chinese, slowly at first but then rapidly. I knew enough Chinese to hear him tell her, 'He asked me to go with him.'

She looked furious. 'Glen, it's very important that you let me know your plans,' Ms Liu said.

'Fine.'

We walked over to the bund where I was introduced to Ms Liu's husband and some of his friends. The 'beautiful thing' I was supposed to see was a fireworks display on the river, but it was cancelled thanks to the rain. Ms Liu and her entourage were going to a teahouse instead, so Byron told her that we would walk around first and then figure out our plan. She didn't like that, but we bid her adieu anyway.

As Byron and I ambled along the bustling bund, he expounded on its past. 'A vital port since the Song dynasty, Ningbo grew into a thriving hub following the opium wars. Foreign traders made their home here, Brits and Dutchmen alike.' He gestured along the curving walkway. 'This promenade itself was once called *Lǎowài tān*, meaning "Foreigner Beach"—a place built by and for outsiders.'

Ducking into the chic boutiques, I was reminded this was no local's haunt. Price tags gave me pause, each digit inflated for tourists. A notebook fetching 380 kuai—nearly sixty dollars—made me balk. Still, window-shopping offered its own allure. Marvelling at gleaming silks and jade sculptures, I absorbed the upscale aesthetic, if not the price point.

I kept mum about my Chinese studies, finding humour in what unfolded when they assumed I was uncomprehending. 'The foreigner is shocked by the high prices,' Byron told a wary shopkeeper, as I feigned wide-eyed wonder. Their hushed exchanges swirled around me, assessment and speculation encoded in each syllable. But I bit my tongue, allowing their perceptions to hold, my language skills a hidden card to play later. For now, I relished my anonymity, another observer people-watching from the fringe. Only the glint in my eye might have betrayed the inner smile, delighting in my unspoken game.

Byron pressed cigarettes on me as we rested in a waterside gazebo, conversing as dusk settled. He radiated national pride, though Ningbo left him ambivalent. 'I am from a Shaanxi coal town. Though dirty, it remains home,' he said. The landscape of his youth starkly contrasted with this glossy port city. As our cigarettes dwindled, word arrived it was time to rejoin the group. With a tinge of reluctance, Byron and I abandoned our momentary refuge and headed back.

We ended up at a bar on the dock and who else but Ms Liu stood there, staring us down. Upon seeing me, she proclaimed, 'Glen, I think you are not tired.' I didn't respond—I just looked down. Guilty as charged.

She was in the middle of eating a banana-split sundae and was delighted to have me back in her control. I took my seat in the chair next to her, feeling like I'd been caught and playtime was over. If I'd been Chinese, she probably would have made me write the character for 'liar' a thousand times on a single sheet of paper.

Our chat yielded intriguing revelations about Ms Liu's

past overseas stint. 'The government dispatched me to Dubai to oversee Chinese workers,' she said. 'Two hundred women, far from home, speaking no English—I was the go-between.' Buffeted by the clashing demands of executives and employees, she longed for her posting to end. Yet despite profound unease, she persevered, bound by duty and a refusal to lose face.

As we strolled back to the hotel, I felt less and less guilty as it seemed that Ms Liu and I had made up from my unauthorised time with Byron. The next morning, we met for breakfast in the hotel restaurant. Everything seemed normal before we headed to the daylong exhibition.

On my last day in Ningbo, Ms Liu called me on the phone and apologised that there wouldn't be time for sightseeing that afternoon.

'Glen, if you can make it, visit the Tianyi Pavilion. It houses the oldest library in China,' she said.

'Thank you so much, Ms Liu. I will try. You have been an amazing guide this trip.'

Ms Liu told me that if I liked Ningbo I should come back and she would get me a job at the university. Then she started talking about her boss and how she tried to keep track of all the things she had to do. She still wasn't certain he appreciated her. Translation: 'Compliment me to him.' I promised to email her a message of gratitude once I returned to Beijing.

I stood alone in my hotel room, the rivers sparkling in invitation below my window. I sank into the desk chair, booting up my Sony Vaio. 'Came for work, left my heart in Ningbo,' I typed, cursing the construction cranes marring the vista. This city had charmed me, its watery veins running with warmth belying the gleaming high-rises. I hated to leave without unravelling all its secrets. But the taxi would arrive soon to ferry me away. I sighed, taking one last lingering look. These rivers would never let me go.

Time ticking away, I went back to the bund. A mist was gathering. Small raindrops bounced lightly off the water. I stood on the pier and watched the movement in the water. *This is mine*, I thought. *This is what I will take with me. The memory of this moment, of Ningbo in the mist.*

Beijing assaulted my senses once more—the parched air this time. Streetlights muted by smog evoked Pig-Pen and his dust cloud, but filthier. My thoughts drifted to Ms Liu, her nurturing nature seeming so out of place with this harsh landscape. She had meant only to cocoon me, which I'd scorned like a surly expat.

I kept my promise and emailed her. I knew it was important for her to have proof that she was doing a good job and I hoped my short message would please her boss.

> Dear Liu Laoshi: This is Glen. I wanted to sincerely thank you for your kindness, professionalism, and help during my trip to Ningbo. You were such a wonderful guide to me—and a friend. I can never fully thank you for your generosity to me. The university is very lucky to have you work there. Thank you for working at the exhibition. I believe many successful projects will emerge from that event. I really fell in love with Ningbo during my stay. The town is so beautiful and the people so warm. I would like to come back again. May I contact you if I do? Thank you again!

What was your spell, Ningbo, that you so enchanted me?

Was it escape from Michael's shadow, the chance to roam unfettered? Days undarkened by work's simmering dramas?

Or adventure's call—to push eastward, where land meets sea?

The grace of your people?

Your rivers' quiet pulse, balm to one raised in hardened desert.

Soothing waves, your name calming me.

Not one thing, but all. Layers that revealed your heart, mysterious as the tide.

I dwelled only briefly in your embrace—yet you imprinted river-carved channels I'll traverse again.

Your waters will remember me, as I remember you.

MY BEIJING BIRTHDAY

For Beijingers, autumn brought relief. Winter overstayed its welcome, bleak and biting beneath cheerless grey. Fickle spring teased with a glimpse of rebirth, fleeting as a migrant bird's stopover. The endless summer swelter transformed the capital into a kiln.

But come September, spirits lifted as the furnace blast relented. Now the golden gingko leaves beckoned us outside to revel in the seasonal change. Crisp twilight descended, perfect for strolls and alfresco gatherings. This temporary reprieve from extremes etches precious memories, sustaining people through the dreary months ahead.

Coinciding with my birthday, autumn in Beijing felt like a personal gift.

It turned out that my first birthday here coincided with the Mid-Autumn Festival, *Zhōngqiū Jié*. For centuries in China, Korea and Vietnam, the full autumn moon heralded the conclusion of harvest; it became a time for feasts, courting rituals and get-togethers to reunite friends and family. One of China's most famous Tang dynasty poets, Li Bai, wrote an ode to the harvest moon saying, *'I raise my cup, invite the bright moon; facing my shadow, together we make three.'*

In 2007, the festival wasn't yet a public holiday. It became one the following year and offered me a chance, in theory, to eat traditional mooncakes. Many Chinese people found these rich pastries either too sweet or too fattening and so I ended up with a stack of regifted boxes of them—which was fine by me.

My friends considered it quite auspicious that my birthday fell on this particular date. Meanwhile, I went back and forth on whether I should organise a birthday dinner with friends, like I would have done if I were back in the States. Part of my apprehension sprang from the fact that my birthday, September 25, was also the day of the festival itself. I worried that people wouldn't appreciate the burden of an additional obligation.

The second and perhaps more personal reason for my hesitation was that I'd nurtured special relationships with each of my friends. I'd always been one to compartmentalise and this applied even more so in China. I hated commingling my friends as I always had to explain how and why we'd met, as if needing to justify my relationships with each person.

On top of that, many of my Chinese friends didn't like to share me. Having a foreign friend, and an American at that, was a big deal to them. This took a while to get used to but once I understood the novelty of foreigners, and also that my English skills gave my friends the opportunity to improve their grasp of the language (and advance their career prospects), it became a status I secretly relished. It seemed inevitable that they would resent each other.

Mid-Autumn Festival or not, I eventually decided that I couldn't let my first birthday in China pass without a dinner. I knew I'd regret it if I didn't do something. After nearly seven months in Beijing my circle of friends had widened into the dozens, divided between coworkers and my language-exchange partners. I didn't want to invite everyone because it would stress me out trying to make sure everyone was having a good time and all. Not to mention that my friends would likely chat in Mandarin together and leave me excluded.

I settled on MoHan, Colin and Davis and emailed each of them an invitation. I had met MoHan and Colin through an advert for language-exchange partners, and Davis had started talking to me one evening at a bar some months earlier. MoHan hailed from Guangxi in the south, Colin was from Wuhan and Davis was from Henan. None could get home for the holidays. So as the Mid-Autumn Festival was traditionally a family celebration, it made sense to invite them. Each in their own way had become like family to me. With visiting our actual families off the table, celebrating the festival together seemed more mutual.

But how to spend a birthday in Beijing? I had no clue and asked the guys for advice. I naturally loved planning but with less than a year in the city under my belt, I was lost.

Davis suggested that we go to Houhai Lake, rent a paddleboat and eat dinner onboard. It sounded ... very China. I forwarded his email to MoHan and Colin for their opinions. MoHan thought too many people would converge on Houhai for the holiday and suggested we go somewhere quieter. Colin thought that as we were in Beijing we should go to a restaurant for Peking duck, which had become one of my go-to dishes.

Of the handful of English language resources that catered to foreigners, the *Beijinger* was the most reliable. I trawled its website and found a place called Da Dong Duck Restaurant, which readers had voted 'Best for Peking Duck' in the previous year. I emailed the guys, 'Meet me there at 7:30.'

The day before my birthday, Nick called to insist he attend any party. We'd worked together that year and his support kept me afloat during my early months in the city. An ex-soldier, he embraced Beijing more than the other guys. I liked Nick, a native of China's northeast, but initially excluded him, knowing couples came as packages. His girlfriend spoke no English—potentially awkward. Yet Nick had been such a lifeline, I couldn't refuse his request.

'Let's meet outside the Jianguomen subway station at 6 pm and take a taxi from there,' I said, confident that my birthday dinner would go off without a hitch. A little too confident, as it turned out.

That Tuesday evening I sprinted for the bus with jagged breath. Usually a quick ten minute ride to the Jianguomen subway station, today the bus didn't budge, trapped in traffic's chokehold. Horns blared as we sat. Exhaust fumes seeped through cracked windows. My pulse hammered. I was worried I'd be late meeting my friends. Mid-Autumn Festival crowds choked the streets, a sea of people swirling, socialising. I thought I should ditch this motionless bus and walk, even if it took twenty minutes. But stubbornly I stayed put, optimistically watching minutes tick by, willing the bus to inch forward. My foot tapped relentlessly as we remained stalled, no escape from the unmoving queue.

I waited.

And waited.

And waited.

I usually took the 800 bus to the subway station. After half an hour of waiting, I started panicking, imagining my plans falling apart. Then, another bus approached. It was the 674. I thought to myself, *Oh, I sometimes take this bus from home. I can take it to Jianguomen as well.* Again, I learned the importance of this festival—no polite gesturing for the foreigner to board first, no parting crowds, no intrigued smiles. Everybody crammed into the bus. It was the first time that people didn't give me deference on the bus, so I had to fight my way on equally. It made sense. Everyone had family and friends to meet.

No one had an inch of personal space so I tried staying close to the front door. Chinese buses are no specimens of fine design. They have so much underutilised space. I gritted my teeth at how much protective space the driver had around him. He could have easily made room for an additional ten people. But I digress.

I started sweating like a pig. I mean *sweating*. Profusely is the right adjective. It was dripping off me.

Research revealed that people of Asian descent possess fewer apocrine sweat glands compared to those of European lineage. This biological distinction partially explained why consistent deodorant use was less culturally ubiquitous across certain East Asian societies relative to numerous Western nations where body odour historically heightened stigma.

The man standing beside me was a migrant worker, a *nóng mín*, from another part of China. He kept staring at me and I could tell he found my suffering hilarious. He started chatting about me with one of his friends (I just knew it was about me). I couldn't tell exactly what he was saying, but it was either about my sweat or the fact that I had to endure the claustrophobic sauna. He eventually raised his arm to hold on to the bar closest to me. I decided to take advantage of this, so when the bus braked I 'accidentally' bumped my face into his shirt so he could act as a wipe, soaking up my sweat.

Unfortunately, he was clever enough to figure out what I was doing and moved his arm. Damn ...

The bus moved two inches and then the driver slammed on the brakes. It was by far the worst traffic I'd experienced. We turned a block and I thought, I'm almost there. Then we turned another block, and realisation crashed down on me. I was on the wrong bus—the 674, not the 684, so we were going in the opposite direction. I was so stressed I boarded the bus without thinking. I started to panic. What if this was a long-distance bus? What if I ended up at the Great Wall? What if I had to stand, drowning in my own sweat in this mobile kiln for three hours? Or even the entire evening?

Fortunately, it wasn't a long-distance bus and relief came sooner than I'd expected. I got off at the next stop, which had a subway station right there. I sent a text to Nick and said I would meet him at Exit B in about five minutes. He responded and said that was fine. At this point, he and his girlfriend had waited for me at the subway station for more than forty-five minutes.

I got on the subway and needed to go only two stops to get to Jianguomen where I raced through the station and up the escalator. But when I got outside, no Nick. I looked all around, then I called him. 'Hi, I just got here. Where are you?'

'We are here,' he said.

'Where? I can't see you.'

'My office.'

'*What?*'

Nick's office was about a ten-minute walk from the subway. Why on Earth he interpreted 'meet at Exit B' as 'meet me at your office' I'll never know. We were finally united about ten minutes later and started walking to catch a taxi. Yes, we were still that naive to think we could grab a taxi and be on our merry way. Trouble was, we had to move locations three times before we got a taxi. After another thirty minutes of wandering, we saw a taxi stop in front of the Moscow Restaurant across the street. Nick's girlfriend screamed at him (I think she was getting hangry), and in a desperate attempt to claim it, he ran through traffic and secured the taxi. Finally!

Beijing taxi drivers were usually warm and jovial but this one was not at all friendly. At my request, Nick told the driver that it was my birthday because Chinese folk always warmed up once a birthday was involved, but he didn't react. He probably hated having to work on a night of celebration. Why should he entertain the musings of some strange foreigner?

Against the odds, we arrived at Da Dong, situated prominently off Beijing's North Third Ring Road. Hordes of hungry diners clustered outside, proof of the renowned roast duck within. My friends, Colin and MoHan, had beaten the crowd, securing our spot on the lengthy waiting list. An opening neared after fifty minutes—finally a chance to sample Da Dong's famous fare.

Earlier I had asked Tan Lu to book us a table, but no dice—Da Dong was crammed for the festival. My Chinese friends always balked when I found new 'foreigner-friendly' joints, convinced I'd get ripped off. And Da Dong didn't run cheap, especially on my budget. Yet roaming the sleek interior, admiring the artful plates emerging from the kitchen, I knew I'd pay extra to experience this craft. No doubt my Chinese friends might not get it, but I'd found a worthy splurge for my birthday.

Da Dong was no ordinary Chinese eatery, but haute cuisine. It took familiar working-class dishes and elevated them to artistry. Too often, Chinese described their traditional food as greasy and wanting—clichés this kitchen obliterated.

I asked MoHan if he had told the staff that it was my birthday. He said he hadn't and within two minutes of him doing so the waiters whisked us upstairs to a private banquet room. I told you about Asians and birthdays, right? 'That's so nice of them,' I muttered to my friends.

The imperial Asian decor was intoxicating and we quickly settled in.

Davis was running a few minutes late, as he often struggled with directions, but he finally made it. Nick left the room for a while and returned with a panicked look on his face. He started talking in Mandarin at top speed and everyone around me started speaking in raised tones. I gaped, my eyes darting between each of them. What could I say?

Welcome to China!

I finally intervened. 'What is going on?'

Colin sighed and said, 'He needs to know.'

The private room carried a 200 kuai price tag— bombshell dropped. No shock really, given the perks: swift seating, an oasis of quiet and privacy worth paying for. Trying to quell any unease, I volunteered to cover the cost. My friends blinked back, faces blank. My nonchalance confused them. Sure, Da Dong was spendy by local standards. But this was my birthday feast.

The ordering began in earnest. The signature roast duck commanded 158 kuai—standard fare for a bird done right. For 20 kuai more, you could hand-select your fowl. An amusing frill, but we declined. MoHan and I made judicious picks, then passed the menu around. Nick's petite girlfriend set promptly to work, ordering with abandon. Dish after dish, my eyes bulging at the mounting tab. Biting my tongue as etiquette demanded, I surveyed her delicate frame wondering where she stashed such appetite.

Here among friends, our awkward dynamic simmered. Each relationship different, disjointed. Anxiety bubbled up, no distraction amid close quarters and stilted small talk. This was a mistake. In the main dining room, we could have hid in the hubbub.

The private room sealed us off. Servers glided by with practiced airs, noses tilted. I missed the main dining hall's lively chaos—the drunken shouts toasting strangers, spirited chatter washing over each table. Out there I'm a spectacle, spotlight always finding me. A zoo animal on bad days, but good days bring camaraderie, feeling the convivial energy.

Silently, I judged future friends who suggested Da Dong for dinner. The best Chinese fare shunned pretence, like the people. No frosty servers or menus in English. Simply honest food mirroring honest souls. I yearned for the cramped eateries of back alleys, loud with life, where the real Beijing dwelled. Not this carnival.

Mounds of food piled up, our table groaning. But no matter—tonight called for indulgence. And sampling every delicacy let me fully experience Da Dong's range. Each new flavour a gift on my birthday, no matter the ultimate cost.

Once we had our Yanjing beers, I wanted to toast everyone for coming. I started by telling them how they would never know how much they'd all helped me adjust to life in Beijing and how much I valued their friendship. But as I spoke, the tension became palpable and they all looked desperate to change the subject.

Even as I spoke, the birthday song erupted, rushed and perfunctory. Glasses clinked in haste to conclude the requisite ritual. So quintessentially Chinese—loath to bare emotion in public, they hurtled through moments meant for savouring. I recalled accounts of foreigners departing China, farewells devoid of tears or embraces. Such open sentiment was shunned and denied its due. Now it was my turn, birthday wishes expressed like obligations to be ticked off. No chance to breathe in the warmth.

I started telling them about my recent trip to Ningbo and how much I had enjoyed it. Colin jumped in and said, 'You know, Ningbo is close to Shanghai. I think if you liked Ningbo, you would like Shanghai.' Recently, he had developed an obsession with Shanghai and eventually wanted to look there for job opportunities.

I teased him and replied, 'No, Shanghai is awful. It's big and dirty. The people are terrible. I hate Shanghai.' Well, guess what Colin had got me for a birthday gift? A book on the history of Shanghai. *Remove foot from mouth,* I cursed inwardly after I unwrapped it. I should have known when he didn't smile back.

The roast duck arrived with ceremony, carved tableside by an artist in surgeon's garb. With deft flicks of his razor-sharp blade, he sliced the bird into a mosaic of mahogany and ivory, his motions as mesmerising as a magician's card tricks. Then, the first succulent bite—crisped skin giving way to tender meat, fat layered just so. Each mouthful sang with spices married to the essence of duck. Chewing thoroughly was required, but no chore when flavours were so symphonic. The height of the chef's craft, executed without pretension, needed no garnish beyond a steamed pancake. In the end, the food told the true story.

MoHan leaned in, professional. 'Peking duck's pedigree stretches back centuries, once reserved solely for royalty.' His hands swept outward. 'After the Qing dynasty fell in 1911, finally the commoners could savour this treasure.'

He pointed out the crisp bronzed skin, perfectly smoked. 'Da Dong trims all fat, their birds leaner than most.'

I nibbled a slice, eyes closing. Crisp gave way to tender meat, flavour singing.

MoHan continued. 'The usual accompaniments'—he tapped the scallions, cucumbers, hoisin. 'But Da Dong adds crushed garlic, sugar, turnips.' He frowned at two bowls. 'These pastes remain a mystery to me.'

I watched MoHan, so earnest in his lesson. With each sample, Peking duck's layers unfolded. My appreciation deepened, glimpsing its proud history.

'You are right, so impressive,' I agreed, smiling.

My friends smiled and nodded along. Did they agree with me? I wasn't sure they did. Could they tell the differences between a Da Dong duck and a duck joint down a dirty alley? I didn't know, but it didn't really matter.

'In the West, we celebrate birthdays with cakes and candles. What about in China?' I asked.

After a few months there, I instinctively knew that cake wouldn't feature in any traditional birthday setting in China. Although the Chinese were rapidly developing a sweet tooth, thanks to the import of Oreos and Snickers, desserts were better left to the simplicity of fresh fruit and cups of herb tea.

Colin started speaking in Mandarin to one of the servers. As if on cue, a bowl of noodles was presented to me. Cake this was not. But cake it had become in my head.

'Here, you get a bowl of noodles. You have to slurp one long noodle into your mouth. It represents long life,' Colin said.

Like many things here, I didn't see the significance but went along. Noodles had always been a precarious dish for me in China, as I was still mastering the use of chopsticks and slippery objects or meals presented a particular challenge. But I managed it, which was no easy feat under the intense gaze of my friends and the servers standing by in the room. When I finished, everyone clapped at my accomplishment. I didn't know when I clapped too.

The check arrived as expected—black leather folder concealing the damage within. Da Dong overlooked no detail, even this final flourish oozed luxury. The folder sat untouched, all eyes averted, tension mounting. Servers paced, impatient for its reveal. Finally I reached for the switch, bracing as I flipped it open. The total detonated like a bomb, eliciting gasps around the table.

Eight hundred and thirty-four kuai. Shock widened eyes around the table. Had we truly indulged so grossly? There must be an error ... that sum could feed a local for half a year, not vanish in one decadent sitting. Dismay gripped my friends, the bourgeois prices inducing disbelief.

I sheepishly passed 200 kuai to MoHan, trusting him to aid dividing the bill. My friends stared, apparently expecting me to shoulder the full birthday tab. I cringed, baffled. Had my invitation implied this dinner was my treat? With a monthly salary of 5000 kuai the costs of intensive language lessons loomed as a burdensome investment relative to my income. At home, sharing birthday costs was customary.

I pulled out 400 kuai and asked Nick for 100 kuai. I mean, his girlfriend *had* over-ordered all that food after all. Trying to de-escalate the situation, Davis suggested that we go downstairs to sort it all out. MoHan ultimately put the entire thing on his credit card (Da Dong was unique in that they also accepted foreign credit cards, which typically only international hotels and luxury brands accepted). As a graduate student doing an internship far from home, he had way less money than most of us, so I felt bad. Either oblivious or trying to skirt their share, Colin and Davis never reached into their wallets. It was an awkward and unfortunate conclusion to the evening. Coming to this restaurant was akin to taking struggling interns to a Michelin-starred restaurant and handing them my bill.

We emerged from Da Dong into lunar radiance, the night aglow for my birthday and mid-autumn revels. That celestial face gazed down, bigger and brighter than I'd ever seen, its magic undimmed by ages of human gazing.

'Can you see the beautiful goddess Chang'e on the moon?' my friends asked.

I explained Western lore told of a man, not a goddess. They nodded knowingly. 'Ah yes, Neil Armstrong.'

Colin added that America had been first to tread the lunar landscape. 'I think I read that somewhere,' I replied, smiling inwardly.

Through Beijing's haze, the moon glowed dark yellow and beige, a hybrid shade uniquely of this place. Despite dinner's tensions, camaraderie kindled as we gazed upward together. I was reminded of childhood stargazing, wondering who else saw the same cosmic glimmers. A lifelong passion for the heavens, and now my first China birthday coincided with a celestial celebration. No gift could be sweeter.

TAIPEI LANGUAGE INSTITUTE

After months of meeting partners for 'language exchanges', which inevitably resulted in me giving free English lessons, I knew I had to buckle down. I didn't even know how to spell things in the romanised version of Chinese, *pīnyīn*, which is key for learners to master the tones for intelligible pronunciation. In the autumn, I enrolled at the Taipei Language Institute (TLI) to advance my Chinese studies. That way, I could hop on a bus in Chongwenmen after work and arrive at its location in the Interchina Commercial Building in Dengshikou, not far from Wangfujing.

Loads of private schools catered to foreigners who wanted to learn Mandarin and it took a lot of research to discern the best of the bunch. I'd seen ads for TLI in a few expat magazines, and I liked its straightforwardness. It seemed serious and less focused on such gimmicks as learning the language by making dumplings. TLI had operated in Taiwan for more than fifty years and started offering courses on the mainland in the mid-1990s. I opted for private classes, which cost more but seemed like a better option than group classes. Considering all my business trips, the scheduling seemed so much less complicated and I wasn't too eager to sit in a classroom of other foreigners who spoke Chinese better than I did.

First, I had to meet the head of the centre, a middle-aged woman who tested my current level. She seemed a bit taken aback when I insisted on having a male teacher. 'I can hear the tones more clearly when it's a deep voice,' I explained.

There was some truth to that. But more than anything, I'd had so many mixed signals with Chinese women that I didn't want to go down that path again, especially if I was paying.

My tutor was a young man named Yang Yang. He was a twenty-four-year-old native Beijinger who had a diligent demeanour. He carried a gold purse ... er ... bag that always had several tubes of ChapStick in it. Young Chinese men had already started to defy conventional gender roles and in a few years the skincare and cosmetics market for men would surge. Needless to say, my gaydar pinged furiously every time I saw him, but we never discussed it. I sensed that while he knew he was different, he may not yet have realised how.

Yang Yang's preparation as a teacher made you feel you were getting your money's worth, especially considering the pace of his classes. He wanted to serve it all up. Meanwhile, I always came into class a bit frazzled. Working all day and braving the journey on those crowded buses often drained me.

Yang Yang eventually revealed that he was moving to Australia to pursue a master's degree in finance, a prospect that excited him no end. On the flip side, he had his guard up about the West. He felt that American horror movies had 'some basis of truth' and worried about American society. Many Japanese women, he informed me, had absorbed Western values and went around 'looking for one-night love'. When he asked me questions about America, he never let up eye contact, aside from the occasional blink as he processed what I told him. I looked forward to Yang Yang's journey Down Under, because I felt he would grow a lot as a person.

He told me rather defiantly that he wouldn't go to 'any parties' in Australia unless they were organised by his university.

I privately thought, *Oh, Yang Yang, you're not going to get invited to* any *parties unless they're organised by the university*. For all his fastidiousness as a teacher (and probably as a pupil), he was a wet blanket socially, unsure and unconfident. Despite Yang Yang's obvious suspicion of the outside world, he told me he would likely try to stay in Australia after graduating. He felt he would have more career opportunities there. Moments like that always gave me pause. Wasn't China the future? I mean, that's why I was here. Yet some of the best and brightest still intended to go elsewhere.

One evening, he entered class rather exasperated. Apparently, he and his mother were taking care of his sick uncle, who was in the hospital. He told me that his uncle's daughter was a 'son of a bitch' who didn't care about her father and switched boyfriends 'every day'. He resented that he, his mother and his 'auntie' had to do everything. Yang Yang had a deep sense of responsibility and I suppose that's what made him a good teacher.

What Yang Yang most delighted in was standing at the whiteboard, writing something down, and barking orders. 'You will write this down,' he'd say.

One time, as I copied the notes off the board, a little acronym tripped me up. 'What's SV mean?' I asked.

Whipping his head around, he sternly replied, 'I will explain it later.'

Ooh-kay.

After a long while, he explained that it stood for 'stative verbs', whatever those are. How little did I understand then that the student was never to ask questions. But despite his strictness, he didn't stick rigidly to the textbook—no, I appreciated Yang Yang for his cultural lessons. For instance, he taught me what sneezing in China means: If you sneeze once, someone misses you. If you sneeze twice, someone is saying something negative about you. If you sneeze three times, someone is just talking about you. If you sneeze four times, you are getting sick. I figured those were reasonable enough.

Despite having started to study the language before moving to China, I still hesitated to use it. After class, I usually went to the McDonald's next door. On good days, classes pumped me up, made me eager to use my Chinese. I would point at the menu to order my *zhīshì hànbǎo* (cheeseburger) and yes, I wanted to add Coke and fries for a set meal, or *tào cān*. Being in a touristy area like Wangfujing meant that even if I mangled my tones, the cashier would act impressed by my 'fluency'. When the order was understood, I rushed back to the bus stop feeling on top of the world. The nights it didn't work out so well, I wondered why I bothered.

To send Yang Yang off to Australia, I treated him to a dinner across the street from our school. It was the most relaxed I had ever seen him—I'd never even seen him out of the classroom—and yet he obviously didn't want to get too personal. We never touched on topics of marriage or dating. But he did tell me that his uncle was the president of a well-known hotel chain. He'd asked for a job once, which his uncle and mother deliberated about. While he assumed that his fluency in English and Japanese would land him in the concierge department, they assigned him to the housekeeping department instead. The funniest part? He loved being a housekeeper. He struck me as having a mild form of OCD and he said he loved making the rooms sparkle. The other housekeepers hated him, he said, because he often checked their rooms and made changes. Once, he had seen his uncle go into the men's room and put his bare hands in the urinal drain to check the cleanliness. It taught him to take pride in everything he did.

After three months, he was promoted to the concierge department. And he despised it. He found it boring and missed the action-packed life of housekeeping. After that, he realised that his uncle and mother had put him in the 'lowest' position so he could learn the meaning of working his way up the ladder.

As I bid Yang Yang farewell that evening, I warned him to prepare for culture shock, and he nodded seriously as he listened. I had no idea what kind of reception a Chinese person moving to Australia would have. What I knew for sure was that he wouldn't get the red carpet experience I'd received here. I worried about my friends as they embarked on these overseas sojourns and hoped they would meet their expectations.

A few weeks after Yang Yang arrived in Australia, he sent me an email. He told me that some of his Chinese friends had told him that when he got off the plane in Sydney he would never want to return to China. 'In truth, I have no such feeling. People here don't go outside and play cards after eating. Although Australians look civilised, I don't like the life here. I guess having such an experience will force me to grow up.'

After Yang Yang left, the TLI staff had a problem. They knew I'd insisted on a male teacher but they didn't have one. I went a couple of weeks without classes before they contacted me. They had found someone but his English wasn't the best and he didn't have that much teaching experience. He did have a deep voice, though. Deal!

Ivan couldn't have been more different from Yang Yang. True, they were both native Beijingers, but that was about it. As soon as I saw him, I realised he was an artist. He wasn't really a Mandarin teacher but he had spent a decade working as an announcer at a radio station, which meant that his Mandarin pronunciation was impeccable.

Right away I saw that Ivan wasn't a teacher of the same quality as Yang Yang. Our first class was a disaster. He ran through the material too quickly and seemed to have no idea how to present it. He started by drawing a giant family tree on the board and teaching me the terms for different relatives. That lent me an interesting cultural insight—unlike English where a grandmother is simply a grandmother, Mandarin had all these different terms that helped to map out the relationships. You couldn't call your mother's mother the same thing as your dad's mother. I knew that family was central in Chinese culture, but seeing how it presented itself in the language illuminated a lot for me. It was also depressing. It meant I had that many more words to master. Because I had a younger sister, I first mastered the word for that, *mèimèi*.

In time, I developed a rapport with Ivan. As I was his only student he invested more time in me. Using his radio background, he prerecorded lessons at his home studio and created individual MP3 files for me to take home. He even made a CD for me, full of his favourite music. In retrospect, I think he did these things to make up for his stumbling English and lack of experience as a teacher.

I worried about Ivan. He didn't look very healthy. His skin was pale and he looked like someone with a naturally unhappy disposition. That unhappiness presented itself in every aspect of him: his slouch, his walk, his face. I wanted to know more but sensed that I never would. What did he yearn for that seemed out of reach?

At thirty-one, Ivan dreamed of moving to London to earn a master's degree in multimedia arts. His English was not nearly as good as Yang Yang's so he thought of creative ways to bridge our language barrier. During one session he shared with me about a hundred photographs he shot on his cell phone. The skyline of the Chinese capital, the hushed interiors of museums, the fleeting expressions of strangers caught unawares on the street—each frame was a masterclass in composition and form. His photographs had a simplicity that instantly appealed and yet challenged conventional notions of technique.

I asked Ivan what it was like for him studying Chinese characters as a child. 'Awful,' he replied without hesitation. As hard as it is to fathom, there are eighty thousand different Chinese characters. A single character conveys so much in terms of feeling and emotion. 'You only need eight thousand characters for day-to-day life,' he said. *Only?* I thought. He said that as children they had to write the same characters endlessly. If they made an error, the teacher made them write the character an additional three hundred times. I was immediately grateful for the twenty-six letters of the English alphabet.

One evening Ivan invited me to dinner at a nearby restaurant. He explained that the government only paid for children's education up to nine years old. After that, their parents had to pay for middle school and beyond. When he was seventeen, his high school sponsored a ten-year-old boy from Guangxi Province to help fund his continuing studies. Ivan became pen pals with this boy and now, fifteen years later, they still kept in touch.

After the boy graduated from high school, he wrote Ivan a letter and said that he wanted to go to college but he was torn because he also felt he should start working to help support his family. Ivan immediately wrote back and told him to go to college, sending along half the amount required for his first year's tuition: 4000 kuai. The following year, Ivan bought him a new computer. That young man was then twenty-four and would soon graduate with a degree in architecture. What I found most interesting about the story was that Ivan and this young man had never met. Ivan's weekly phone calls kept him apprised of the happenings in the lad's life from romantic endeavours and academic pursuits to other noteworthy events.

It was a heartwarming story and confirmed my instincts about Ivan's character. What kept Ivan from pursuing his dreams in London was a lack of money, yet he continued to help support his old pen pal financially. I urged Ivan to travel to Guangxi Province when his friend graduated to finally meet him.

Ivan invited me to see a 'drama' with him. I hadn't gone to a play in China yet and was curious. The show had three lines of dialogue in it. The rest was pantomime, some kind of 'experimental theatre'. While I struggled to understand the meaning of the play, it was an honour to go. I was the only foreigner there. During one part of the play, two beggars emerged and started pleading for money with hand signals.

The audience exploded into raucous laughter, which confused me. Ivan leaned over at another point and told me that the person on stage was acting like the conductor of a bus. I was stunned. How could he ascertain that person was the conductor? I took the bus every day and couldn't make that judgment. *Culture is key*, I thought to myself again. There are many things you 'get' only when you've lived in a society long enough.

I noticed a photograph of Ivan in the playbill. He responded with a nonchalant shrug, a gesture that I came to know as quintessentially Ivan. With a casualness that belied his talent, he revealed that he had graced the stages of several productions before.

Ivan's invitations opened doors to myriad artistic events, each offering a glimpse into a previously unexplored world. Gallery openings became a staple of our shared experiences, a testament to Ivan's deep immersion in the creative undercurrents of the city. I first met his eclectic circle of friends at these gatherings. They formed a tribe of individuals who existed on the fringes, each with style and substance. Their fierce independence truly set them apart.

The truth was I liked Ivan very much, but he was the wrong teacher for me. He did not have the teaching background that a beginner like me required. I suspect he took the job because he wanted to save up for his London dream, but I think a part of him felt guilty about working with me. Ivan would have been a perfect instructor for a more advanced student, but I needed more support. I remember leaving class one evening and on my walk back to the bus stop to return home I burst into hot tears. Despite my fervent desire to learn Chinese a trifecta of obstacles—my age, my full-time job and my personality—all combined to impede my progress. 'Fail fast' is one of the best pieces of advice to give a language learner, but I was too scared to apply it to myself.

When I drift back to those formative days at the Taipei Language Institute, it is not the gruelling tone drills nor the intricate contours of characters that confounded my untrained hand. Instead, what surfaces first is the melodic laughter of Yang Yang and Ivan, echoing through McDonald's as we shared French fries.

I can still picture Yang Yang's delicate fingers, pushing his glasses up the bridge of his nose with a quiet hesitancy that belied his inner strength. And Ivan, once liberated from the confines of the classroom, would don a cloak of bravado, his every gesture a silent rebellion against tradition.

Though they may not have realised it at the time, Yang Yang and Ivan were imparting a lesson far more profound than any textbook could contain. Through their very being, they were teaching me that language is no mere collection of static rules and rote phrases but a living, breathing entity that moulds itself to the unique intricacies of each speaker's soul.

When I cast my mind back to those halcyon days, watching my teachers navigate the waters between tradition and modernity, I begin to understand the true complexity of the Chinese people. They are not some faceless mass, interchangeable and indistinguishable, but a tapestry of individuals, each grappling with the weight of history and the pull of progress in their own deeply personal way.

BARRY

One evening, as I walked into my apartment building, a five-year-old boy caught sight of me in the hall. He shrieked, 'Hello,' and then bolted away. As I didn't stay home too often, I never really made any connections with my neighbours. I was the only foreigner living in the building and if any other English speakers lived there, none had introduced themselves.

Most Chinese children learned English in school, but not much—but apparently enough to holler a half-hearted 'Hello'. What I knew for sure was that my native English skills made me valuable, so perhaps I could parlay them into getting acquainted with a neighbour.

I asked Nick to type a note in Chinese that I could tack to the building's bulletin board. It explained that I was an American who lived in the building, that I had an interest in Chinese culture, and that I'd love to join my neighbours for breakfast one morning. While I had experienced numerous lunches and dinner, Chinese breakfast was largely undefined for me. What did the Chinese eat to kickstart their day? In return, I could help coach their children in English. It was kind of funny, because after Nick sent me the note, I put it into the translator to see what exactly he'd written. Chinese people were direct and this note epitomised that. He wrote that I would only 'interrupt' the family between 6:30 and 7:15 am. With a chuckle, I realised that Nick probably thought this was another one of my stupid ideas. The day after I posted the note in the lobby, Nick got a call. I now had a plan to meet a family in my building on Saturday morning.

The man who invited me, Barry Liu, was an all-around great guy. Slender and polished, in his early thirties, wearing glasses and with the whitest teeth. He was attractive to me in a 'daddy' sense. Originally from Hunan Province, he stood out as one of the few who refrained from continuously reminding me that Chairman Mao came from the same region. He went to Ningxiang No.1 High School in Changsha, Hunan's capital city, and graduated at the top of his class. As we rode the elevator from the lobby to his apartment on the ninth floor, I asked him about education in China and if it was true that most of it simply came down to rote memorisation. He said that, for decades, memorising facts and the correct stroke order of Chinese characters had been the norm. Yet education was transforming, but not nearly as fast as it needed to. His wife worked as a Chinese teacher at a primary school and the teachers had begun asking the kids for their 'opinion' after they read stories. This was a sea change compared to the way things were run in the past. Education had never been interactive before. It didn't surprise me that this would be happening in Beijing. But what about smaller locales?

I was stunned to see how modern his apartment was, so much nicer than the bare-bones environment I lived in. His wife had recently given birth. In addition to his wife and the now two-month-old daughter, his parents and his mother-in-law also lived there. It must have felt tight at times, though I didn't detect it during breakfast. The wife wasn't super friendly, but could you blame her? She'd barely left the hospital and her husband decided to invite some stranger up to breakfast.

Barry's father also seemed distrustful of me. He eyed me, wary—probably convinced that I'd become another mouth to feed.

The breakfast spread before me was an unapologetic carbohydrate fest, complete with a tall glass of milk, bread reminiscent of yellow cake and a fried dough concoction called *yóutiáo*. Rounding out the homage to all things starch was a pomelo, its tart flesh providing a counterpoint to the richness of the fried dough, and a few boiled eggs. While this combination of dishes wouldn't necessarily be my first choice for breakfast, the food was almost an afterthought compared to the friendly vibe that surrounded us.

I learned more about Barry's background. He had graduated with his bachelor's degree in pharmaceuticals from the Ocean University of China in Qingdao, one of the top programs in the country. Then he moved to Beijing and received a master's degree in pharmacology from Peking Union Medical College and the Chinese Academy of Medical Sciences, an elite and highly competitive program focused on preparing graduates to work in regulation, research or corporate roles. He was now a vice president at Damgo Health Consultancy, a niche PR and advertising firm focused exclusively on promoting domestic and multinational pharmaceutical products in China.

He told me one of Damgo's major clients was Shanghai Dahua Pharmaceuticals, the maker of Postinor-2—commonly known as the 'morning-after pill'—which had just been approved for over-the-counter sales in urban pharmacies. Another key account was Guangdong Lingrui Pharmaceutical, producer of the leading anti-fungal spray for athlete's foot. I could see why these products would have potential in the

Chinese market. Demand was growing rapidly for previously unavailable healthcare goods for family planning, personal hygiene and lifestyle improvement. And in China's increasingly competitive pharmaceutical landscape, specialist agencies like Damgo played a crucial role in branding, consumer education and navigating complex regulations around marketing these sensitive product categories.

While I didn't know much about Hunan Province then, Barry struck me as an example of the upward trajectory that the whole country was riding. Hunan hadn't grown as prosperous as other provinces—if anything it was most revered for its fiery country cuisine and its revolutionaries like Mao Zedong. Yet Barry had a master's, a lucrative job and an apartment that could rival a flat in a Chicago skyscraper. What was the secret of his success?

'One of the most important things in China is the college entrance exam, the *gāokǎo*,' he said. 'But there is a wide disparity in how these exams are weighted in China. It's an intense three-day exam and your whole future rides on it. Kids from Beijing and Shanghai don't have to score as high on the *gāokǎo* to be admitted to college. But kids in poorer provinces ... I grew up in Hunan, so I had to score very high to get the chance. If I hadn't done well, I would probably be a peasant today.'

Thinking about how much depended on this one test amazed me. No wonder so many Chinese parents invested so heavily in their children's education. Competition was fierce. As Barry held his daughter and encouraged me to speak to her in my 'native English', I realised that he was already trying to give her a head start on her education. And she was two months old.

Excited to have a chance to practice his English again, Barry told me that he'd like to take me out. For me, the best part of knowing an English-speaking neighbour was that I finally had someone nearby who could help me if I got into trouble. While the reception from his wife and extended family was less than hospitable, I was grateful for that morning.

After a few days, Barry emailed and asked if he could visit my home. The day we had breakfast, he had informed me that I would 'invite' him to my apartment at some point. That caught me off guard because I didn't know what he meant. Was I supposed to prepare a meal for him? I didn't know. When I asked my friends, they said he wanted to see where I lived and that when someone allowed you to visit their home they expected you to invite them into yours as well. *Ooh-kay.*

He came over that evening and I think he wanted to get to know me more. I offered him some bottled water, but he didn't want any. We went into my room—the living room didn't have an air conditioner—and talked for a couple of hours on my bed. I gave Barry a doll I had bought for his daughter and he seemed touched. Offhand, I told him about my struggles to obtain a monthly pass to Longtan Park and he surprised me a few days later by getting me one.

For the duration of the year I lived in that apartment, we would meet on weekends at my apartment or at Longtan Park. It was a win-win for both of us. He got to reawaken the part of him that loved English and I got to learn more about China. As a working husband and father, it was a generous thing for him to do. And his age and experience meant that he illuminated a side of Chinese life different from that of my younger friends.

As pleasant as Barry was, there was some tension in our talks. He wanted to know what exactly my life plans were.

'My plans?' I asked.

'You moved to China,' he said. 'What's your next step? How are you going to build a career? Buy a house? Buy a car? Get married? Will you stay here forever or go back to America?' A sceptical look would creep across his face.

I often deflected these questions with a laugh or an 'I don't know' because they made me uncomfortable. This was another of those in-your-face cultural moments. Chinese people had their lives planned for them by their parents from the moment they entered the world. Everything was predetermined. The only question was, how hard would you work to make it? Would you rise to the top like Barry, or would you drift, rudderless?

For Barry, my decision to say, 'Fuck it,' quit my career and move to China must've seemed irresponsible at best. Had I been a graduate on a gap year, he might have given me more leeway. But as Barry and I were about the same age he felt I ought to make decisions more like his own. These conversations made me wonder if I had made the wrong choice by coming here. For many Chinese people, my decision meant I was less on an adventure and more likely running from something. This only deepened my resolve to prove everyone wrong. I would build something solid out of this China chapter.

'Do you want some advice?' Barry asked one afternoon at Longtan Park. Knowing that I would get it whether or not I solicited it, I agreed.

'I think you should become a teacher. You're from America, you speak excellent English and the parents would love you.

English, but perfect English,' he said.

Teaching had become a recurring theme for me. Barry wasn't the first to suggest that I be a teacher. My grandparents on my mother's side spent their careers as public school teachers. Maybe it wasn't that bad of an idea. A country obsessed with English and education probably meant that I would have an 'iron rice bowl'—a job for life—that harkened back to when everyone worked in state-owned enterprises.

I nodded. 'I'll think about it.'

DELL ENGLISH

The year had raced by faster than I realised. I had learned and grown tremendously. Beijing had captured my heart. But with only a few months left on my contract, I refused to renew for another year at AITA.

I'd had the same desperate conversation with many friends, fishing eagerly for a lifeline. Was there anyone in this city who offered jobs to hapless foreigners like me? The unexpected path came from the most unlikely of characters—my colleague Andy.

A native of nearby Hebei Province, Andy was among the most traditional of all the Chinese people I'd met. While my other friends spent their time lapping up episodes of American TV or scheming on how to get ahead in their careers, Andy always seemed content. He went to college for a science degree and then worked for a few years as a traditional Chinese medicine (TCM) doctor. Though I had anticipated experiencing traditional practices like TCM more often in China, this was my first personal encounter with it. But 2007 Beijing was moving on—at least temporarily—from these ancient ways.

'Let me see your palm,' Andy said, grabbing my hand across the table. He traced the creases with intense scrutiny, like a fortune teller at a carnival. 'Hmm, interesting. I predict you will not marry until age thirty-five, but theirs will be everlasting love.'

I laughed. 'Surely my love life can't be foretold in the wrinkles of my hand?'

'Doubt me if you wish, but I have yet to be proven wrong,' he said. 'Now, let's discuss your digestion. All this oily food cannot be good for your stomach or spleen ...'

And so it went every lunch hour, Andy relishing opportunities to diagnose my ailments and lecture me on anatomy or Eastern medicine. He claimed too much thinking damaged the lungs. Acupuncturists could supposedly diagnose by examining one's face, feet, even ears. I nodded along to his soliloquies, interjecting an occasional 'hmm' or 'fascinating' to placate my pontificating physician friend.

One afternoon at a Sichuan restaurant, Andy clicked his tongue as I ordered the *gān biān sì jī dòu*, a spicy green bean delicacy. 'Far too hot for you, I fear.'

I smiled slyly. 'I'm from New Mexico. Spice is all we know.'

When the greens arrived, glistening in a sheen of ginger oil and peppercorns, I swept my chopsticks through eagerly. As I chewed the tender beans, Andy watched me expectantly for signs of discomfort. But the gradual numbing tingle of the Sichuan pepper only delighted me more.

I cleaned my plate without flinching once. 'Like I said, we eat Hatch chiles more scorching than this for breakfast.'

Andy raised his eyebrows, finally impressed by the ironclad endurance of my intestines.

As we waited for the bill, I asked him how he planned to spend the weekend. He said he would go back to his university and see his 'half girlfriend'. It begged the question, 'Which half?' He said that they were in 'negotiations' about whether to formally date. Like many of my unmarried Chinese male friends, lack of financial means posed barriers to finding a romantic partner. Andy resorted to living in a traditional courtyard, or *sìhéyuàn*, with six other families. Though he got his own room, he described the overall property as cramped. I could imagine.

'I need to tell you something,' he said, leaning forward. 'I've started working on the weekends at an English training centre to make extra money. We need more teachers. I think you would be a wonderful teacher.'

Andy enticed me to teach at Dell English by explaining that I could teach at night, after work, or on weekends. Importantly, these were adult students who already spoke English and only wanted to improve. Simply being a native speaker—and an American, to boot—made me qualified. The pay? One hundred and fifty kuai an hour.

'Okay, I'll try,' I replied, a bit unsure.

Andy arranged for my class to meet at their Fangzhuang location. This was perfect because it wasn't far from AITA, just over the bridge from where I lived in Chongwenmen. My class would take place on Wednesday and Friday nights from seven to nine. The course I would teach would last eight weeks. Simple enough.

Andy and I took the bus to the centre after work. The classroom was narrow with a group of metal chairs in a half circle, a whiteboard and a lectern for me. He told me I could borrow a TV and DVD player from the front desk if I ever needed it. Dell English didn't have a curriculum per se. The teachers essentially owned their classes' two hours and it was up to them to fill that time. I didn't know any teachers in China, so I relied on the internet for ideas. I overprepared and came with dozens of ideas and notes brimming in my backpack.

My Fangzhuang class had about fifteen students. Because they were a bit older, they liked my methods. One of them told me that I taught like a Chinese teacher because I was a bit more formal, whereas the 'training centre' model was more about playing games and having fun. As we had no syllabus or oversight from management, it all came down to the teacher's personality and what they brought to the classroom. As long as students didn't complain and renewed their tuition, the teacher had autonomy. I found this appealing.

The truth was that I took teaching seriously, and I wanted my students to gain something from it. Preparing for one class took about four hours. Teaching was hard work. When I did the math, though, I realised I was barely making any money at all. Slowly, I started prioritising preparation for my English classes over responsibilities at AITA. I invested more hours researching engaging topics to present and games to captivate student imaginations.

Prepping for the classes also enhanced my knowledge about China's development. An article in the *Wall Street Journal* detailed how a decade earlier, China had the worst aviation safety record of any country. As a result, the government devoted more resources to training and by 2007 the country had an almost-zero crash record. I used this as an example in class to inspire students in their language learning.

While a couple of younger students were considering immigrating to other countries, most focused on their families. I had a married couple in their early thirties. I asked if they needed to use English at work. They laughed and said no, they worked at very local companies. They had a six-year-old son and they wanted to give him an advantage with his English studies. And as their own English wasn't perfect, they figured studying it again could help them improve his scores. It was a poignant reminder of the two central elements of Chinese culture that I'd come to discover: family and education.

I wanted my students also to have a better understanding and appreciation of Western culture. For example, during the week of Halloween, I brought some bite-size candy and explained the concept of trick-or-treating.

Honestly, I felt like I should have paid my students. I was theoretically teaching them English, but they also taught me Chinese culture. I often dropped some hint of a stereotype that I had heard about China and they would gently correct me. And as I was studying Chinese, they taught me as much as I taught them. I loved sharing English slang and idioms and discovering that Mandarin often had its own equivalents. I looked forward to each class, thrilled to gauge my students' opinions on that day's news or learn about their aspirations.

'No more writing,' the students teasingly chorused when I announced the weekly writing assignment. Their eyes implored behind forced smiles—could I not relent on this one requirement amid their already hectic lives?

I clasped my hands, endeavouring to explain my rationale yet again. 'Writing solidifies your English language skills even as we focus on verbal fluency in class.'

'But we just want to speak better English,' Li Chen interjected. 'Our writing is not so bad already.' Murmurs of agreement stirred.

'I understand, yet writing presents you with different challenges.'

Their faces fell as my words found their target. I continued gently, 'And for those more reticent to speak up, writing offers a judgment-free space to build your confidence.'

This resonated with the class wallflowers. They sat a little taller, empowered by the realisation.

'So then, shall we begin?' I flourished a whiteboard marker. 'This week's essay topic: What does success look like to you thirty years from now?'

Pens scratched earnestly. Li Chen's brow remained tightly furrowed. As they wrote, my mind wandered …What dreams filled those pages? How might their ambitions in this era reshape the flows of human history? I itched to understand it all, my students' hopes as much as my curiosities about China itself. This assignment might unveil it in their unfiltered and uncorrected words and verve as shown in these extracts:

> What things you need to accomplish in the next 30 years? I don't know what the life would happen in thirty years. Maybe I only need for a good health and it's the most important for me when I'm fifty-five years old. Talk about my job. I'll be a software test engineer and plenty of experience will be got together. So I should have my own company. Sometimes the boss of Microsoft want to treat me to have supper, but I have refused him because I'm too busy to consort with my family. My wife should be fair for me and I'll have a son. Weekend he may help me to wash my car. When he is young I'll teach him everything that I liked. Painting,

swimming, calligraphy, driving, guitar, etc. I think he will be able to buy some roses to his girlfriend. When he is about twenty-five years old although I don't know how many girlfriends he has sent the flowers. I wish everything would be true. It's not a dream and need for my effort. — Osorken

This year is golden pig year, also is my 30 years old. Yesterday night I thought my last 30 years very long time and the time flying. I haven't do anything what I think it is so successful thing. I think it is not you do/save much money, but I am healthy. I am peace and our family is happiness and we are love each other. In next 30 years my life successful is my English level it is very well. Second I will marriage who love me and understand me. Also I expect we have a lovely baby and we have comfortable home. Whatever we do we are so happy and know thanks for everything. Thanks for every people. — Sarah

It is in thirty years later Oh, what a fine day today! It's 1 Jan 2038 on the calendar. How time flies, it looks like we just finish the english lessons, but it's 30 years ago ;) Now I have to get up and go out for the morning exercise. There are lots things come into my head while walking in the garden. Thanks to Glen who was our english teacher several decades ago, thanks to I went to learn english, other we could not live and work here comfortably, you know, Australia is an english speaking country, communication is the most important, so

I thanks. After finished the dell english lesson, my english ability had a real improvement and I received the header's recognizes in the company, and we got a chance to go abroad for a global project in Australia. I found it's really very nice and beautiful and people are friendly and so many Chinese people there. My wife and I used to talk about moving to Switzerland, which is one country in west-central Europe and be famous for its peace and etiquette, but we finally decided to settle here after the compare and long time consideration. Now, we find that the choice is right! We like the environment for living and working, as well as my son and daughter. Though our parents and relatives still live in China, we can go back to see them during the holiday and they also come here to spend their leisure time, I know it's my perfect life, it's the result of our efforts.— Peter

The compositions were revealing. The students had little problem in stressing their desires. How would I fare, I wondered, if circumstances called for me to write such a personal essay?

Looking back, I have many regrets about my first foray into formal English teaching at Fangzhuang. My stiff approach strayed too close to the way a Chinese teacher would teach an English class. I was overprepared, serious without being stern and not personable enough for the students. And I acted too 'holier than thou' about the English language.

One of my favourite students, Cindy, was a woman who had started studying English to help her daughter with her homework. She spent all day doing homework and prepping for class. On one occasion, I had given the students a quiz, and one of the questions I asked Cindy was, 'Would a native English speaker describe a wedding as 'beautiful' or 'glorious'?'

Cindy considered and then confidently answered, 'Glorious.'

I looked toward the floor, disappointed, and corrected her. 'Beautiful.'

Cindy cringed, ashamed. She hadn't studied hard enough, evidently.

That exchange has haunted me for years. Who cares how a native English speaker would describe it? What matters is what comes from your heart.

Regardless of level, my students shared some particularities. Pronouncing the words 'veterinarian' and 'entrepreneur' was difficult. 'Usually' often sounded like 'you-really' and 'clothes' was 'clo-the-ses'. Because I hadn't received training in teaching English to non-native speakers, I was often perplexed about how to help them. I was a native speaker but didn't know the rules of my own language. They often wrote down the syllables of certain words they'd learned in school and asked me how to pronounce them. I had to say, 'I'm sorry, I don't know that system.'

The funniest thing was how my students would ask me again and again how I'd learned English. 'Um, just listening to my parents, I guess.' They pried into what methods my teachers had used on me as a kid and I couldn't think of anything specific. It wasn't until years later that I realised how much effort Chinese pupils put in at elementary school, not only to learn how to write characters but even how to properly pronounce Chinese words without a regional accent. Even native Mandarin speakers couldn't just 'pick it up'.

People put in thousands of focused hours on the path to fluency. Every Chinese person I knew believed their English abilities were lacking, which never failed to unnerve me when I compared their fluency to my own rudimentary grasp of Mandarin. Even as they apologised profusely for their 'terrible' English, I could only marvel at their intricate vocabulary and largely accurate grammar. Meanwhile, my tongue tangled in tones.

My students often asked personal questions. Many assumed that I'd already been married as I was older than thirty. I kept tight-lipped about my personal life, but found that some of the most popular teachers were open books. They gave their students explicit details about themselves, including their sex lives. But that wasn't my style. I was lucky that my students liked me enough to accept my dry lessons.

As Christmas approached, the students suggested that we do our final class as a dinner. Initially, I thought they'd suggested it because they wanted to learn more about how foreigners celebrated the holiday. Only in retrospect did I come to appreciate that they recognised it was my first year abroad, that I was alone, and that Christmas carried the same significance to me as Spring Festival did to the Chinese. They didn't want me to feel lonely.

We went to Der Landgraf, a German restaurant I had discovered a few months earlier around the corner from Dell English. One thing that distinguished the restaurant was the service. When dining in small Chinese restaurants, patrons usually had to deal with apathetic service and yell for attention. Here, the all-Chinese staff were polite, efficient and always a step ahead. Servers would ask at the conclusion of the meal in perfect English, 'Would you like coffee or dessert?' The downside to all this? Expense. A meal for two could easily cost four hundred kuai.

As I became a regular at Der Landgraf, I learned a great deal more. The Chinese owner had trained in Germany for some time and also owned a large restaurant in Cologne. He was an uncommon gem, taking exceptional care of his employees, providing a staff doctor and salaries exceeding industry norms. The restaurant catered all Air China's first-class flights and served the German national women's football team when they stayed in China for competitions.

The Chinese adored German culture. Already boisterous, Chinese patrons became even more raucous when indulging in ten-pint flights of beer, speedily downing each glass. But it was the ambience that I thrived on. We drank steins of Kölsch, a top-fermented beer from Cologne, and ate German sausages and authentic 'homemade' bread.

I explained to my students that many foreigners living in Beijing felt that good service wasn't possible in China because of cultural differences. I pointed out that Der Landgraf proved that wasn't true. With a bit of training and some care from management, anything was possible.

As the beer flowed, the formality of our classroom ebbed away. Instead, there was laughter and lots of photo-snapping. But mostly there was nonstop discussion: the differences in holidays between China and the West; gossip about families, children, careers; President George W Bush; and if I thought watching *Prison Break* was better than watching *Friends* for learning English. At some point, I forgot that my students were Chinese as they easily conversed in English. The dinner table had an air of casual comfort that was often lacking in the classroom setting. Over mugs of frothy German beer, the conversation flowed organically—quite unlike the stilted interactions that sometimes occurred during lectures. If only Dell English had allowed me to provide a round of Bitburger to make every class this much fun.

One of my students, David, was a native Beijinger. He insisted on walking me to the bus stop after each class. I felt guilty because I knew he lived in the opposite direction and I was only going to make him later for work. Whenever I protested, he insisted that I was his teacher and that it was his duty. Such extraordinary heart. He worked in the sales department of the China World Hotel in Guomao, selling banquets to customers.

Though a native Beijinger, first-tier city status didn't alleviate his pressure. He had a girlfriend he hoped to marry, but her parents disapproved of the match because he did not own an apartment. Despite their pedigrees as native Beijingers, his prospects dimmed without this marker of stability. His story was one I'd heard repeatedly—love was not sufficient for young people to overcome traditional expectations about home ownership before marriage.

He quizzed me about how Americans handled such matters. David's jaw dropped when I described American parents granting a simple blessing and then leaving young couples to choose their life partner. In China, elders directed marital decisions. His own wedding plans hinged on parental approval—not only of the bride, but also of mortgage matters. Though he eventually married his girlfriend after three years' courtship, they resided with her family until financially ready for their own place.

As we left the restaurant on that blustery evening, David again insisted on standing with me at the bus stop. But that day, I put my foot down, patting him on his shoulder. 'David,' I said, 'you really don't need to do this. It's freezing and you know I know how to take the bus by now.'

He looked at me with reverence. 'It is my duty.'

At the end of those eight weeks, I had improved so much as a teacher. Standing in front of a group of people twice a week and having to think on my feet gave me new confidence. There was no place to hide. I had learned how to anticipate problems that came up and I took pride when I saw my class progress.

The moment Dell English informed me that the majority of my students had chosen to renew their enrolment for another course, I felt a warmth bloom in my chest. It was a stark contrast to the drain I so often felt at my desk job at AITA, where the hours seemed to stretch on in an endless monotony of paperwork and emails.

But in the evenings, when I stepped into that classroom and faced the eager, expectant faces of my students, I felt a crackle of electricity. Each session was an adventure, a journey into the unknown where anything could happen, and I found myself invigorated by the unpredictability of it all.

As I looked back on those eight weeks, I realised I had become something more, something I had never dared to imagine for myself. I had become an English teacher, a guide and a mentor, a shaper of minds and a cultivator of dreams. And in that moment of realisation, I knew that my life would never be the same again.

AMERICAN

Living or travelling outside my country for a long period of time provided me with awareness about where I came from. Moving to China made me realise many things about America that I hadn't before. While English was a global language, I discovered that Americans had distinct turns of phrase for other things from the rest of the world. American English extended beyond words to entirely different, if not outright dated, thinking and logic.

I became aware of the peculiar systems America clung to. When people asked my height or weight, I didn't know how to tell them in kilograms or metres. Clothing sizes are often measured in centimetres instead of inches, distance is measured in kilometres versus miles, and volume is measured in litres rather than gallons. In addition to Americans not using the metric system, we used Fahrenheit instead of Celsius for temperature. We don't tell time in military time (not to mention the inanity of daylight savings time). And what size is a men's twelve in the rest of the shoe-buying world?

Besides units of measurement, I discovered other differences. I was floored when I saw that milk and yogurt were sold in the dry goods section of grocery stores without refrigeration. I learned that due to differences in pasteurisation and processing standards, food products beyond dairy are often required to be refrigerated in the United States, even though the same products can be safely stored at room temperature or cooler in much of the world. Though I had long viewed America as pioneering and cutting-edge, certain manifestations of 'American exceptionalism' led me to see my homeland as sometimes backward thinking and stubbornly independent from global norms.

I struggled with imposter syndrome. My Chinese friends viewed me as a sophisticate there to enlighten them. Certainly, I had arrived in China with a degree of haughtiness about my nationality, career accomplishments, and the feeling that I wasn't like 'those Americans'. I had always thought I knew America, its manifest truths as self-evident as amber waves of grain.

Through living abroad I came to view America in a new, more critical light, seeing areas where we lacked compared to others. Meeting Europeans who were multilingual, Chinese friends who chatted with ease about international events in even the most distant parts of the world, and a broader worldview made me reconsider American society. There were elements I appreciated and clung to ('We're nicer!'), but it also opened my eyes to what was missing. For example, the Chinese emphasis on education was admirable.

'There's so much happening in China that I want the wider world to know about,' was something I ruminated on. I was never ashamed to be American then. Indeed, the Chinese venerated many aspects of American society. For me? I felt a void.

It was a recurring pattern on my travels through China: as soon as locals discerned my American origins from my accent or dress, their eyes brightened with interest. 'America,' they would exclaim with a thumbs-up. While its politics may have stymied them, its soft power was alluring. From *Friends*, which showed a group of adults hanging out in a café and fancy apartment in New York, to the raunchiness of *American Pie*, the Chinese were entranced. Things must be better in America, right? Right?

I had no doubt that part of the warm reception I received in China stemmed from the fact that I came from a country that most Chinese people admired greatly. But what troubled me was the sinking feeling of, *I hope they don't become too much like America.* I wasn't worried about mass shootings in a country where firearms were forbidden. I was worried about waste, excessive consumption and so many of the other 'first world' problems with which America was grappling. Chinese people viewed many things in the West, like owning a car, as a sign of upward mobility. I understood that. But I knew that many elements of the American lifestyle weren't sustainable for the planet or even the people themselves. Credit cards were starting to emerge widely across China. Would people start drowning in credit card debt as they funded their new lifestyles? There was simply too much about America that they didn't understand.

To most Chinese, America was a technicolour dream. As seen through America's pop culture exports, even ordinary Americans enjoyed spacious castles with green yards and endless blue skies. The apartments sprawling on shows like *Friends* seemed impossibly large, unlike the crammed high-rises of Beijing, where a few hundred square feet cost a fortune. In America, so it appeared, every school was Harvard or Yale, opportunity served up like ripe peaches at a roadside stand. Decent jobs grew on trees, there for the taking, theirs for the choosing, a stark departure from the intense competition back home.

I admired so much about the Chinese way of life. There were hidden problems that I didn't see or couldn't comprehend the scale of, but there was much to admire in the way Chinese people led their lives. For all its challenges, I wished more people had appreciated what Chinese society had to offer.

EXIT STRATEGY

The American Embassy in Beijing would like to remind all American citizens to carry valid identification at all times and to ensure that all immigration documents, such as Chinese visas, are in order.

The embassy has learned that the Exit and Entry Administration Bureau of the Ministry of Public Security seeks to ensure that foreigners in Beijing are in possession of valid documentation. Police are asking foreigners to produce documentation on demand and visiting homes to see that foreigners are in compliance with all regulatory procedures.

Please be advised that current regulations state that the penalty for overstaying a visa is 500 RMB a day of overstay, not to exceed 5000 RMB and detention. The period of detention can range from five to thirty days depending on the severity of the violation. Detention may be longer than thirty days in the case that the authorities believe that the foreigner was involved in criminal activity. The embassy is aware of several recent detentions of American citizens relating to visa overstays and violating the terms of their visas.

Americans in China, who are not staying at hotels, including Americans who are staying with friends or relatives, must register with the local police as soon as they arrive. Otherwise, they may be fined up to 500 RMB a day.

— US Embassy Consular Notice

Beyond my visa, the passport papers I carried ruled my life. At AITA, our focus was on sending Chinese delegations to Australia and New Zealand but we constantly grappled with the Australian embassy in Beijing, trying to understand why it rejected so many of our Chinese applicants.

It's hard to fathom the visa struggles the Chinese faced back then, considering the established image today of Chinese tour groups splurging on luxury goods in Paris or hitting the Vegas casinos. Embassies worldwide demanded stacks of paperwork from Chinese hopefuls—bank statements, housing deeds, marriage licences—even for tourist visas.

The bureaucracy only worsened considering that in these booming economic times in China, many applicants were first-time visitors or tourists planning a trip on the spur of the moment. Overseas trade shows or chances to take part in official delegations were business opportunities many Chinese entrepreneurs couldn't ignore. Applying for a visa a day or two in advance wasn't unusual for these people, but their destination countries had other ideas.

Since 9/11, the US and Canada had become increasingly stringent in their visa application procedures. In some cases, the rejection rate for Chinese applicants could run as high as fifty per cent. To the frustration of many Chinese people, the procedures seemed arbitrary. One day someone would go in and get approved and the next day someone else with a nearly identical application would be denied. As an American who enjoyed visa-free privileges in so many parts of the world—except China, of course—it was a wake-up call to the reality of what people of other nationalities faced on a daily basis. I found it ironic that Americans could enjoy broadly convenient international travel if they chose to, yet many didn't even have a passport.

I heard about a Chinese man who applied for a tourist visa for Italy. The Italian embassy in Beijing requested several documents to ensure that he had enough reason to return to China and not overstay his visa. Frustrated by the number of documents he needed to produce in such a short time, he decided not to complete the process. But because he did not, the embassy officially marked him as 'rejected'. Turns out, many countries shared information about visa applicants to ward off fraud and undesirables. When he discovered this, it had become nearly impossible for him to get a visa to many countries.

A few months later, I had a wake-up call about how precarious my own visa situation was. Previously, I felt a false sense of security, believing I would never have to endure the experience of the police conducting a visa spot check on me. After all, I resided and worked in Chongwenmen, a distinctly Chinese neighbourhood, separate from the foreigner enclaves like Chaoyang District. However, fate had different ideas, as one ordinary morning when Jess and I innocently crossed the street on our way to work, oblivious to what lay ahead.

As our footsteps echoed on the pavement, a voice pierced the air from behind us.

'Hello.'

Startled, we spun around, only to find ourselves confronted by three towering policemen. Their stern expressions and authoritative presence sent a shiver down my spine.

'Passport?' one of the officers demanded. His voice cracked like a whip, authority dripping from each syllable.

I patted my breast pocket out of habit, feeling the hard edges of my passport. Jess stood beside me, his nonchalance slowly collapsing as his hands rifled through his own pockets. His eyes met mine, an admission of guilt.

'You know, in China you need to carry your passport with you at all times.'

Jess's knuckles whitened as his hands closed into tight fists. His face darkened, the last trace of his casual aura vanishing beneath a storm cloud of frustration.

'It's in my flat,' he choked out through gritted teeth. 'How should I have known to carry the bloody thing everywhere?'

The officer eyed him coolly, Jess's outburst no more remarkable than a fleck of dust settling on his crisp uniform.

Silence as the officers exchanged disapproving glances. Their unspoken judgment hovered like a dark cloud over us. Instead of challenging Jess's explanation, they redirected their inquiry, asking if we had registered our address with the police. With a flicker of relief, I reached into my pocket, producing a copy of our registration form. One of the officers withdrew from his pocket an expensive-looking lacquer fountain pen and brandished it with purpose. He diligently transcribed every detail from the registration form into his notebook. Meanwhile, the other two officers scrutinised my passport and accommodation registration, their actions under the watchful gaze of passersby on their way to work. The attention we attracted only heightened the tension as an uneasy sense of vulnerability settled upon us.

Although the officers maintained a demeanour of calmness, politeness and respect, I couldn't shake my growing unease. Each passing moment felt like a tightrope walk as they probed deeper into our lives, questioning our purpose in Beijing. The knowledge of our illegal visa status weighed heavily on my conscience. I began to fear the unknown lurking beneath the surface.

With the aura of folktales, the expat community whispered stories of police swooping down upon foreigners who dared to work illegally. The imminent threat of the snuffing out of my burgeoning adventure, especially with the Olympics on the horizon, intensified my anxiety. It couldn't end so soon, not when the world's attention was fixed on this city of wonders.

The officer handed back my papers, his eyes giving nothing away. I slid them into my pocket but felt no sense of conclusion. Jess and I uttered quiet thanks as we withdrew. We continued our walk towards the office. I knew this wasn't the end of the affair.

The next morning crept in like a cell door clanking shut. Jess and I exchanged hollow looks over our Nescafé instant coffee as policemen materialised in the AITA lobby. Michael led them wordlessly into the conference room. The repetitive ticking of the clock mirrored the pulses in our chests. The not knowing was its own special torment.

My hands moved ceaselessly, rubbing together with nervous energy as I shifted in my seat. I had always fidgeted when anxious ever since I was a child. It was a tendency my friends knew well and gently teased me about. Jess seemed equally restless in the seat beside me. His gaze flitted between the clock and the window, brows furrowed as he bent paperclip after paperclip out of shape. The tiny scratches and clicks of the metal punctuated the heavy silence hanging over us while we waited. Though we didn't speak, our shared anxiety was apparent in Jess's twisted handful of metal and my reddened, friction-burned palms.

Michael's face was unreadable as he stepped out of the conference room. The pit in my stomach deepened as I waited for the news that could make or break us. I needed to understand what had happened, but I was getting nothing. Quiet and cryptic. Had they grilled him in there? Had he somehow played innocent? Had he slipped them money under the table? The details stayed buried; that door stayed shut. Somehow, we were still standing at the end. In that instant, I knew I was meant to be in China right then. By whatever luck or astrology, they had let me stay for now. Those encounters with authorities kept my visa status in the forefront of my mind—no visa meant no China.

I started doing my research months before my contract at AITA expired. I refused to leave before the 2008 Beijing Summer Olympics. But the process worried me—I had only just embarked on my China journey. I didn't want it derailed by bureaucracy. My weekly meetings with Calvin thus took on a new focus, revolving around the tangle of visas. As a former college student in Canada, Calvin knew the challenges foreigners faced when abroad, making him my perfect source of information.

*

The crackling of my footfalls echoed down the icy hutong as I made my way to meet Calvin. Beijing's early winter had swept across the city, coating the twisted alleyways in a silvery rime. Tendrils of woodsmoke scented the frozen air, fading remnants of the day's bustle.

I pulled my coat tighter against the chill, marvelling at the ancient courtyard homes rising around me. Nestled among them, an oasis of light and warmth beckoned—the Red Capital Club loomed before me.

Stepping into the entryway, I felt transported back to the 1950s. Chairman Mao memorabilia and posters from the early PRC era decked the hall. A glossy limousine from that age sat parked by the door, once used to ferry party dignitaries. Through an archway glowed a traditional courtyard, glazed tiles glittering beneath red lanterns. There in its heart stood Calvin, grinning as I approached through the frozen night.

'This place is incredible,' I exclaimed. The chill in my fingers was already forgotten.

Calvin smiled knowingly. 'I know, right? One of my favourite spots for dinner. And you'll really love the food.'

We fell in behind a server dressed in a crisp Mao jacket as he led us deeper inside, past lovingly restored antique furnishing and fixtures at every turn.

The menu spanned pages, a tome chronicling dishes steeped in Chinese Communist Party history. One entry featured the Marshals' Favourite—massive green peppers bursting with a spiced pork filling, the sear of Sichuan peppercorns teased by rich fattiness. I learned it had fuelled China's ten marshals during the Red Army's gruelling Long March.

Another dish featured Deng's chicken, lustrous cubes of tofu and poultry lacquered in a savoury broth. Flanked by two cats carved ornately from root vegetables in slick black and white, they depicted China's paramount leader Deng Xiaoping's proclamation that outward form mattered less than functionary purpose: 'It doesn't matter if a cat is black or white, as long as it catches mice.'

Every plate encapsulated some morsel of the last fifty years, from communist edicts to tales of the civil war. The menu was a tapestry woven from such vibrant threads, each dish a glimpse into the living pulse of history.

Over dinner, I shared my concerns. With the Olympics coming up next year, I had heard rumours that visa renewal might prove difficult. Calvin chuckled, shaking his head. 'No, no, it has nothing to do with the Olympics. There's a five-year communist party congress setting the stage for the party's future leaders in October. It's a highly sensitive time.'

I nodded, feeling a little out of my depth. 'I see. When does it start?'

'Mid-October, but there's so much secrecy surrounding it that no one knows the exact date,' Calvin said.

He went on to explain that during such momentous events, purges of officials, breakups of organised crime such as prostitution rings and other clampdowns were common, helping to remind everyone who was in charge. Foreigners were simply collateral damage and not a significant focus of Chinese officialdom. (By the time the congress ended on October 21, Xi Jinping had been appointed to a high-ranking spot on the politburo standing committee, indicating he would succeed then-president Hu Jintao as the next leader of the country.)

The alcohol burned going down, doing little to calm my rattled nerves. I set the glass down with a trembling hand. 'I had no idea it was so complicated.' I took another fiery sip. The rules could change at any time.

Calvin smiled. 'Don't worry too much about it, Glen. Make sure you stay on top of your visa situation, and you'll be fine.'

We raised our glasses of *báijiǔ*, toasting to our friendship, and continued the evening with more drinks and stories. We took a tour of the Red Capital Club's wine cellar, located in an old bomb shelter built during a time when the Chinese feared a Russian attack. That night, I was grateful to have someone like Calvin, with his insider knowledge of Chinese politics and culture, to guide me through the complexities of life in China.

My F-type visa, on which I'd been working illegally all these months, could be renewed when it expired in March, but a new wrinkle stymied me: I couldn't renew it from within mainland China. This immediately sent a ripple across the dozens of questionable visa agents who catered to the foreign community. Would I have to fly back to the States to apply for a new visa? I was reluctant to do that. Not only was the cost prohibitive, but I didn't want to leave for that long. And what would happen if I did go all the way home, only for the policy to change overnight? My China dream would end early.

I diligently spent those last months at AITA combing the various forums where foreigners shared tips with each other. This opaque system baffled me and it was hard to parse the truth. I even messaged some of the visa agents. I wanted to believe them when they assured me they could renew my visa for a few thousand kuai—especially the ones who claimed strong government connections—but I couldn't help my scepticism.

Finally, my research paid off. I wouldn't have to go all

the way to the US. I could also apply at Chinese embassies in nearby Mongolia, Hong Kong or South Korea.

I started to put my plan into action and decided when my contract expired, I would visit another Asian city: Seoul.

BEYOND THE PAY CHEQUE

Phoenix, Sally, Judy and Nick all left AITA before my contract ended in March 2008. But by then much had already changed. Michael had relocated Jess and me from our office near the conference room to the space outside his office—the worst location to sit. We couldn't come in late, take a few extra minutes at lunch or sneak out early. And worse, I ended up with the seat right outside Michael's door, in his direct line of sight. I couldn't tell whether he considered it an honour to get this close to him or if it indicated he trusted my work ethic even less than Jess's.

Then there was Kathy. Our encounters sparked ideas as much as headaches. This new colleague was from Wuhan, wrapped herself in a big purple coat no matter the weather and wore glasses that constantly slipped down her nose. She had a gummy smile. Her role was to handle anything that fell under the all-encompassing term 'business development'.

She focused less on the overseas delegations and visas that were AITA's bread and butter, and more on trying to partner up Australian businesses with similar companies in China. Often these were fool's errands but even a single deal might yield profit for AITA. Not a bad return on investment, considering Kathy's paltry salary of 2000 kuai a month.

As much as I bonded with most of my colleagues, Kathy presented a new challenge. I'd lived in the country for a while now so perhaps some of my disenchantment with her was that I simply didn't see things with the same charmed awe as I did when I got off the plane. Maybe I was starting to burn out?

Though she knew how to get things done well enough, Kathy had zero decision-making capacity. She agreed with whatever a person with authority said. Her intellect was evident, but her appearance fell short compared to her female colleagues. This likely contributed to Michael's more stringent approach towards her. Ironically, Kathy's irrational and inflexible disposition was a perfect reflection of Michael's own shortcomings. Blind allegiance and unquestioning rationale were par for the course for any Chinese employees who wanted to remain in Michael's good graces. Kathy merely followed his lead, adhering rigidly to his way of operating. Through her, Michael's managerial shortcomings and flaws shot to the surface. She served as the perfect proxy for his brand of ill-conceived leadership.

She tapped me on the shoulder at least ten times a day. Nothing made me shudder more than to hear her say, 'Hi, Glen.'

Every time, I would turn in my plastic chair with a fake smile. 'Hi, Kathy …' I'd grind out.

Whenever someone tried to reason with her, she listened and then responded with, 'Yeah, but …' and insert her preprogrammed rebuttal. That was her trademark. Yes, she got some results and spoke advanced business English, but she was impossible to reason with. Jess and I dreaded working with her; though she had good intentions and could have been effective with the right tutelage, it always ended up being a lose-lose for us.

Dispensing unsolicited medical advice was common practice among Chinese friends. Typically, this didn't bother me. As Nick and I grew closer, he offered the occasional health tip—like boiling Coca-Cola and adding ginger slices when I had a cold. His offbeat suggestions often proved helpful.

Kathy's advice was another story entirely. Her grave warnings grated on me. If she saw me at the water dispenser, she declared solemnly, 'Cold water is bad for health.' My morning apple elicited another stern notification: 'Eating apples in the morning is bad for health.' I knew she meant well, as such advice-giving was a Chinese custom. By then, however, I had lost all patience for her bothersome bulletins. Eventually I stopped responding altogether, unable to appreciate her cultural sign of care.

When Jess sneezed at work one afternoon, Kathy sent both of us an email:

From: Kathy
To: Jess, Glen
November 8, 2007
3:07 pm
Subject: how to cure cold with Chinese traditional way?
fry egg, walnut, green Chinese onion and ginger sheet together, then drink them with they are hot, it is a very good way to cure cold, when i was young and live in a village, my grandmother cure my cold with this way. it is really food and keep fit,

Jess, glen, please drink more hot water, don't drink soft drinkings (*sic*), hot water is good at health and could kill virus, what's more, more than 70 per cent water in each person, but they run off very quickly, so we should drink more hot water.

thank you!

Kathy was draining, but Maggie—Maggie was joy. Kathy dampened our spirits; Maggie lifted them.

She was twenty-four years old and from Henan Province. Something about her personality reminded me of a rabbit. She spoke to me only when the others were out of the office, but had an uncanny emotional intelligence. Maggie always delivered and her outgoing personality made her a joy to work with. But her youth and lack of belief in her English skills meant that she never stood out to others in our company.

Maggie's role was less defined. She was supposed to jump in and help here and there. We often spent our time translating documents between English and Chinese. Maggie excelled at consulting her digital translator and finding the corresponding vocabulary, though this early tech often used antiquated terminology.

Maggie once asked me if I thought someone in our office was a 'good person'. I described him as 'so-so' and asked her opinion. She explained that he kept trying to make himself look better by subtly criticising others to his superiors. Sensing an opportunity to learn more, I asked Maggie what Chinese organisations were like in general. What did bosses value? In reply she told me about two concepts I had not so far heard of: *jūnzǐ* and *xiǎorén*. She put these terms in her digital translator and presented me with the screen. The first translated to 'man of honour'. She said Chinese bosses like employees who do what they say they will and who are honest and straightforward. This type of employee also avoided office politics as much as possible.

At the same time, Chinese bosses liked 'petty people' or 'flunkies' around them—*xiǎorén*. These fed the boss gossip and served as the eyes and ears of the company. They didn't do much work and didn't need to be that good at their job as they mostly spied for the boss. Many 'petty' employees tried to take down the 'honourable' ones at work to maintain their positions. It fascinated me to no end that Chinese bosses valued slimeballs as well as honest employees to achieve their goals.

Michael had two deputies who played significant roles in AITA: Ms Xu and Mr Zhao. While they were both highly competent, their approaches and leadership styles differed greatly, creating an intriguing dynamic within the workplace. Ms Xu exuded a serious air, often sporting an Anna Wintour bob hairstyle. Unmarried and in her forties, she displayed an unwavering professionalism. Compared to Mr Zhao's team, hers seemed more adept at completing projects, though her group suffered from higher staff turnover. Unmarried women in leadership positions in China were known for their strong work ethic and dedication to their careers, often sacrificing personal lives.

Ms Xu appeared to rarely clash with Michael, most likely due to her methodical and deliberate approach to business. She possessed a keen understanding of Michael's expectations and knew how to deliver results or come remarkably close. She built a formidable inner circle comprised mostly of men to achieve her demanding expectations. As a woman, Ms Xu faced a slight disadvantage in terms of relating to Michael and networking in the same way as Mr Zhao did. The prevailing social customs made it more challenging for her to suggest casual after-work activities with Michael. Nevertheless, it was evident that he respected Ms Xu for her abilities and contributions.

Whenever Ms Xu spearheaded a successful new deal,

Michael made sure to highlight her valuable efforts in meetings, publicly praising her negotiating talents which had won over partners.

Though curt with other managers, Michael patiently entertained even Ms Xu's most tedious budget requests. During heated arguments, he would stand firm against all opponents but gradually defer to Ms Xu's perspectives. In the way he looked to her for guidance—and rewarded her counsel—it was clear Michael respected and relied heavily on Ms Xu's proven capabilities.

Mr Zhao embodied the opposite of Ms Xu. With his tall stature and wide, goofy smile, he resembled the late Premier Zhou Enlai but came across more like some friendly village mayor than a big city executive.

In meetings, he leaned back casually in his chair, cracking jokes that sparked waves of laughter. Female colleagues found reasons to hover by his desk, smiling at his breezy banter as he asked after their weekends. His relaxed, engaging air drew people like particles to a magnet—especially the women, who blushed and stammered if he so much as said their names. His charm was like gravity—inevitable and irresistible.

Though he uttered only one or two words to me during our meetings, his manner and grace, most definitely a product of generations and moments I could never fully grasp, gave me a favourable impression, despite the language barrier that stood between us.

Moments arose when he seemingly failed to sway Michael fully to his vision, unlike the consistent counsel Ms Xu provided. I ascertained that a few ventures proposed by the charismatic Mr Zhao did not yield hoped-for profits and progress. Ultimately, he and Ms Xu complemented one another in true yin-and-yang fashion. They represented the twin forces within AITA—the order and scholastic restraint of Ms Xu balancing the affable guile of Mr Zhao. They were Michael's right and left hands, chosen not despite but because of their opposing styles.

I might not have had a great salary but the benefits—or as my Chinese friends always called them, 'welfare'—were plentiful. While AITA would fade substantially in my rearview, the lessons learned there would travel with me long along the open road ahead.

NORTHWEST

As we stepped off the plane at Lanzhou Zhongchuan International Airport, a spark of excitement flared in my chest. The thrill of the unknown was what I loved most about our business trips. I didn't bother asking where we had to go this time around; it was all part of the adventure. But as we piled into the car, my eagerness waned. We had a three-hour drive to Tianshui ahead of us and it was already late at night. I wanted nothing more than to collapse into bed.

The interminable road unfurled ahead of us like a snake as we roared through the desolate night. The tyres kicked up dust that glowed silver in the headlights. In the distance, the mountains slept, not a light winking in the far-flung villages tucked in their folds. Still we charged on. Behind us, Beijing was far away. Ahead, the wild promise of the future this endless road would present to us come daybreak. Where it would lead, I could not guess. But the coming miles would surely teach what no book could, that much I knew.

I sat in the back seat, trying to make small talk with one of Michael's senior managers from Inner Mongolia, but the language barrier proved too great. Michael and his colleague chatted away in Mandarin, their laughter and exclamations echoing through the car. I couldn't shake the feeling they were laughing at me, that I was merely a prop in their game of business. I was their white monkey trained to hop and dance around the office to illustrate that AITA was a thriving business for potential clients.

When we arrived at Tianshui, it was well past five in the morning. But my exhaustion paled in comparison to my growing resentment of Michael and his team. I couldn't stand the way they treated me like an outsider, a curiosity to be trotted out to impress their Chinese clients. But as I settled into my hotel room, lying on top of the plush white quilt of my bed, I reminded myself of the opportunities that lay ahead. This was China, a land of endless possibility and adventure. I'd come here to seize it, no matter the cost.

A tourist map in my hotel room gave me a bit of context to where I'd ended up:

> Tianshui was the main stopping point on the Silk Road from Lanzhou. Its history dates back even further than this. However, a number of sources cite the banks of the Wei River were the 'cradle of Chinese civilisation.' This region has been inhabited since Neolithic times, excavated relics have a history of 8120 years, and maybe it is the heart of prehistoric China. Fuxi, the earliest Chinese ancestor, was born here. A stop here is highly recommended.'

Tianshui dazzled the senses like a spin through a kaleidoscope. Colour and scents collided from every angle. Red paper lanterns jostled with yellow signage to outshine one another, while spice-laden air pressed against me, urging my nostrils to drink in the heady perfume of chilli, mustard, vinegar and garlic. The streets seemed to vibrate with the skittering of cyclists, of vendors pushing apple carts, and machinists, construction workers and factory employees striding around in coveralls, while gold, crimson and blue silken banners rippled with the ghosts of long-gone silk traders.

We had nothing planned for that day, so while Michael and his colleagues slept through the rest of the morning, I got only about five hours of rest, after which I ventured out alone. I plunged through markets crammed with silk tapestries, wool shawls, cityscape paintings and copper pagodas. The scents of *Tiānshuǐ miàn* drew me irresistibly forth until I stood over bubbling vats that swirled with plump wheat noodles. They were ladled into bowls and swam in an umber sauce that crackled on my tongue, numbing and electrifying at once—a feat of dinnertime alchemy.

As I feasted, fireworks of chatter and commerce resounded all around. Tianshui flirted with every sense. The smells had me salivating as the choir of city noises serenaded me, mesmerised by the modern and historical sights and stimulated by the feel of swatches of textiles and bewitched by its beguiling Silk Road history. Few cities could so masterfully fuse past with present into something so intoxicatingly bold and unabashed.

'Better turn in early, you'll need your rest for tomorrow morning,' Michael said when I encountered him in the hall on the way back to my hotel room.

'What's tomorrow?' I asked, working to keep the irritation out of my tone. He hadn't briefed me on any morning-related events yesterday.

'We're going to attend a ceremony to honour Fuxi.'

'Fuxi being?'

He grinned at me and I couldn't tell if the smile conveyed mockery or excitement. 'A legendary figure from Chinese mythology. You'll find out.'

That's all he said before sliding his keycard in the door's electronic lock and disappearing into the darkness of his room, the door shutting behind him with a quiet snick.

Admittedly, my knowledge of Sinology was rather basic, hence not knowing about Fuxi. As Michael didn't seem to think it urgent that I knew I decided against researching it that night. A thought flickered through my mind that he might be acting nonchalantly to lure me into that mindset as a trap to see me embarrassed. I quickly dismissed it. Though I didn't necessarily trust him not to pull that, if he did, surely he would be the ass for doing so. I was his subordinate after all.

At about ten in the morning, all of us in Michael's group joined an immense gathering in front of the Fuxi Temple in the city's downtown area. The heat produced by the thousand-plus bodies surrounding me made the otherwise chilly morning bearable as we all gazed at the majestic structure.

It was styled in the manner of an ancient Chinese palace, with wide stone steps leading up to an entrance comprising tall, sleek red pillars on each side. A silk banner with silver Chinese characters ran across the front, each end tied to the roof. At the top of the steps stood a man and a woman dressed in exquisite crimson costumes with intricate golden embroidery and elaborate headpieces of the same colour scheme. In front of them were red drums to match their clothing and the temple.

A hush came over the crowd as the two each lifted an arm, drumstick in hand, and brought them down with a resounding thud on their instruments. Then the deep boom of a tolling bell reverberated through the air and the gathering came alive as the festivities unfolded.

These included a dance of worship, its performers lined

up, side by side, half in costumes of moss green, teal and royal blue and the other half wearing outfits of varying shades of pink. They stood behind a row of small, round tables covered in silky golden cloths topped by piles of colour-coordinated fruits. Yellow pomelos occupied their own table, as did bright red apples, persimmons and kumquats. Everything about the scene was a feast—for the eyes and the ears and our stomachs.

The rituals continued with sacrifices being made to a statue of Fuxi. Later came the reading of a eulogy. Through all this, it became clear to me Fuxi was a cultural hero who had contributed immensely to the foundation of Chinese civilisation.

With a serpent's body and a human head, Fuxi was considered a divine yet earthly being. He was credited with many inventions, such as the trigrams of the *I Ching*, which modern Chinese people still used, as well as crucial cultural artefacts like writing, fishing, hunting and cooking. Together with his sister and consort Nuwa, he created the first humans out of yellow mud and taught them the skills they needed to survive.

A carnival atmosphere infused Tianshui as locals celebrated the mythic founder who had paved their way through history. Cheery crimson banners of the man/serpent deity fluttered along streets festooned for the occasion and a great fanfare accompanied the parading of a dragon-shaped effigy.

But the true stars were the locals themselves. Young and elderly alike joined the festivities with gusto, their smiling faces mirrors of ancestors who had walked this soil for centuries before. The rich bonds of generations past and present were visible in their shared songs, stories and sustenance. Even bees seemed irresistibly drawn to the positive energy and tantalising fare of ceremonial meals.

Despite living in a small town, at least by Chinese standards, the people of Tianshui carried themselves with refinement. The mayor dressed like a Wall Street executive and the locals were polite and well mannered. Despite being the only foreigner in attendance, I did not feel like an outsider. Instead, they treated me like any other guest, which I found quite refreshing.

Our immersion in legend continued as I was guided through aged temple halls, where votive candles and coils of sandalwood smoke paid ongoing homage to the ascended Fuxi. Kneeling devotees channelled fervent dreams and appeals through flickering flames to the rhythmic throb of drums. That perpetual lifeblood between mortal pleas and divine ear seemed amplified in these shadowed inner sanctums.

As dusk enfolded Tianshui, we were feted at a lavish banquet whose never-ending courses we punctuated with customary toasts. We were treated to *guōkuì*, crispy fried pockets stuffed with pork and celery and seasoned with soy sauce. Next came mutton broth with glass noodles and carrots and seasoned with peppercorn. For dessert we had persimmon cakes layered with sweet glutinous rice and dates. An emptied glass quickly spirited away afforded the opportunity for myriad gracious salutes between tables as attentive waitstaff replenished our cups with wine. The welcome shown towards this foreign stranger proved as bottomless as the fetching wine jars lining our long, happy table.

My interpreter, Rong, and I visited at least fifteen such tables brimming with new-met friends. Over a sea of red wine, I strode table to table, greeting the locals and receiving warm and gracious welcomes in return.

Inebriated and high on the communal spirit, I was

dumbstruck when the meal suddenly ended mid-bite and mid-laugh. With our glasses still full and plates mounded with unfinished cuisine, conversations ceased in response to some unseen signal and everyone filed out of the room.

I never discovered what prompted such an abrupt, synchronised departure, the wine and camaraderie flowing one minute and vanishing the next. But the glowing imprint of Tianshui's boundless hospitality lingered long after the last mysterious guest had gone.

My visit to Tianshui left me with wonderful memories, but the next morning ground me into paste as we embarked on another three-hour drive to our next destination, Baoji. The traffic came to a standstill due to a road construction project and we had to sit there for what seemed like forever.

I hadn't expected to come across such a lush and tropical climate in this region. The greenery and humidity gave off a vibe that felt more like South America than Asia. As the traffic crawled by a line of hills, terraced for farming, we passed by some mining projects. I couldn't help but worry about the safety of the workers; none of them wore any protective gear. It was painfully clear that the slightest mishap could prove fatal.

My Inner Mongolian coworker couldn't stop leaning over to examine my Danish Skagen watch. He seemed fascinated by its intricate design. Despite the language barrier, he had seemed friendly enough. A person's eyes revealed so much. At one point, he pulled my arm towards his face to examine my watch even closer. I admired the insatiable curiosity among Chinese people about things that I would have considered ordinary back home. As I read my book, he leaned over my shoulder and even read a few sentences aloud, which made me feel connected to him in an odd way.

Soon, though, the driver grew increasingly frustrated with the traffic and started driving on the wrong side of the road, blaring his horn. It reminded me of a scene from *Romancing the Stone*. The jarring impact of the vehicle plunging into endless potholes made rest elusive. It didn't help either that there were toll booths every few miles and the driver had to stop and pay five kuai at every single one to continue our journey.

Finally, we arrived in Baoji, but with one look I wasn't impressed. It felt more industrial than Tianshui and the people didn't seem very welcoming. When we met the mayor, he proudly told me that Baoji was the birthplace of the Ming and Qing dynasties. Still, I preferred Tianshui.

A young woman, Ru, acted as my interpreter, as was often the case on my trips. I always felt important when I had an interpreter with me, but the best part was that she could actually answer my questions about what was going on. After our introductions, we visited a modern, fully automated dairy-processing plant.

The company's president had put up metal signs all over the grounds, each displaying one of his personal maxims. My two favourites were, 'It is good to not be fooled by flattery but be wary of the man who is not criticised' and 'It takes twenty years to build a reputation and five minutes to destroy it. Think about this as you handle your work.'

A few servers approached our delegation at the end of the tour to offer glasses of strawberry milk, which I struggled to drink because it was lukewarm. I explained to Ru that

Americans chilled their milk. She told me Chinese people got upset when served cold drinks as Chinese health beliefs emphasised that cold water shocked the stomach and harmed digestion. Many carried kettles on their overseas trips to 'purify' water, she said.

The next morning, I headed downstairs for breakfast with Michael and the rest of the team at the appointed hour, my stomach rumbling in anticipation of the morning meal. As we walked into the restaurant, the sweet aroma of steamed buns and savoury dumplings wafted through the air.

A middle-aged waitress with a warm smile motioned for me to take a seat at a wooden table near the window. I'd hoped to indulge in the buffet breakfasts that were the norm in China, but this hotel was too small to have one. Instead, another waitress appeared and handed me a menu printed entirely in Chinese characters, without any photos.

My heart sank as I realised ordering from this menu would be impossible. Michael was already seated at the table and halfway through his meal. He could see the situation but made no move to help. The waitress—who definitely did not speak English—and I were waiting for Michael to step in and handle the order for us. But he didn't.

'Glen, tell her what you want,' he said, his tone sharp and unyielding. The waitress and I froze, looking at each other in confusion. A sense of embarrassment and frustration washed over me, knowing that Michael was intentionally putting me and the waitress in an awkward situation.

'I ... I don't know what to order,' I stammered, trying to keep my cool.

'You need to figure it out. This is China, not America.

You can't always rely on people to speak English,' Michael replied, his words laced with impatience.

I hated him in that moment. He had no empathy for the poor waitress who wanted to serve us, and he was embarrassing me in front of the team. I muttered something about not being hungry as I handed the menu back to the confused waitress, who trudged away.

'Glen, you should eat breakfast. What do you want?' he asked again, his voice now tinged with annoyance.

'I'm fine,' I said, my voice barely above a whisper.

It wasn't until later that I realised what Michael intended to do. He wasn't being cruel for the sake of it. He wanted to push me out of my comfort zone, force me to rely on my own abilities and adapt to this way of life. As someone who had lived in China for a while now, I needed to start experimenting and taking risks, even if it meant embarrassing myself.

Michael remained a puzzle that I wished circumstance had allowed me to piece together. AITA's enigmatic overseer was quick with a cigarette for the driver yet sparing with praise for colleagues.

I thought of the young man who had once traversed disparate worlds to claim his Australian identity—tales of blundering through Aussie slang, stoking courage against small-minded ridicule. Had he flinched at the first taste of Vegemite? Michael could have been more of a guide and mentor to me. But it wasn't meant to be.

After a few hours in Baoji, we drove to the major city of Xi'an, the capital of several ancient Chinese dynasties, including the Qin and Tang, home to many important historical sites and artefacts. The city's modernity floored me. It rivalled Beijing in terms of construction activity. Everywhere you looked, new developments were taking shape, from the burgeoning aviation industry to the sleek, modern skyscrapers that dominated the skyline.

As we walked through the ancient city of Xi'an, our guide, Tu, enthusiastically shared with us the history and culture of the area. I couldn't help but feel a little disappointed that we wouldn't have time to visit the famous terracotta soldiers. But then Tu brought up an interesting tidbit about President Clinton's visit to Xi'an in 1998.

'The locals loved him for choosing to visit our city before Beijing since it demonstrated a willingness to engage with China on a cultural and personal level rather than only a political one,' he told us, beaming with pride.

I couldn't resist chiming in, 'Oh yeah, I remember reading about that in a Smithsonian exhibit back in the States.'

Tu's face lit up. 'Really? You've been to the Smithsonian? That's amazing.'

I grinned, quite pleased with myself. But then I made the mistake of revealing that Xi'an was our last stop on the trip.

Tu's expression immediately changed. 'So we're last?' he asked, sounding pained.

I quickly tried to backtrack. 'No, no, not last. You're ... um ... you're the grand finale.'

But I could tell it was too late. I had unintentionally insulted his beloved city and he was now looking at me with glum disappointment.

Tu led us to an airplane manufacturing centre and as we stepped inside I couldn't contain my awe. This was no ordinary factory—it was a powerhouse on par with Boeing, and the central government was clearly investing in its success. The showroom boasted dozens of detailed airplane models that had not gone into production yet. Even for a city on the cusp, this was the room of the future.

'Xi'an is third, after Beijing and Shanghai, in the number of universities it has; its programs are focused on aviation and software,' Tu explained.

As we toured the facility, my mind raced with possibilities. Could this be the birthplace of the next generation of aircraft? Could Xi'an become a hub for space research and exploration? The potential staggered my mind and I felt a thrill of excitement just being there. While major hubs like Shanghai and Guangzhou stood out for their economic prowess, I believed the future drivers of growth and innovation would arise in places like Xi'an, which foreigners considered only as a graveyard for terracotta warriors.

To my surprise, when we set out to explore the city I found a thriving coffee culture in Xi'an, with charming independent cafés and shops dotting the streets. The city blended the best of East and West with tea parlours alongside coffeehouses, and Chinese architecture next to Italian designs and all with a refined, polished vibe that felt aspirational and exciting. Locals walked with the confidence that came with being associated with such a strong tradition.

A sense of gratitude washed over me. As an expatriate, I had been blessed with the chance to call Beijing, China's capital, my home. Life in the city was filled with excitement and endless discoveries. In the months leading up to my move to China, I had immersed myself in books and articles, eagerly devouring every piece of information about this vast country.

The Silk Road, a legendary route of ancient trade and cultural exchange, had captivated my imagination. Little did I know then that my journey would lead me to traverse these very paths, to witness the echoes of history firsthand.

I couldn't help but marvel at it all—the mesmerising landscapes, dotted with arid deserts, majestic mountains and quaint oasis towns. The opportunity to explore this part of China was a gift I'd never anticipated.

As we ventured towards the ageless embrace of the Xi'an City Wall we came to stand atop a relic steeped in ancient whispers. Constructed in 1370 from brick and earth, it loomed twelve metres tall, an impervious ring guarding the old city. I thought of the legions of labourers who toiled to erect this colossal barricade more than six hundred years ago, entirely by hand without modern machinery.

I felt insignificantly small against its impressive scale. Yet I sensed not foreboding but comfort beside its weathered bulk, as if the substance of ages long past now accompanied me on my stroll. Looking outward beyond the moat-girdled sentry walk, the modern metropolis bustled under my gaze. It was an intriguing juxtaposition of new against old.

But while ground-level glass towers and neon lights prevailed, from my elevated vantage I witnessed humble corners where Xi'an's enduring heritage persisted quietly. Wandering the fourteen kilometres encircling the great walls transported me through eras. Soldiers and scholars, peasants and artisans may have all passed through time immemorial where I now stood. The walls bounded more than a city; they bounded the ages together.

Our sojourn through northwest China had been an odyssey

of revelations. From unearthing the primordial tales of Fuxi, their echoes entwined with Judeo-Christian lore, to beholding Xi'an's modern visage, China remained an enigmatic tapestry. A reservoir of knowledge beckoned, vast as the horizon's expanse. A lifetime could scarcely quench this thirst. I had become enamoured, entangled in China's allure, bewitched by its spell.

MICHAEL'S RECKONING

Michael was relentlessly forward-thinking in his business pursuits. His mind was in perpetual motion, constantly churning out ideas for the next venture, even before the ink had dried on his current deals. There was rarely an opportunity to revel in success.

AITA's 2007 Australia-China Investment Trade Forum in Beijing stood as a testament to Michael's uncanny ability to bridge the divide between East and West. In a landscape where securing the attendance of overseas officials was akin to finding a needle in a haystack, Michael had struck gold. His persuasive powers were legendary and he wielded them like a master craftsman, convincing sceptical Chinese clients that he could deliver, even if the meetings themselves yielded little more than a few handshakes and photo ops.

But hints of change were popping up through China and collaboration was becoming increasingly rocky. The government's crackdown on corruption, wasted funds, and malfeasance sent shockwaves through the business community, leaving Chinese partners in the public and private sectors looking over their shoulders, wondering if they would be the next to fall under the scrutiny of the authorities.

This new reality required Michael to bring even more establishment figures to China. He assembled a delegation from the parliament of the Australian state of Victoria, carefully selecting individuals whose collective expertise and authority would command respect and create new opportunities. He chose Ken Smith, the shadow minister for local government and Acting Speaker, known for his far-reaching influence; Martin Dixon, a versatile strategist handling a diverse portfolio; and Matthew Guy, a detail-oriented visionary. Michael further strengthened the delegation with the inclusion of Helen Shardey, the previously mentioned highly knowledgeable health expert, and John Vogels, a specialist in the primary industries crucial to the nation's economy.

Ken Smith stepped to the podium, straightening his notes as he gazed out at the gathered delegation with an affable smile. 'I am proud to say that the Australian International Trade Association has been an invaluable bridge spanning Chinese and Australian interests these past years,' he began, eliciting an energetic round of applause from attendees. Michael edged forward in his seat, eyes alight as if seeing a long-held vision crystallise before him.

Two highlights of the forum included the signing of a Memorandum of Understanding (MOU) by the Shenyang Province Electricity Board for a major investment project in Australia, valued at 40 to 70 million RMB. Through that, the company expressed interest in leasing or purchasing land in Australia for building greenhouses. AITA had to locate potential partners for the project.

But the MOUs distracted from where the real money lay for Michael and AITA. We'd begun co-organising BusinessWeek 2008, an event to take place in Melbourne in May. By successfully delivering the Aussie officials to China, Michael secured participation in the event from two organisations among others: the Shanxi Provincial Council for Promoting Small and Medium Enterprises Development and the Promotion of International Trade Hubei Sub-Council (CCPIT). Yet despite the upward trajectory, Michael's unpredictable style would not change.

Although working alongside Michael often left Jess and me with a bitter taste, we couldn't deny his acumen. The man knew how to make money. Who could deny his influence all across the Pacific Rim? He seemed unstoppable. But on 28 January 2008, as Jess and I were monitoring Australian media reports, we made a startling discovery—an investigative report exposing Michael Guo's misdeeds. As it came across our screens, it signalled his comeuppance had arrived in dramatic fashion.

Whether it was Jess or me who stumbled upon the article first, our shared realisation at that moment pierced the air. The headline 'Unmade in China' glared at us from the screen, an open invitation to explore the dark underbelly of Michael's activities. This article in *The Age*, a major daily newspaper based in Melbourne, included startling revelations from a whistleblower, named as Peter Magerl, a former Australian police superintendent employed under an AITA recruitment scheme. He detailed an assault within our office that demanded the Australian embassy's involvement. The story laid bare the extent of Michael's government connections in Australia. Michael's brother was even an elected official there.

For almost a year, we had dismissed Michael as a typical Chinese boss. Only now did we see him for the man he was, unscrupulous and willing to cross almost any line for his own gain. Ruthlessly ambitious and drunk on dreams of an empire stretching from Beijing to Brisbane, Michael barrelled ahead with no thought of the wreckage left in his wake, poisoning partnerships and friendships along the way.

Peter Magerl's heart had raced with anticipation when AITA offered him a job teaching English in Beijing. The opportunity seemed like a dream come true but he had no idea what chaos awaited. Upon arriving in Beijing, Magerl's excitement quickly turned to shock as he discovered that AITA was not the trustworthy organisation it claimed to be. The company operated without adhering to the principles of a not-for-profit organisation, lacked a legitimate board of directors and disregarded Australian law. Magerl also witnessed the appalling treatment of AITA's employees, with Michael verbally abusing and threatening everyone around him. The teachers they brought to China often had no qualifications and taught while intoxicated if they showed up at all.

Driven by his sense of duty, Magerl confronted Michael only to face a terrifying outburst of smashed teacups that left him and two other Australians trembling with fear in a locked conference room. Realising the danger Michael represented, Magerl made a beeline back to Australia, shocked by the turmoil he had unwittingly stumbled into when he had only signed up to teach English.

Determined to expose the truth, Magerl launched a relentless campaign, reaching out to politicians, trade and educational organisations and government bodies to expose AITA's dubious activities. He hired a private investigator and tirelessly pursued the faceless members of AITA's elusive board. Eventually, the New South Wales attorney general's office took legal action against the company for its failure to produce the required paperwork to prove its supposed nonprofit status.

Another exposé headlined 'Blacklisted Pair Exploit MPs' unveiled a troubling new dimension in the affair, tracing alarming links between AITA and the upper ranks of Australia's political elite. Documents showed AITA executives and advisors improperly influencing parliamentary heavyweights from across the ideological spectrum. Among those entangled with AITA's interests, the report revealed: Julie Bishop, deputy leader of the opposition Liberal Party; Labor government parliamentary secretary Laurie Ferguson; and Liberal shadow minister for veterans' affairs Bronwyn Bishop. Even Prime Minister Kevin Rudd appeared on the margins of AITA's questionable Chinese deal-making operations.

Prompted by the reports, probes and warnings had now come from the Australian Competition and Consumer Commission federal regulator as well as the Victorian consumer protection bureau. The critical question remained: how high up Australia's political ladder did this scandal reach?

With Australia's trade and political relationships with China at stake, all eyes turned to the coming Australia-China BusinessWeek 2008 event. Initially, the Melbourne City Council's logo appeared as a sponsor on the event's website, only for the city swiftly clarifying it had neither endorsed nor sponsored the event, fuelling the intrigue surrounding AITA's deceptive practices.

As the investigation continued, the true extent of the company's activities came to light. Inquiries were launched into potential violations of Commonwealth laws, and concerns were raised about AITA's involvement in facilitating employment in China with illegal work visas. Michael brazenly claimed that AITA's actions ultimately benefited Australia, hinting at a multimillion-dollar project in South Australia without revealing any concrete details.

I understood the murky links between official businesses and lobbyists. But Michael's approach was so brash that it threatened the very politicians and organisations he relied on to buy friends and influence.

A torrent of worries inundated Jess and me as we anxiously tried to grasp the magnitude of the allegations against Michael. Our minds raced uncontrollably over the implications this scandal could have on our own fates while we desperately attempted to piece together how his house of cards could collapse so suddenly. *The Age* had interviewed Michael for the article, so he knew about its impending publication. We couldn't afford to stray from business as usual, lest our behaviour aroused suspicion.

Worse, though, was the potential impact on AITA's ability to conduct business. Would delegations cancel? Securing appointments with Australian agencies and businesses had already proved tough and the article threatened to exacerbate the situation. I had wanted my final weeks at the company to slip by as smoothly as possible, but that didn't seem likely now. I did feel a sense of gratitude that the articles would at least help prospective employees with due diligence in the future. In the weeks leading up to my own employment at AITA, my Google searches had resulted only in links to AITA's website.

That afternoon, Jess and I opted to skip lunch, preferring to remain within sight of Michael's office, where we did our best to project an image of calm focus. But the moment five o'clock rolled around we dashed for the exit and meticulously dissected the details of the exposé over dinner. Although much of it resonated with our own experiences, at least physical assault had never featured in our individual ordeals. Though when Michael had threatened to fire me back in August, I'd always sensed physicality was a real possibility.

As we spoke, we stood in line at Origus, a pizza buffet chain we only went to because it was cheap. The usual array of pizzas, stacked high with toppings, stretched out before us. Cheese cascaded in gooey rivulets, pepperoni sizzled and the colour of the vegetables in the salad bowl beckoned with false cheerfulness. We felt nauseous. With trembling hands, we each hesitantly grabbed a slice of pizza. Grease oozed from the crust, staining our fingers in a brutal reminder of the slippery slope we had to climb. While the side dishes tempted us, our tongues tasted nothing. The French fries lacked their usual crunch; the chicken nuggets seemed artificial. Each tasteless bite accused us of what we had unknowingly entangled ourselves in.

The restaurant's noise faded into a distant buzz as our minds swirled with the many questions that plagued us. There could be no mention of AITA on our résumés or LinkedIn now. As an American, the consequences might impact on me less, but for Jess it spelled the end of a dream. This job should have ushered him on to something greater, a stepping stone towards his long-time aspirations. That possibility now lay shattered before him, nothing more than a mirage.

We exchanged glances, defeated and frightened expressions mirroring each other's. The company apartment that awaited us suddenly seemed like a sinister trap, its walls closing in, harbouring the imminent threat of Michael's presence.

Jess's voice broke the heavy silence. 'I've made a decision.'

A surge of anticipation and anxiety coursed through me. What was he going to say? Had he found a way out of this maze? His eyes met mine.

'I'm leaving when your contract ends.'

From there, we devised a plan. The weeklong break for Chinese New Year festivities loomed next month and we knew it would be our best chance to solidify our escape. We agreed to maintain the charade until then, to continue acting as if nothing was wrong, as if we still trusted Michael and cared about AITA's success. It was a dangerous game, but one we had to play to ensure our safety and the success of our getaway. We would simply bide our time until March arrived.

At that moment, I felt incredible gratitude for having Jess by my side. I clung to it, a source of solidarity amid the madness.

THE YEAR OF THE RAT

Beijing thrummed with anticipation as its residents eagerly prepared for the biggest holiday of the year. The sound of fireworks and scent of gunpowder intensified with each day, wafting through streets as the Year of the Rat approached. Smoke mingled with aromas from the grills of street vendors roasting sweet potatoes and chestnuts, their caramelised sugars a perfect counterpoint to the brimstone bite. The air buzzed with expectations of festivity waiting to burst forth.

When I arrived in 2007, the Year of the Pig was already in full swing, but February 2008 marked the advent of the new year. In Chinese astrology, the rat holds a revered position as the first sign in the zodiac, imbuing its years with a spirit of industriousness, ceaseless activity and abundant renewal. Rat years hold a pivotal role in the calendar, with the 2008 Beijing Olympics highlighting this one.

The magic of Chinese New Year, what locals called Spring Festival, pulled at me like a kite on a string ever since I was small. Television offered tantalising glimpses of this cultural extravaganza, stoking my desire to experience it firsthand. Scenes of the celebrations captivated my imagination, and I couldn't wait to witness the vibrant festivities in the heart of Beijing. The kaleidoscope of red lanterns and weaving dragons I had seen on TV largely derived from the Chinese diaspora, not mainland China itself. Mesmerised by the festive scenes, I mistakenly assumed they originated from Chinese cities rather than far-flung outposts ranging from sultry Singapore to the spirited Chinatowns on the West Coast. Only later did I grasp that these vibrant traditions had spread and taken root around the world, perpetuated by overseas Chinese communities. The Cultural Revolution had erased certain elements of these traditions, condemning them as archaic or superstitious so that they no longer appeared in mainland China.

My journey eventually took me to the south closer to Hong Kong, where I would encounter the lion dances that still echoed with the spirit of the Old World. Meanwhile, the reality of Chinese New Year in Beijing made a stark departure from my whimsical imaginings. For a bachelor expatriate like me, it could be lonely.

Much like Christmas in the West, Spring Festival in China is a cherished family holiday. As it approached, a great migration wave swept through the country, sending millions on a journey back home. Each year, this mass movement of people swelled the trains beyond capacity, weary bodies pressing together in intimate proximity, tickets having sold out even before the first snowmelt. Throughout the journey, silent prayers were uttered for the blessing of an empty seat, heads nodding off on shoulders once unknown but now as familiar as old friends. Stories were bartered like currency to maintain sanity, memories of the previous year's stowing away in cramped compartments still vivid but already blurred in anticipation of new tactics and manoeuvres for that year's return voyage. By early February, Beijing had hollowed out into a ghostly shell, a huge portion of its inhabitants back in their hometowns, although the holiday didn't officially start until February 8.

On that first night, I chronicled my experience in my journal with a mix of awe and annoyance:

It's only 7:54 pm and I already have an ENORMOUS headache from the firecrackers. These people started setting off firecrackers in the DAYTIME. This will go on for the next several days. Why didn't I buy earplugs? The air has that strong chemical smell that you get after lighting a firework. Sharp and sulfurous! People are doing it right outside my bedroom window! My God ... Just go back inside your apartment! It's freezing out there!

The sheer number of shops that closed during this festive period caught me off guard. As more and more locked up early for the holiday break, I found solace in small pleasures—like stockpiling fiery spiced peanuts from my go-to place before it too closed. It was a small victory amid the sea of loneliness surrounding me.

It was disheartening to find myself enveloped by celebrations of renewal while feeling completely detached from the joy. For the first time since arriving in China, the full weight of my outsider status bore down on me. Any Chinese person unable to travel home would have shared my sentiment, but I did not know that then. I could only imagine how a foreigner must feel in America around Thanksgiving or Christmas, alone in the midst of a country immersed in celebration.

I scoured the *Beijinger* to find which parks hosted temple fairs, those week-long lantern carnivals that brightened winter's gloom. Longtan Park blazed on the map so off I went, bundled against February's bite. The chill soon left me as I was surrounded by hundreds of people, welcoming me into their festive celebration. Crimson banners snapped overhead while dragon dancers wove down the paths, the percussion's *boom-ta boom-ta* refusing to be drowned by laughter or calls for roasted chestnuts. Vendors' cries mingled with birdsong and temple bells. The world outside the fair transformed into a stage where dragons undulated with grace, stilt walkers defied gravity and acrobats wove intricate tales of daring. Traditional Beijing street fare beckoned; I discovered *tánghúlu,* skewered, crystallised fruits that brightened the scene with their bold colour.

As the drums' frenzied beats fuelled the festivities, firecrackers exploded through the night, their sharp bursts echoing the ever faster drumming of my heart. Again and again they rang out, those hungry beasts. There was nothing to do but surrender. The firecrackers only added to the city's already poor air quality. Maybe if I'd had a family to light them with myself, I wouldn't have resented it so much.

Undeterred, I remained at the temple fair, lingering until the darkest hours of the night. The bitter wind howled, making the paper lanterns sway precariously on their strings above me. I hunkered in the shadows, my breath freezing into icy plumes as I eyed the red orbs warily. Buffeted by gusts, the lanterns dipped and twirled in a hypnotic dance, at times threatening to break free of their tethers and plummet earthward as the wind tossed them about like demons taunting me from the darkness. I feared one would break free and strike me. A father hoisted his bundled boy onto his shoulders, eliciting a chorus of laughter from the surrounding kin. I pictured myself in that child's place, safe and secure. The drums and cymbals heralded the next performance, but I turned up my collar and retreated farther from the celebrations, banished to my post on the fringes as an observer.

After walking back home and crawling into bed, I surrendered to the onslaught of firecrackers, drifting into a realm where dragons danced among lantern-lit dreams.

GEORGE

The normally staid offices of AITA pulsed with youthful vigour, a sea of eager twenty-somethings filling the desks. The average employee age skewed young, with a few seasoned exceptions that anchored the team—Michael; Vicky; managers Xu and Zhao, fonts of institutional knowledge; Tan Lu, the steadfast office manager who kept things running smoothly; and, of course, the driver. A thought nagged at me as I glanced around—where were the seasoned managers in their fifties, the ones with a wealth of experience? Surely there were more humane alternatives to Michael.

The answer soon dawned as I delved more and more into history books from the Beijing Bookworm. The Cultural Revolution had irreparably damaged the education of individuals born between 1945 and 1955, a scar China's schools had borne during their forced closure from 1965 to 1975. During this period, universities and schools shut down and academic institutions faced severe disruptions. Intellectuals, professors, and students were targeted and often subjected to persecution, imprisonment or forced labour. Many individuals who should have pursued higher education during that period couldn't do so due to the upheaval. Decades later, I witnessed the lingering effects as a generation of leaders had no chance to join this business landscape.

Amid this backdrop, George emerged as a man of distinction. In his early fifties, he stood out from the youthful crowd with his remarkable experiences working in Germany and Hong

Kong, being fluent in both German and Cantonese. He joined AITA during my final months and his arrival breathed life into the office. He was more of a consultant and the looks on his face frequently revealed that he thought Michael's decisions were as loony as I did. At last an experienced mentor was on hand to guide my well-meaning yet green colleagues whose unseasoned eagerness I had grown accustomed to.

We were meeting with trade attachés from the Australian embassy about expanding wine imports when one let slip an impolitic truth over instant coffee: that Great Wall, China's bestselling wine, was nothing more than leftover Aussie juice bottled up behind the Great Wall label to tickle the unsophisticated palates of China's newly rich. Michael tensed while Jess and I exchanged uneasy glances, but George was inscrutable as ever, preserving the peace by taking meeting notes in his small deliberate hand.

After the awkward talks ended, Michael unfurled his next scheme—why not beat the Chinese at their own game? Import Australia's *cheapest* wine, then disguise it as some Asian elixir to fleece nouveau riche Chinese wine lovers still too ignorant to know swill from shiraz.

His smile grew slippery as he envisioned the margins, paying little for wine few self-respecting Westerners would consume. Rebrand it as Forbidden Palace or Emperor's Reserve, he crowed as George placidly transcribed, no flicker of judgment creasing his broad face. He would carry out whatever scheme Michael ordered, even if it went against his personal values. The boss was the boss.

George was a lifeline for me in those fraught final weeks. I was already on edge about the media exposé, about which only Jess and I knew and we dared not share with anyone at the office. When Michael's antics darkened my mood, I knew I could pull George into one of the cramped meeting rooms that no one used. Behind the closed door, his stoicism washed over me, easing the knot in my chest.

He sat there contentedly, his face betraying nothing as I paced and fretted, railing against Michael's questionable ethics or my own powerlessness. George listened without judgment as frustrations spilled out that likely confirmed his suspicions of Michael's misdeeds. He was a human pressure valve, absorbing my anxious energy until I steadied. In George's presence, the office would recede for a blessed half hour. His reliability anchored me as everything else threatened to unravel.

One memorable evening, the air in Beijing was tinged with anticipation as George extended an invitation to Paulaner Bräuhaus in the exquisite Kempinski Hotel. The establishment's grand entrance beckoned us inside, whereupon a vibrant symphony of sound greeted us. The hum of conversations mingled with the clinking of glasses and the cheerful laughter of patrons, created a vibrant ambience.

George guided me with an infectious enthusiasm through the bustling crowd towards the centre of the pub. As we settled into our seats, he leaned in, his eyes infused with excitement. As the taproom attendant poured the amber lager into my half-litre stein, he set the glass down with a solid thud. 'My friend, allow me to properly introduce you to a Paulaner original.' He slid the frothy brew across the polished wood. I raised it to my nose, awakening to aromas of sweet biscuit and grassy hops that mingled and married. As that first sip met my tongue, hints of caramel and nut arrived at the party to linger on my palate. George grinned with pride. 'In Munich, they call this liquid gold, still brewed under the same Bavarian purity law. But you don't need to take my word for it ...'

His words brought to mind the image of skilled artisans meticulously crafting their brews with unwavering dedication. Yet another testament to the multicultural richness of experiences that Beijing had to offer, exposing me to a world I would never have encountered otherwise. I'd never been to Europe, but there was so much I could discover about the whole world by living in Beijing.

As the night wore on, the enticing aroma of freshly poured German beer filled the room, awakening my senses. Those hulking steins may as well have been filled with liquid gold the way the luminous brew seemed to mock the tavern's muted lighting, radiating brilliance that had me instantly spellbound. With my first taste, those centuries-old brewing secrets unfolded across my palate—rich complex flavours swirling in a sublime dance. I was transported, the embodiment of Germany in a sip.

The beer loosened my tongue and I began pouring out my plans to George. The clinking of glasses provided a gentle accompaniment as I told him I planned to flee AITA in a few weeks. George not only agreed with my decision but shared the same disbelief at the company's prevailing management style.

'Glen,' he confided, shaking his head, 'it's truly astonishing how this place is being run. It feels like we're trapped in the Beijing of the early 1980s.'

His words validated the doubts that had lingered for so long. I realised then that the issues I had observed at AITA were not solely a reflection of 'Chinese management' style but also the direct consequence of Michael's unconventional and flawed approach to running the company.

Among the many concerns I harboured about Michael, one stood out: his condescending attitude toward those around him. Michael always exuded an air of superiority, whether harassing humble waiters who had migrated from the countryside or terrifying his entire staff. As the boss, the *lǎobǎn*, he revelled in his prestige, a notion highly esteemed in Chinese culture. Yet Michael's personal narrative, whatever it may have been, of acquiring Australian citizenship and owning the company fuelled his delusion that he was above everyone else. This attitude clashed with my values, leaving me unsettled.

Adding to his behaviour, Michael had a peculiar manner of asking if someone knew something in Chinese. While the commonly used structure in China at the time would be *'Zhīdào ma?'* Michael employed a different form when speaking to our office employees: *'Zhī bù zhīdào?'* Slowly and patronisingly, he would pose these questions, sending shivers down my spine whenever he put my Chinese colleagues on the spot. His unpredictability extended beyond language as he would carry out surprise inspections without warning, checking which websites we were surfing. Every choice he made, even in his use of language, helped him to assert his superiority and make everyone else feel inadequate.

A few weeks before my contract expired, I received an email from Michael. Reluctantly, I opened it, only to find effusive praise for my performance throughout the past year. In truth, I wasn't sure if Michael had intended to renew my contract. He had Jess now, so I had less to offer, and after working with me for nearly a year Michael could tell I was no fan of his. He asked me to stay, offering a significant salary increase that would skyrocket my monthly pay from 5000 kuai to an astounding 20,000 kuai, accompanied by generous bonuses. It wasn't an offer to dismiss lightly. A substantial raise like that would be hard to find elsewhere in Beijing, especially after only a year of work in the country. I thanked him for his generous offer but requested time to deliberate.

The following day, a middle-aged woman materialised at the office. I had seen her working there before but, like many others, she had vanished one day. She sought refuge in Tan Lu's office, probably to collect her long-overdue salary. It didn't take long for Michael to discover her presence. He stormed into the room, his bulging neck veins betraying his pent-up fury. He unleashed a tirade of incoherent anger at the woman. She yelled back and scrambled for safety, moving quickly to the other side of the table, ensuring it stood between her and Michael. At that moment, my lingering doubts shattered into dust—there was no way I could continue working at AITA.

Despite my criticisms, I couldn't help but admire certain aspects of Michael's character. One particular trait stood out—the unwavering belief that, like Adidas' ad campaign, impossible was nothing. This mindset echoed the shared philosophy of all successful entrepreneurs. It was here that I recognised Michael's true Chinese nature. He refused to confine himself to preconceived notions of how things should be done. Instead, he embraced the breaking of norms and the challenge of conventions. For him, growth, experimentation and pushing boundaries were the very essence of progress.

But it was people like George, with their unique experiences as Chinese expatriates abroad, who infused a sense of progress into their homeland. They were the bridges between cultures, carrying the best practices and knowledge they had acquired from their international endeavours. George, with his global mindset and deep understanding of Western and Chinese business practices, was a shining example of this transformative force. His ability to adapt and blend the best of both worlds let me leave with a glint of hope for a brighter future.

It would be years before I fully grasped how profoundly Chinese society and economy benefited from integrating foreign traditions and cultures. Not wholesale adoption mind you, but rather selectively taking this and that—the best parts, sometimes even the underappreciated parts—and adapting them specifically for China. The more time China spent carefully studying and analysing other cultures, the better it seemed to be for the country overall.

FAREWELL

When I first arrived in China, I was a different person—timid, work obsessed and ignorant of life beyond my American bubble. Seeds of change had taken root in the span of a single year in this remarkable country.

Through unexpected friendships and illuminating conversations, my narrow worldview expanded into panoramic understanding. Moments of courage sparked new confidence I never knew lay dormant inside. I discovered a deeper acceptance of who I was by opening myself to diverse cultures and perspectives.

China asked much of me, pushing me far past familiar limits. Yet for all the growing pains, what it gave back was beyond measure. Where once I saw only work and deadlines, now I saw vibrant community and interconnection. In place of old fears, new fortitude emerged.

That final morning, nostalgia swelled. I opened the cupboard door and took out the money I had carefully saved over the past year. The creaking hinges seemed to bid me farewell. Each month I had received a modest 5000 kuai, along with bonuses Michael handed me in rare bursts of generosity. Fortunately, money had never hindered my experiences here. Free accommodation eliminated worries of rent and generous friends had spoiled me. I avoided the extravagant bottomless brunches and happy hours of the expat scene, preferring to immerse myself in the local culture instead. Scarlet and Jess were my only non-Chinese friends.

Jess had decided to stay in Beijing and build a life with his girlfriend. The day before, Michael had called me into his office and handed me my 20,000 kuai end-of-contract bonus. This would help fund my voyage to South Korea. Jess would not receive such a reward. I stood before his door and knocked, rousing him from his slumber. His eyes met mine, filled with unspoken questions. Words felt inadequate. Instead, I reached into my pocket and retrieved an envelope containing 10,000 kuai, pressing it into his hand. Our eyes locked and understanding passed between us. It was a gesture born not from obligation, but from the depths of my heart—a small token of the gratitude I held for my friend. In that moment, we both knew it was not just the right thing to do; it was the only thing to do.

I harboured zero regrets. The currency that mattered most couldn't be quantified on a balance sheet. Serendipitous moments revealed it—laughing over lamb skewers as the night market came alive, exploring sexual discoveries with intriguing partners, sitting in a classroom to learn Mandarin. This modest apartment had nurtured adventures beyond my dreams.

One final sweep of the apartment to ensure I had left nothing behind. I taped up another box, joining the ranks of transplants who briefly lived here before moving on.

As I packed up the last of my belongings, each item took on a sudden significance. I absorbed its essence, etching every detail into memory. The dormant television caught my eye—once full of promise, now eclipsed by the vivid experiences beyond these walls. In the kitchen, the little coffee grinder sat idle, a relic recalling shared mornings. Jess grasping a bag of Sumatra beans, their earthy musk wafting as I fiddled with dials. Whirring, sweeping, then reducing the treasure into powder. Inhaling the nutty aroma, our bleary eyes meeting. Anchoring our nerves before braving another workday. One small ritual cementing resilience forged shoulder to shoulder, facing each trial as brothers.

I scanned the room, reflecting on the profound personal growth these four walls had witnessed. The textbooks and flash cards from intensive language classes, the piles of Chinese history volumes dog-eared and annotated. Each artefact testified to my growth.

Before coming to China, I had known of Chairman Mao but not Deng Xiaoping. Now I understood the monumental legacy of China's great economic reformer. When I first arrived, I was as green as the foreigners long-term expats poked fun at, those who after a month believed they grasped China only to confess confusion after six months. It took me a full year living here to finally admit the truth that, in many ways, this country remained an enigma. The complex, rapid changes shape-shifting modern China from its insular past had humbled many an arrogant newcomer. My first months may have been spent convinced I had unlocked ancient mysteries, but genuine awareness only began once I accepted how little I truly understood. Now, still learning each day, I tread carefully, knowing the depth behind outward appearances.

I rose from the bed, bags in hand, ready to embark on the next chapter of my life. Jess and I had been meticulously planning our exit strategy behind the scenes. Unknown to Michael, we had subtly laid the groundwork for this pivotal moment. This was the day we would finally leave AITA on our own terms.

Jess left the bedroom window slightly open, tossing his house keys inside through the gap. I had a fresh SIM card ready to swap into my phone as soon as our final shift ended. To Michael, I was just another foreigner soon to be on a plane back to America. And Jess? Well, he would surely return to work on Monday as usual. Or so Michael thought.

He didn't know about our last vengeful act. On that final day, Jess and I discreetly tucked away into shared drive folders news articles exposing AITA's misdeeds. Our hope was that someday, when Michael inevitably needed to hire more foreign staff, unsuspecting new recruits would uncover the buried truths about AITA's dark side. Consider it a parting gift for our future replacements, a cautionary trail of crumbs we hoped would guide them towards escape.

Michael had arranged a farewell banquet, assembling the usual team—Jess, Ms Xu and Mr Zhao, our stalwart driver, and a medley of colleagues. As we threaded through the bustling streets of Chongwenmen, the awkwardness of strained conversation permeated. We ducked into the restaurant, welcomed by a lavish spread Michael had orchestrated to send me off in style. But underneath the superficial fanfare, awkwardness lingered. Words were left unsaid, tensions quietly bubbled. Michael's toast rang hollow. Xu and Zhao's smiles failed to reach their eyes.

I had never been to this restaurant but it quickly became apparent how prestigious it was when I saw the final sections of the menu, dedicated to cigarette purchases. Diners could light up and indulge as tobacco was a state-owned product (with no warning labels, a perk of being a monopoly). None of us in our group smoked, except for the driver, so we refrained.

The steaming bowl of wheat noodles arrived at our table, the tantalising aroma reaching my nose even before the server set it down. As I lifted my chopsticks for the first bite, thinly sliced flank steak and chewy rice noodles peeked out beneath the surface. Slurping the spicy soup, my companions and I locked teary eyes as we subtly competed to withstand the rising heat. The fire danced on our tongues, the peppercorns once again pleasurably pricking the mouth. Empty bowls represented a triumph of sorts, proof that one had braved the flames and emerged victorious.

Sitting across from Jess and Michael, I felt my mask slip off as our lunch wore on. With each forced grin and hollow words about how much I would miss everyone, I was putting on a performance, an actor reciting memorised lines. Jess tried to smooth over the awkward pauses with a stilted chuckle here and there, though the discomfort lingered. Michael was stone-faced, his silence speaking volumes about his displeasure over my imminent departure.

As we stepped out of the restaurant into the glow of a March afternoon, the sun's rays wrapped around us in a farewell embrace. Sensing the significance of the moment, we huddled together for one final group photo, smiles masking the uncertainty. I did not know how long my time in China would be but I knew I would forever cherish the people I had met here, brought together only by the magic of Beijing.

I would remember my lovely AITA coworkers, Scarlet, Nick, Judy, Sally, Jess and all the others who had guided me with such care. And friends like Calvin and Davis who had shown me the wonders of this country. While the names of my students would inevitably fade over time, their spirit and hunger to learn would continue to inspire me. Then there were the strangers imprinted on my memory in fleeting moments, the taxi drivers who corrected my Mandarin, the woman in the park who showed me a shortcut, the children who eagerly called out 'Hello!' when they saw me. Though I grasped their hands but briefly, crossing the bridge of this life together for mere steps, never could time erode how they had touched my spirit.

Even as the sun dipped below the horizon, I carried these people and moments in my heart. Beijing had woven an unbreakable thread between us. Wherever my path led, I would remember.

Beijing was the place where the future seemed unwritten and alive with possibility. As I walked its streets, I felt the energy that only exists on the cusp of change. This was a pivotal point—for China, for the world, and for my own inconsequential life.

In this city, poised between its storied past and an uncertain future, I experienced a profound sense of belonging. Beijing had claimed me as its own. Fate demanded that I stay.

EPILOGUE

I lived in Beijing for another twelve years. Through an ironic twist of fate, my new apartment was even closer to the AITA office, which constantly reminded me of the past I desperately wanted to leave behind. In those initial months of freedom, I lived in a delicate balance between hope and fear, always aware that Michael might discover I had never truly left China. Every day I worried about our paths crossing again and I couldn't bear to imagine what he was capable of if he recognised me. Every time I ventured outside, I frantically scanned for any trace of his presence.

It was on Gui Jie, Beijing's iconic dining street adorned with vibrant red lanterns and the very one on which Michael had hosted my welcome dinner, that my senses sharpened, aware of the shadows whispering his name. And there he was.

My heart slammed to a stop, time losing meaning as a tall figure whipped around, the ghostly lanterns carving the familiar sadistic features I had hoped were gone from my life forever. Had fate delivered Michael to find me here? The world around me blurred with uncertainty. It was too late to escape, too late to shield myself from his gaze. However, in a moment of relief, it became evident that this was not Michael after all.

As my racing heart gradually settled, a newfound determination took hold of me. I vowed that I would no longer allow this fear to consume me. I refused to let Michael Guo hold me hostage any longer. In that moment I resolved to leave him behind forever.

Months later, one of Michael's trusted deputies, Mr Zhao, and I bumped into each other. Working full-time as a teacher took me to the far-flung corners of that sprawling metropolis each day. From morning classes in one district to afternoon classes in another, my life became a whirlwind of subway rides, bus journeys and taxi escapades. One sunny afternoon, as I hurried up the stairs at Jianguomen station to catch the next train, there stood Mr Zhao. His eyes lit up with recognition and a warm, genuine smile appeared on his face.

We exchanged greetings in Mandarin, and I saw the approving glint in Mr Zhao's eyes. I transformed myself in the months since fleeing AITA. We forged an unspoken pact between us then. I had no doubt that this kind gentleman would not betray me to Michael.

With a smile, I bid Mr Zhao farewell and stepped onto the awaiting Line 2 subway. As the train left, I felt an overwhelming sense of gratitude for the remarkable souls who had crossed my path, those like Mr Zhao, who silently understood me. These connections meant the world to me.

I took great pride in my connections with Australia and genuinely learned a lot about the region through my work with AITA. Although I hadn't fully appreciated it at the time, that first year taught me so much about myself and the larger world. As much as I had embraced Chinese culture with zeal, part of me felt undeniably Australian too.

There is merit to the argument that Australia leaned too heavily on China, developing an economic dependence that left it exposed. However, in an interconnected Pacific region, Australia's cultivation of Chinese trade and tourism was a rational, calculated strategy, though debated by some as overly ambitious. Seeking to capitalise on burgeoning Asian markets, Australia positioned itself not only as a source of raw materials but also as an aspirational destination for China's rapidly expanding middle class. Integrating Chinese consumers into Australia's economic future aligned with geographic realities and wider Asia-Pacific trends. The core question remains whether Aussie strategists overplayed their hand.

While on the surface Sino-Australian ties had blossomed economically, simmering political tensions were threatening this relationship so vital to Australian trade. The year 2020 ushered in a marked deterioration. Australia's call for an independent probe into the origins of Covid-19 provoked Beijing. In reprisal, barriers arose at Chinese docks for Australia's barley, beef and above all, its wine. The message exacted economic pain, a stern warning to Canberra over the limits of critique. For an Australian wine industry elevated by Chinese thirst, it was a reminder that their preeminence could no longer be divorced from diplomatic whims.

In a more personal twist, Chinese authorities held my colleague, news anchor Cheng Lei, a naturalised Australian citizen, under residential surveillance on murky espionage charges. Watching relations deteriorate so rapidly and acrimoniously saddened me. I remembered the Australian officials who had eagerly tried to strengthen connections at all levels. When I worked at AITA, it was hard to imagine that these ties would ever reach such a stage. However, relationships between countries, much like those between individuals, are dynamic and ever-changing.

In March 2024, China announced it would lift the tariffs on Australian wine that had been in place since 2020, signalling a thaw in the previously frosty relations between the two nations. The decision followed months of diplomatic rapprochement, which began with the election of a new Australian government in 2022. Prime Minister Anthony Albanese welcomed the move, noting that his administration had successfully lobbied for the removal of duties on Australian barley and continued to press for the elimination of remaining trade barriers on products such as beef and lobster.

The Australian government's calm and consistent approach to engaging with China yielded tangible benefits for the nation's economy. The lifting of the wine tariffs, which had exceeded 200 per cent, offered relief to Australian winemakers who had lost access to their most lucrative export market, valued at A$1.2 billion at its peak. Although the industry had pivoted to other markets during the dispute, it struggled to sell the same volume of wine and faced a significant glut. The restoration of access to the Chinese market provided a much-needed boost to the sector, even as winemakers acknowledged that regaining lost market share would require concerted effort.

As I reflect on my time at AITA and the tumultuous years that followed, I am struck by the profound impact that seemingly small decisions can have on the course of one's life. My experiences in Beijing, at the agency and in the years after, taught me invaluable lessons about resilience, adaptability and the power of human connection. The relationships I forged during that time have left an indelible mark on my soul.

In the end, my journey from AITA to the present day has been one of personal growth, of confronting fears and discovering inner strength. It has taught me that while we cannot always control the circumstances that shape our lives, we can choose how we respond to them. We can find the courage to leave behind that which no longer serves us, to forge new paths and embrace the unknown. And we can do so with the knowledge that, no matter where life takes us, the connections we make along the way have the power to sustain and inspire us, to remind us of our shared humanity in an increasingly chaotic world.

ACKNOWLEDGEMENTS

Writing a book is akin to crafting a mosaic, with countless voices shaping the final form. As the author, I bear responsibility for merits and weaknesses in these pages. However, I am deeply grateful to all who helped refine *Beijing Bound* through reading excerpts or full drafts.

In our interconnected world, producing a polished book is a global collaboration. From those flagging disruptive phrases to those bolstering me during struggles, individuals worldwide elevated this work. Regrettably I cannot thank each one, but know this achievement is shared.

I profoundly thank Ellie Nalle for refining my unwieldy first drafts into engaging prose. Under your talented guidance I've grown tremendously as a writer.

Sincere gratitude to Richard Caldwell, John Herzfeld and Kim Yoonmi for invaluable insights, and early readers Jaysen Henderson-Greenbey, Barbara Kyle and Ethan Gilsdorf for honing resonant themes.

Thanks also to Nam Cho whose striking cover art captures the city's modern zeitgeist, and to Annegret Richter for charming maps that transport readers.

To you, dear reader, thank you for exploring these pages. Please consider supporting this work by sharing it widely and providing honest feedback to shape future cross-cultural narratives. In today's publishing landscape, your voice and advocacy help deserving stories break through. With your readership and counsel, the next work can dig deeper still.

ABOUT THE AUTHOR

Glen Loveland lived in Beijing from 2007 to 2020, working for such companies as Pearson and the Walt Disney Company.

He became the first foreigner hired in the human resources department of state broadcaster China Global Television Network (CGTN), where he had oversight of expatriate recruitment.

He currently works at the Thunderbird School of Global Management.

Loveland graduated from the University of Massachusetts-Lowell and studied Mandarin at the Beijing Language and Culture University.

Beijing Bound is his first book.

www.ingramcontent.com/pod-product-compliance
Lightning Source LLC
Chambersburg PA
CBHW020134130526
44590CB00039B/163